9 1/2 YEARS BEHIND THE GREEN DOOR
A MEMOIR

A Mitchell Brothers Stripper Remembers Her Lover Artie Mitchell,
Hunter S. Thompson, and the Killing that Rocked San Francisco

by

Simone Corday

9 ½ Years Behind the Green Door – a memoir:
A Mitchell Brothers Stripper Remembers Her Lover Artie Mitchell,
Hunter S. Thompson, and the Killing That Rocked San Francisco

Copyright by Simone Corday, 2007.

Mill City Press, Inc.

Mill City Press, Inc.
212 3rd Avenue North, Suite 570
Minneapolis, MN 55401
1.888.MILLCITY
www.millcitypress.net

ISBN 978-1-934248-62-1
ISBN 1-934248-62-2
LCCN 2007940543

Cover photo © Charles Gatewood, used with permission
Set in Arno, by Dzyn Lab.

For Artie Jay Mitchell

and

For the Girls of the O'Farrell

ACKNOWLEDGMENTS

Thanks to everyone who has given me valuable advice, shared their stories and insights, and particularly to those who inhabit this story. A special thanks to Rita Ricardo and Charles De Santos, for their continued friendship and support, and their belief in this book from the start. Thanks to Dave Patrick, and Gene Ross for first putting my words in print. I am also grateful to Charles Gatewood, for the use of his unforgettable cover photo of a dancer from his "Post Modern Pin-Ups," available at charlesgatewood.com.

✳ *Please Note: The cover model is not the author!*
The cover photo was chosen to represent the numerous alluring women who give the sex business vibrance, and enable it to thrive.

Table of Contents

PREFACE

"There is no such thing as risk-free anything. In fact, all
valuable human things come to us from risk and loss ... Part of
the sizzle of sex is the danger, the risk of loss of identity in love.
That's part of the drama of love."

– CAMILLE PAGLIA, IN SEX, ART, and AMERICAN CULTURE.

This book is a true story. It began as a journal I kept when I started
dancing at the Mitchell Brothers O'Farrell Theater in 1981—a decade after
the Mitchells shot their breakthrough porn film *Behind the Green Door*.
In the fullness of time, I chose to pursue a complex love affair with Artie
Mitchell, an infamous, flamboyant pornographer and one of the last true
outlaws of the Western World. I loved Artie because he was uninhibited
and challenging. I could love him because our relationship ebbed and
flowed—times we were together were balanced by times apart.

Falling for a bewitching pornographer with a radical imagination had
many moments of ecstasy and times of maddening frustration. Since
I worked at the theater which Artie co-owned, the balance of power
between us was far from equal. He was a hard-living outlaw, and our
relationship was strained when he disappeared on binges. Although
much of what I went through as a result of his drug use and advancing
alcoholism may seem diabolical, it went with the territory of being
significant in his life. In many ways, Artie and I lived poet William
Blake's line "The road of excess leads to the palace of wisdom." I count
myself lucky to have ridden passion to the ends of experience. Although
agonizing at times, the connection I had with him was truly erotic and over
the years the bond of love between us became steel.

After Art's death I began transcribing my journal, towards the end of writing a book. Dates, events and conversations are accurate to the best of my recollection, and names of the major players are unchanged. The characters of some of the dancers and other minor figures are composites. Their names and identifying details have been altered to protect the real people I worked with. The setting of one non-Mitchell Brothers movie was changed, for the same reason. Compressing ten years of life into a readable manuscript was like assembling a Chinese puzzle, and events of lesser importance are not included. Details surrounding Art's death have been drawn from grand jury transcripts and published accounts, and represent my earnest efforts to portray what actually occurred.

The O'Farrell Theater was a wild place, where the compelling emphasis was on sex. I had some wild experiences, which I describe realistically. It is my hope that the reader will also be able to focus on the more serious parts of this story, and hear my perspective.

When Art was depicted as a monster at the subsequent murder trial and in the media, I realized how important it was to tell my story--the truth about the Art I knew, about me, and about our world--in all its ugliness, its comedy, and its beauty.

I have never regretted my choice of Artie, or my time behind the O'Farrell's "green door." In truth, I bought the ticket, and it was a spectacular ride.

Simone Corday
San Francisco, California
August 2007

PROLOGUE

April 1991

South of the Golden Gate Bridge, worlds apart from Chinatown, North Beach and The City's romantic fog, stands Mission Dolores, the oldest building in this lovely city of contradictions. Finished in 1791, the sturdy little mission and the grander basilica face Dolores Street, stately with its center aisle of palms and overripe trees that shade the churches and sleepy Victorians along a two-mile stretch to Market Street traffic and the deserted U.S. Mint. The Spanish founders and other early San Franciscans are buried under cold tombstones with sorrowful nineteenth century inscriptions in the mission's remaining tiny graveyard, while five thousand Native Americans lie anonymously under the nearby buildings and streets. Streets like Sixteenth, so alive with cars and people, graffiti and the air of possibility, the music of Selena and Tupac Shakur, cobalt blue hair and piercings, sexuality and attitude. Much more than churches, I have loved the district's pre-Christian festivals—*Carnaval* for the living, and *Dia de los Muertos*, when marigolds and sugar skulls decorate altars in the storefronts, and a troupe of skeletons dance through the candlelit streets celebrating the souls of the dead. I was at Mission Dolores only once before, drawn to one of those sanctified places whose tough walls affirm the ongoing power of life.

Weeks following Artie Mitchell's death, when I am still reeling from the impact, on a gloomy afternoon I am back here. Heartbreaking grief—everyone who has lived it knows the feeling. My stomach clenched into a taut rubber ball, my body tightened and recoiled, in the tearless candle glow my whole being hardens with one question. After years of loving Artie, why was our relationship severed by his murder? Why was he killed in the middle of life, at forty-five, a father of six children? Why was he shot to death by his brother? It was a crime as old as Cain and Abel, but so uncommon I never saw it coming.

I have searched every street of the city for my lover's face, all the grand and poor neighborhoods, and cannot find him. None of the explanations I am hearing for his killing brings me any peace—so I am on sacred ground, confronting God and all things holy. Never have I felt so full of rage, and so powerless.

In the silence of the basilica, in the crystalline stained glass light and the frozen stares of the saints there are no clues. I will have to look back, back to what happened at the O'Farrell, in our lives, and into myself, for the answers.

Part 1

CHAPTER 1:
Flesh and Fantasy

AUGUST 11, 1981

Was I really gutsy enough to do this? I asked myself all
afternoon—just parking at the edge of the Tenderloin and walking
into the Mitchell Brothers O'Farrell Theater's formidable blue building
seemed dangerous. I heard the place was the best club to work as a
dancer in San Francisco, and that it was wild, but since moving to
the city I had been too wrapped up in my own interests to notice
stories in the news about this edgy theater and the Mitchells. The
O'Farrell's marquee, and its doors and windows of shiny one-way
glass were modest; although the building was adorned with a mural
of whales adrift under the sea, and delightful painted waves lapping
at its roof. In the warm California sunlight, the place sparkled with
presence. What goes on inside? I wondered. Mitchell Brothers didn't
look menacing—not like a topless nightclub with a barker and cheap,
glaring signs hawking women like freaks in a sideshow, not like the
sinister strip bar in *Touch of Evil*, not at all like a Barbary Coast den
of iniquity where a savvy young woman like me could get shanghaied
from her soul.

A couple of my friends had worked as strippers at the long defunct
Follies when they were going to college, and told me dancing paid well
and could be fun. I pictured the old movie *Gypsy*: a brave, luminous
Natalie Wood taken under wing by worldly strippers in elaborate
spangled gowns; while footlights would glow on filmy chiffon and

17

shimmering rhinestones. A cavernous, Gothic auditorium would have a phantom or two in the wings; and a well-paying, appreciative audience in row upon row of seats outlined in shadow. Time warp images. Did the O'Farrell's pleasing exterior conceal such a scene—or would its mirrored doors swing open on a replica of a decadent cabaret in Sally Bowles' Berlin, or some more modern, dark forbidden city?

I was looking for a job that would support me while I studied art history, painting and design at San Francisco State. I needed something that would pay better than my $8.oo an hour part-time secretarial stint with three criminal lawyers. And though my young bosses were hip and generally kind, there was an undercurrent of condescension that was a nagging reminder of just where an office worker with an artistic bent stood in wealth and position-driven San Francisco, that cut me to the core. How delectable it would be to drop out of a nine to five tedium that I would never truly fit into. Maybe I could dance a couple of nights a week for awhile and make some extra money—until I found some work I liked, or could make a living with my clothing designs again or with some other craft—I had thought, scanning the papers, finding an interesting ad.

In the early evening a faintly salty, brisk wind whirled up Polk Street from the direction of the bay, as I turned the corner onto O'Farrell Street and took a few more steps to the theater's entrance and my new life. "Burning with curiosity," Alice went down the rabbit hole to Wonderland—I wandered into the O'Farrell.

"I'm here to audition," I told a fat man in a tuxedo-style, ruffled shirt at an open counter that served as the theater's box office. With a wry smile, he asked me to wait in an area off to the side that had a few cushy chairs, near a little neon sign that read Ultra Room. Wearing a print dress under my coat and a gold heart-shaped locket, I was excited and afraid, expecting the other women would look like models out of some magazine like *Glamour*. Then two attractive—but not model-perfect—girls in their twenties joined me who were also there to audition, and I felt calmer. One of them was a blonde from Nebraska who wore a quirky outfit from the Salvation Army and had brought along a heavy backpack. The other was a black woman who was dressed like she had spent the day sightseeing on Fisherman's Wharf, in shorts with a polo shirt and a denim jacket. Along a ledge hung numerous framed 8" x 10", black and white photos of dancers in costume. A slowly revolving, backlit display showed off some much larger color pictures. Two were of great-looking stars that would appear at the theater soon as feature attractions. The third large still was of a pretty girl in a black leather bikini. With a slender black ribbon around her neck and a cascade of straight brown hair, she was advertising the Ultra Room. In time, I would find out she was my future lover Artie's cunning second wife, Karen Mitchell.

At 7:30 p.m., one last straggler arrived for the audition; someone hit an electric buzzer, and the big man from the box office pushed open a massive dark wood door and led the way. Up a long flight of stairs lay a couple of brightly-lit dressing rooms, and we were shown into the largest to get ready for the amateur contest. Costumes of every color and a couple of feather boas hung against the wall, while bags of lingerie, gloves, and other mysterious things bunched together on a floor dusted with cast-off sequins and glitter. The counter spilled over with makeup, brushes and curling irons, and the shimmering depleted champagne and wine bottles along the top of the mirrors and some casual lipstick kisses on the walls gave the place a reckless feel. A locker door clanged shut out in the hall, and a rapid shuffle of bills in a dancer's hand came closer as she counted her money. Two of the contestants knew each other and talked warmly, but the whole scene was too foreign for me to say much. As hairspray and perfume blended in the warm air, the box office guy carried in a hat, and my little group of amateurs drew numbers. The black girl from the lobby, who said she was from Ohio, took off her shorts and shirt to zip herself into a tight lavender gown, cut out to expose her entire ass—a style that seemed a bit over the top, to me. She would be Contestant Number One.

In the shadows of the tech booth upstairs where the DJ was running the lights and music, I waited for the contest and watched the New York Live show dancers and the audience below. When the first woman slinked onstage, earthy and bored and beautiful, the audience was spellbound, and in her power. With the warm powdery lights glinting off her auburn hair, she seduced, even in a plain evening gown. Like an ancient goddess come to life, she finally unhooked a black g-string with a little elastic on it, and let it fall. Down in the New York Live audience, dancers wearing body suits and lingerie bobbed up and down on the guys' laps, in a red carpeted palace, with a T-shaped stage at its core.

A gorgeous, icy blonde, Lisa Adams, who had starred in porn movies, danced next. Lisa was aloof from the crowd, but at the end of her show pinched flesh between each thumb and forefinger to lift her breasts. It looked like it would hurt, or something. But so sexual. Lisa was destined to eventually become Jim Mitchell's third wife, and was a key player in the tragic events leading to Art Mitchell's death.

Then it was time for us amateurs. Although you didn't have to win the contest to be hired, someone from the management chose the winner and awarded the $75.00 cash prize by the applause of the audience. That night this responsibility fell on the senior DJ, Rob, but I didn't notice him until the whole thing was over. Once the dancer in the lavender gown was onstage, I made a last-minute dash to the dressing room to check my dress and makeup. A pretty black woman who had arrived last went on second. She ended her show with some sultry floor work, like a pro from another club. Next was the blonde, who tossed a naked rubber baby doll around during part of her show, and for the finale stood on her head naked and played "Turkey in the Straw" on the violin. I did a simple dance and striptease, my impression of what the regular dancers had done half an hour earlier. When the revealing spotlight in the center of the room was on me, the guys leaned forward hushed, serious and staring. Being on stage felt comfortable, since I started ballet at three. I always loved dancing. I adored sex. People clapped for me. I won. How unbelievable!

Afterwards, all us contestants went back to the office. Rob, casually dressed, in his thirties, and authoritative in a relaxed way, wanted to know how old we were. We asked what you did in the audience.

"Well, I don't want to see any handjobs or any blowjobs down there," Rob said. "You'll do a lot more for a five than you'll do for a one." Those were the rules. The Mitchell brothers weren't into making rules, they were into breaking them.

Rob gave us the number to call for an appointment if we wanted to work there. Later in the week I went to an office in a sleek modern building to meet with the Mitchell Brothers accountant, a humorless woman in a conservative suit, to fill out employment papers and present my ID. She looked like the last person on earth who would be working for a strip club.

On my way out I asked, "Is it possible the theater could get busted?"

"No. That hasn't happened for more than a year," she said, giving me a glance full of contempt. "Since then, they made some changes in the shows."

⌒⌐

Working my first shift, I was petrified. Even the other women being at ease hanging out naked or nearly so in the dressing room seemed odd to me. One girl, a bit heavy with a real short haircut and a hostile edge noticed. "Don't be afraid of us," she said. "We're only strippers."

Mitchell Brothers served up the sizzle of fantasy—not the steak. The O'Farrell dancers earned their pay sitting on customers' laps for tips (lap-dancing) in-between dancing on stage, or performing in other scheduled shows. At first, it was a bit shocking to be dressed only in lingerie and heels when I was sitting with the customers in the big, twilight auditorium watching dancers on the radiant stage of the New York Live. No alcohol, soft drinks or other refreshments were served like they do at strip bars or gentlemen's clubs, so the dancers never had to hustle drinks, and the customers were better behaved since they weren't drinking liquor on the premises. The men in the audience were mellow, like amused guests at a lighthearted party. Most of them were well-behaved yuppies who rarely got out of line, and the guard at the back of the room gave us security.

Talking to so many different people fascinated me, and it was a kick to have the upper hand in such an outrageous situation. Many of the men were attractive, so the flirting could be fun. In the main O'Farrell show, the New York Live, we sat on the customers' laps in theater seats. Depending on what the customer wanted and what the dancer agreed to, looking around the audience most women would be sitting sideways talking with the guys, getting hugs or making out. Others would be facing away from the guys and rocking on their laps. Some women went further than others, but in the comfortably dim lighting, who really knew. Walking back to the packed audience in the New York Live show, you could feel, unprecedented and magical, the steam of sex.

Guys who didn't even want to fool around were turned on and intrigued by the atmosphere, so Mitchell Brothers was crowded. What each stripper earned was different each shift, and depended on her appeal, her ability to hustle, on her luck and her mood. In the early

80's many dancers averaged from about $100 to $300 in tips per shift, supplemented by a check from the management that ran about $15 each shift. But there was always the occasional terribly slow night, or bad spell, when customers were sparse and money was hard to come by. When I stopped dancing in 1989, the amount of tips had climbed and there were occasional stories of a smitten customer tipping his favorite dancer more than $1000 during a single shift. For a beginning stripper like me in the early 80's, the O'Farrell was a different world and I couldn't believe the money. And some customers who were shy, like Harvey, just wanted to talk. I liked that, too.

～

Outsiders have told me they are surprised I was able to endure the sex business. They wonder how I escaped the fate of strippers in Hollywood movies, and ask, "What about your upbringing made you a survivor?"

My background was not especially unique—although I did start dancing later than most, and had a Masters degree and a variety of life and work experiences before I got into the business. I'd been trying to find an alternative way to earn a decent living for years. I always hated conventional jobs, restrictions, the expectations of other people. When I was born in California, my father had just been transferred to Japan. In a year my mother bravely, but anxiously took her first and only child by ship to Yokohama, then south on the train to the island of Kyushu. Until I was twelve, we moved constantly, lived in New York City, Tacoma, Las Vegas, Hawaii, and Washington, D.C. Being uprooted made me flexible, tolerant, restless, and gave me the detached perspective of an outsider.

When I was beginning junior high, my parents bought a lovely two-story house on a quiet tree-lined street, with roses, camellias and a solitary birch tree in the front yard, in Sacramento, California. Most of the time I lived there with my mother. Stoic, restrained, and very much a loner, my father continued traveling, constant to his other wife, the U.S. Army. I read novel after novel and fantasized about getting out, to pursue adventure after mysterious adventure; to live my life like a fine stream of consciousness novel. The Sacramento Valley has the kind of flat provincial boredom I ached to escape from. The kind of intense summertime heat that fans the flames of restlessness and longing.

My family's lifestyle was hardly typical, but my parents were honest, responsible people who taught me what was important to them. Conscientious hard work and persistence are rewarding, they said, and in some areas I became a perfectionist. Be considerate of other people's feelings, they urged, and I learned to be kind. Their independence and loyalty to each other I absorbed as a basic way of life. My father spent so much time in Europe, Asia, and on military posts scattered throughout the states, for fifteen years of my parents' forty-five-year marriage they lived apart. My mother believed in self-reliance, faithfulness, and having fun. My father taught me integrity, and gave me the heart of a fighter.

I kept many of my adventures—including Mitchell Brothers— secret from my family to avoid confrontation. My parents were never religious, but they were born in 1910 and had Victorian values. Although they were tolerant and generous with me, the generation gap between us was so vast I shared little understanding with them. Since I grew up in the 50's and early 60's, the mainstream culture and my parents' marriage did not lead me to expect an equitable relationship. My parents hoped I would marry someone safe who would support me, not that I would succeed on my own. Soon the world was alive with experimentation and upheaval, and I was swept up in it. During college, I had a short crazed marriage. I followed my divorce with a few extremist boyfriends, including one who went to federal prison for masterminding a drug-smuggling conspiracy fiasco that involved gunrunning. The last thing I wanted was to be trapped in a conventional marriage in suburbia. I wasn't looking for a virtuous prince on a white horse. I wouldn't have liked him. I wanted a renegade.

~

Friday night, as I walked into the tech booth to give the disc jockey my music, two men wearing baseball caps were out there watching the show. The slender man with a beard reached around me elegantly from the back, to run his hands down the thin crepe of my dress over my body with the most irresistible touch. "Who do we have here?" I heard in a rich low Oklahoma drawl that was confident, relaxed, and full of amused enjoyment. "You're not dancing first, are you?" he asked.

I was crimson. I went down and tried to do a hot show as they hooted and clapped for me, and once in awhile I could hear a self-assured, delighted cackle I knew was his. But by the time I got back upstairs to the near darkness of the tech booth, it was empty. He was gone.

If I ever get a chance to make love to that man, I will, I decided. I had never wanted anyone so much.

The next time I worked he spotted me out in the hall and gave me a charming smile. "Hi," he said. "I'm Art Mitchell."

~

Before the night shift started, another dancer and I brought some take-out food to eat in the O'Farrell's TV room. An attractive man with a mustache appeared. After greeting us with "Hello, ladies, how are you?" he started talking to us about diarrhea and shit. "Please, we're eating," I protested. It was Jim Mitchell. He was having fun with my not knowing he was the boss, and watching our reaction to his rudeness. At best, Jim's sense of humor seemed offbeat.

~

Soon after I started working at Mitchell Brothers my mother died suddenly, from a heart attack. Since my father was in his early seventies, I steeled myself for the future—I felt my survival would soon depend on me alone. I was tired of being adrift and dissatisfied. Use the charm you have, Simone, I told myself. Make some money.

The first dancer that would talk to me was Belladonna. I was different: a little serious, an outsider, an ex-teacher and secretary with an MA in English Lit. from a UC, who didn't drink or get high. But all the women who danced at Mitchell Brothers were there for the same reasons: to make money, and to live in a free, unstructured way.

One night, alone in the dressing room with her, I admitted, "I'm thirty-three."

Tall and striking with shoulder-length straight red hair, Belladonna sounded surprised. "You certainly don't look it. You can do this," she said calmly. "You won't have any problem."

Belladonna did a show dressed as a French maid. She had been *so* stoned on smack a couple of years before, that she took a wrong turn going downstairs and fell through the floor over the cigarette machine. She gave me valuable advice—buy costumes that are shiny and wear more blush.

Clearly, we were no longer in Kansas. The diversity of personalities and backgrounds of the women I danced with was stimulating. We relied on each other for information and support. Working with a bunch of strippers was far more amusing than being locked up in some tame high-rise office.

Because the majority of the customers were white-collar guys who were white or Asian, and tended to tip white women better, most of the dancers were white. For many black dancers, it was harder to earn enough tips at the O'Farrell, although some preferred working there, and did make good money in the audience and in the shows. It was rare for Asian women to apply to work at Mitchell Brothers, but a pragmatic dancer from Thailand was quite popular. Years later she would be involved in organizing dancers to protest policies at clubs, and be a cofounder of the Exotic Dancers Alliance.

Many of the shows amazed me. Justine did a pearl act—she would stuff a long strand of pearls up her pussy with a carefully manicured hand, before getting up and dancing. As a finale, she pulled out the pearls. It was *so* dramatic.

Each performer provided her own costumes and chose her own music. Whether the curtain opened to Rick James's "Super Freak" or Grace Jones's "The Hunter Gets Captured by the Game," as long as we stripped by the end of a two or three song set, almost any choreography was acceptable. Most strippers left on a few accessories throughout their shows—heels plus jewelry, maybe a garter belt and stockings, a boa, or the occasional negligee usually stayed on. I spent a little longer on my makeup and styling my dark brown hair. I picked up a long emerald green gown at an outlet and a burgundy turkey feather boa, wore the two together, and danced to the same tapes for a couple of months. I felt so glamorous.

One of the great things about working as a stripper is that it validates your attractiveness and the impact you can have on people in a way few other jobs are able to do. Pouring individuality and mood into the times you are onstage, while earning a good living working a few shifts each week can be as emotionally fulfilling as it is creative. As you perform hundreds of shows, your self-assurance builds in a positive way. In November, as soon as I felt confident that dancing would bring me a good, steady income, I chose a stage name, "Simone." I told the attorneys I was still working for, that I was quitting, to study art.

I was studying art history and painting, with a loose future plan to go back to more conventional work—at some point. It was fantastic to have enough free time and money to continue going to school. That first year I was at the O'Farrell I was only dancing in the New York show a couple of times a week. My conception of things was not very complete. Because Mitchell Brothers had been busted before, I thought maybe it would happen again. I kept my options open, just in case.

~

When I started working at the theater, I was dating a street artist. I met him on Fisherman's Wharf, when I was selling my drawings and clothing I designed and made. A heavy drinker with a mean streak who wrote poetry and made and sold jewelry, he had constant money problems. Although he had been titillated by the idea of my dancing at Mitchell Brothers, he was too jealous to handle the reality of it. I was changing, becoming stronger and more confident. I stopped seeing him. I was ready for someone different. Someone who could accept the business I had chosen.

~

As I walked past the little dressing room, Art was standing in back of a pretty young woman caressing her shoulders, and both were staring into the mirror at their reflection. There was such a heat to it. I stood transfixed until I realized the room was deserted—everyone had left them alone and I should, too. I never saw her again.

~

One night a handsome black man was walking around upstairs smiling to himself. "See that guy," one of the dancers said to me. "That's Huey Newton." I was impressed. The rebel hero of the Black Panther Party dropped by once in a while to visit Art and Jim.

Writers, politicians, and celebrities in entertainment and sports were intrigued by the mystique of Mitchell Brothers. They came to the theater and were cultivated by Jim, and entertained by Art. The mix of visitors varied over the years, and included people as diverse as: Sammy Davis, Jr.; comedians Penn and Teller; journalists Hunter S. Thompson and Warren Hinckle; California State Senator Quentin Kopp; former Sheriff Richard Hongisto; political consultant Jack Davis; underground cartoonist R. Crumb; the entire U.S.C. football team; and the rock groups Guns N' Roses, Aerosmith and Motley Crue.

The mix of eighty dancers was as unique, and constantly changing. "I've always liked to think that Mitchell Brothers is a place for everyone," Art told me.

Justine's costumes glittered with beads and rhinestones and came from New York. She was dating a plastic surgeon.

Valentine looked like the most glamorous of movie stars from the 1940's, was a fireball on stage, toured in Japan. She drank a lot and got fired a few times for doing handjobs and stuff in the audience.

Although she was twenty-three, Glynis had the slender body of a thirteen-year old, and a sharp sardonic mind. She had grown up in exclusive Pacific Heights.

Gail was tall, blonde, and athletic. She looked as wholesome as Doris Day but had the brash manner of a lady jock.

Chelsea was a rebel who did performance art pieces in little clubs around town once in awhile. She chose her costumes and music to make an eccentric impact.

A lovely brunette from Canada, Rita Ricardo, did professional burlesque shows, and was serious about her career. She wanted to do some porn movies to increase what she would be paid as a feature performer on tour.

Rhonda was an elegant black dancer, who had done movies. She came from a show business family, and had a gracious, warm charm.

Rita and Rhonda were solid, dependable women and would become my closest friends.

Most of the dancers were laughing, drinking, getting wild, and making great money. Girls crawled up on stage and did shows together sometimes. It heated up the customers, and they would tip better. The dancers and the customers were having a good time.

~

One Friday night I was sitting on a guy's lap in the front row getting hugged, when Frank, the Filipino security guard who dressed in a cop outfit, pointed his flashlight at me. "You," I heard, "don't get so friendly with the customers."

I was shocked. I thought that was my job—but in July 1982, the heat was suddenly on. The Mitchells knew that the hotter the dancers were in the audience, the better business was—so there was subtle encouragement to be discreetly wild. But whenever there was legal pressure on the theater, dancers could be punished for behavior that had been encouraged a day or week earlier. Women who lasted learned to adapt quickly, not to question the fairness of the management.

By the next day, none of the dancers were allowed in the audience. The Ultra Room, the original live show at Mitchell Brothers, hadn't had windows for the last couple of years, the customers had been touching the dancers, and vice cops had been coming in with infrared cameras to secretly photograph anything suspicious. They mailed the pictures to Art and Jim and said they were taking them to court. There was to be no touching, the Kopenhagen and live Cine Stage shows were temporarily closed, and windows had to be put back in the Ultra Room. The star booked that week was furious.

From porn stars who became established in the 70's like Marilyn Chambers, Serena, Annette Haven, Annie Sprinkle, CJ Laing and Sharon Mitchell to stars of the 80's and beyond, the list of actresses and strippers who have appeared at Mitchell Brothers is exceptional. Nina Hartley, Erica Boyer, Megan Leigh, and Summer Cummings were O'Farrell dancers before they became stars. Mitchell Brothers provided a variety of erotic entertainment. Some weeks a young starlet would appear, like Traci Lords (who was even younger than the brothers thought) in 1985. Once in awhile the most classic of burlesque strippers, Tempest Storm, would appear. The stars were our high-paid celebrities, and were booked for a one-week stint of a few shows per day. When their week ended, they were gone—usually to perform at another theater or do a movie.

The very first porn star I met was a tough-minded survivor. Since she had a reputation for being an obnoxious drunk she was barred from a lot of hotels in San Francisco, so she lived in the little Ultra Room dressing room when she was appearing at the theater. She'd bring in avocados, and wore a wig so the public wouldn't recognize her when she went out. She tried to sell us fishnet body suits and lingerie she'd bought too much of, and was friendly, lonely, and hard.

As soon as they pulled us out of the audience, we weren't making the tips we needed. We couldn't get off the stage or touch anybody. Business was terribly slow and a bunch of girls just left. Being an optimist, I sensed things would turn around. It was scary, but intriguing. Upstairs between the times we danced on stage, there was absolutely nothing to do.

～

AUGUST 11, 1982

I put on a red chiffon blouse and panties, but I wasn't fully dressed for my show. Artie came down the hall from the tech booth, lipstick marks on his cheek. He was drunk and gave me a look that was warm and inviting.

31

"Red is your color. You're so much of a woman. What have you been doing? How about a kiss?"

I kissed him, passionately. He was surprised. I could have given him the most polite peck on the cheek.

"What can I say? Anytime, any place," he said. "What are you, first?"

"No, I'm on fourth."

"Well, that's some time. Why don't you come back to my office. You know where it's at, don't you?"

I went back and put on some black spandex pants, intimidated by the sign on the door leading out to the offices that said, "Girls beyond this point must be clothed. Jim Mitchell."

Art and Jim shared a large office that doubled as a poolroom and was used for entertaining. The space had a relaxed boys' club feel, with an edgy undercurrent. "What's this bullshit?" Art noticed I had more clothes on than a moment before. "I'm going to lock the door. Would you like a Chivas?"

"Oh, no."

"Can I get you a beer? You don't drink, do you? How about some of this?" He offered some of his Heineken and I declined. "What can I do for you, I'm sure there's something . . . ." He took off his jeans, "I'm going to give you a good screwing, something you've been needing." I stripped off my clothes and we sat on the beige flowered couch. And I went down on him.

Artie looked over at me, "You're gonna be my new girlfriend if you keep this up . . . . Don't hog it baby, I want to fuck you." He leaned forward over me, as I shyly glanced at the vintage clock outlined in blue neon.

On the rug he got into me from the back, and grabbed my hair, pulling my head back, like I was a horse he was riding. "No," I said. No one ever pulled my hair before. He let go. Like an Indy 500

32

winner taking a test drive on a suburban street, he tried out a few of the most basic moves, then stopped. It wasn't earthshaking.

"That's a lot for a daddy like me. I hope I wasn't too hard on you, but you seem like you're in pretty good shape."

Daddy, I thought silently, did he have children? A wife?

Then his tone cooled as he dismissed me, "Well, you have a show to do. You'd better go."

They must have been looking for me. Back in the small dressing room, the house manager Paulie came just to the doorway and saw my dazed expression and my attempt to reconstruct my hair, and he knew.

I did my first show. Then the second. During my last song, Art was yelling and he came down to get me. "I've seen some hot shows but that was really hot." He followed me up the stairs to the dressing room. He stared at a heavy-set dancer in the shower close by for quite a while before she saw him and faked a low scream. Coming up in back of me, he slipped his hand under the full skirt of my nylon dress. I wanted him. "Have you ever seen my dark room?" Art took me by the hand into the hallway and into the stuffy, hot editing room. He turned on a standard-looking red light bulb. I had no idea my life was about to change forever.

"Did you think you'd be getting more of this today?"

"I thought I might."

After we started, he intuitively turned me around, and put me down on the floor. Athletic and strong, Art had a rare reverence for sex mixed with cool detachment, that gave him a brilliant instinct for it. I had met my match.

" . . . You're just in heaven with a hot cock in you, aren't you?"

This time the sex was rough and flawless. Art took me down in the most masterful, devastating way. After awhile he was yelling. We had made so much noise the girls in the next room had to have known. After getting dressed I said, "Well, I guess I should go dance. I'll see you later." I kissed him deeply and Art's mouth was still open when I quit. "You're a lot of fun," I said.

"So are you. You're so beautiful," he said. "I'm gonna have to come over and see you. I know you live somewhere in the city."

I touched his arm and looked cautiously out the door, as Art laughed lowly, with relaxed light-hearted grace. The general manager Vince saw me as I left. He looked amused.

After I fastened my rhinestone necklace, and draped my fluffy pink feather boa over one shoulder of my new beaded costume, I was almost ready for stage. Some dancer I didn't know well said to me, "Don't you just hate that man sometimes. He just takes what he wants. Tell the DJ. He knows how it is."

In a beautiful post-orgasmic haze, I missed the tinge of jealousy in her voice.

At the beginning of the next night shift, when I took my place in the chorus line to Olivia Newton-John's "Let's Get Physical," Art was up there watching. I was so happy I glowed. When he came through the dressing room someone asked about the court case, "How's it going?"

"We don't know. We can stay out of jail, probably, we have a couple of appeals going."

Art gave me a wink and said, "The hottest thing about you is you're so real."

❧

In a couple of weeks, we were back in the audience getting tips. The dancers had to wear bodysuits or tights plus lingerie as their audience costume. Even though the rules were stricter, business picked up for the brothers, and the girls were making money.

I went up to this young blond white guy in jeans and asked if he wanted company. Pulling out his wallet so I would see the bunch of bills inside he said, "Sure, I'll try some of that, how much does it cost?"

"We usually stay about a minute for a dollar." I sat down with him, he gave me one dollar and grabbed at my breasts. "No, you can't do that, we have to be really careful because there's a case going on," I said.

"What does my dollar buy me, then, what can I do? My dollar doesn't buy anything then, does it?"

"Yes it does. I can sit here with you and you can have my company."

"What's that worth, NOTHING!" he was angry.

"Oh, come on." I got up and walked away.

A few minutes later, the guard called me out in the hall. One of the house managers, Paulie, stood there, mad. "Listen, this customer told me you told him it costs a dollar. You'll have to tell your story to Vince on Monday and if you EVER get caught soliciting again, YOU'RE OUT and it'll be better for everybody!"

This was my first confrontation with anyone in a year at Mitchell Brothers. Paulie's point of view hardly seemed enlightened.

Upstairs thirty minutes later, Paulie looked calmer, "The guy was an asshole and he was way out of line with Gail."

"I'm sorry and I won't let it happen again."

After that, the guard kept flashlighting me for sitting with guys longer than three minutes. It made me nervous.

When I told Belladonna I got in trouble, she said she always solicits everyone.

Her scar was healing. Belladonna and her boyfriend were playing with razor blades about a month before. She got this horrible long gash on the inside of her wrist. To cover it, Belladonna was borrowing one of my long black gloves.

~

Harvey, who I sat with when I first started dancing, started mailing two or three creepy letters a week to me at the theater. In the spring when he told me God talked to him through the radio, I stopped sitting with Harvey. By September he believed he was telepathically communicating with me, that I loved him, and was destined to marry him. When he came into Mitchell Brothers, I avoided him, worried about what Harvey, now crazed, might do.

Harvey was especially upsetting to me because my ex-husband had gone nuts and joined the Jehovah's Witnesses months before I left him. When I was eighteen, very naive, romantically idealistic, and dying to leave home, I met my ex-husband. He was serious, quiet, seemed intriguing.

After our wedding, I opened the refrigerator in the house we moved into, to find wilted flowers from a funeral held for the woman who lived there before me. It was a grim, cold house. Without joy. Especially for anyone so young.

Among many sources of torment, my ex-husband wasn't sure if he wanted to be straight or gay. Eventually he took to praying, even before the infrequent times we were having sex. "Oh, God, take these images away from me!" he would cry. Towards the end, he began hiding my birth control pills and molding a life-size statue of Christ for our living room, out of chicken wire and plaster. He was one of those mean-spirited yahoos who turned on in the 60's and then strangely became holier than thou.

In the three years I spent with him, I developed a great deal of tolerance—for his depressed moods. It was his theatrical outbursts, shattering the windows in our bedroom, slicing my skirt into tiny pieces, breaking the canvas I painted of a bird, flying away, that terrified me as they began to happen more often and became more dramatic. When he tried to stop me from finishing college, I filed for divorce. The night I left, he was beating on our sectional, screaming that his twenty-one year-old innocent wife was the Whore of Babylon.

"Please don't admit my wife," he wrote to schools I was applying to after I left him. "Her pursuing a graduate degree is against my wishes."

Even though we hadn't been happy together, for five years after I left, my ex-husband followed me all around the area where I was living. Before there were anti-stalking laws, at night he peered in at me through windows like a peeping Tom. He mailed a ton of simple-minded religious material to me. At first I felt sorry for him. Five years later, I hated his guts and moved out of the valley to hopefully lose him forever.

By the time this ordeal ended, the idea of marriage was tainted for me. I was not at all eager to settle into a self-sacrificing career as a schoolteacher either, and was more than ready to enjoy the pleasures of life.

After living in San Francisco for awhile, I was almost glad my ex-husband had been weird. If I had married someone a little nicer, would I still be trapped in some suburb, never to fall into the pornographic talons of the Mitchell brothers, and find my true destiny?

～

In the dressing room, Chelsea put on a black vinyl mask and began cutting it away so it would show more of her eyes and eye makeup. "Could I rob a bank in this?" she asked." You must be in about the same bag as I am. I don't want to go back. You don't want to go back to some straight job, do you?"

"No. No," I said.

"The reason I'm doing this is because at least there's money in it. But in a way I need a job as a file clerk, where I can just limbo out."

"I've tried that. I worked in insurance. It was the worst nine months of my life," I said. "At least when really awful things have happened to me I wasn't bored."

Chelsea laughed. "I sat with a guy tonight who said, Gee, I think you're too smart for me," she said. "Most men are not that bright—especially the men who come in here. Intelligence is a *feminine* quality."

Every shift brought a different set of people into the audience. Some musicians would drift in after playing at the Great American Music Hall next door. That evening, a young guy was telling the dancers he was John Hammond.

We speculated he was a roadie pretending to be a big shot. In time, John Hammond's reputation would continue to grow—as an acclaimed acoustic blues guitar player and vocalist, and a Grammy-winner.

A friendly regular customer who was Italian came in. He was always cheerful and generous. I talked to him for half an hour. A handsome Chinese man in his thirties, who had an import business on Pier 39, was there entertaining a guest.

I sat with a very solid, heavy-set man, in his early forties. Rigid-looking. He said he was from out of town, but he'd gone to San Francisco State. It surprised him, or maybe he didn't even believe me, that I had an MA in English. I had more education than this guy, and he was teaching theater at a junior college. How ironic. He acted afraid to be seen in a place like this, but was curious enough to come in, anyway.

While I was dancing, I blew a kiss to a sheep farmer I'd been talking to. Later he said, "Thanks for doing that. That's the first recognition I've ever gotten from a stage."

CHAPTER 2:
Doing Dracula

OCTOBER 1982

Early in the chilly fall evening, Art came into our crowded dressing room and said he had been fishing. Glynis said she could tell, he looked very "sportiff." I slipped into my blue spandex costume and did the chorus line. When I was upstairs again kneeling at my locker, he came and stood in back of me and asked, "You don't really want to do that, do you?" seeming a little drunk.

Art led me to the basement, way down at the bottom of the O'Farrell. Old signs and pieces of various things were laying around down there. It was gritty and dirty and he took one of the old velvet theater seats and plunked it down, "That's for your knees." Then he said, "You taught at a prison, didn't you?"

"Yes. It was an adventure." Thirty-five hundred male inmates— including Sirhan Sirhan, Dan White, and serial killer Juan Corona— were confined there, mostly for armed robbery, murder, and rape. Since a riot was expected, the prisoners were locked down just before Christmas. For three weeks the teachers worked in the cellblocks as back-up guards. I will never forget being there, watching guards cuff inmates to the railing on the tiers, while they searched their cells. Forbidden possessions were hurled into a dumpster below; choice items were stolen. It was the underside of the American dream. The word "prison" reminds me of black teardrop tattoos and despair, but it also makes me remember dignity, strength, and survival. I couldn't bear working there, though. Prisons produce so much tragedy. I'm too open-minded, too caring, for electric gates, lockdowns, and the system.

Over our heads was the New York Live stage. Gail was dancing to "Eminence Front" by the Who, a glittering song with a relentless beat.

I took off my costume. Art unzipped his pants but still had on a down vest and his shirt, too, soft flannel. "When you were there, did you get fucked in the prison?"

"No."

"But you wanted to?"

"Yes."

Ever the outlaw, Art had no trouble envisioning cellblocks. Against the backdrop of the stark concrete walls, suddenly I had the sense that he and I were playing out our own private scene in a movie—or in a novel! Art has a more developed sense of fantasy than anyone I've ever met, I thought. It was like my own.

"Who did you really want to fuck in there," his voice echoed and gained momentum. "I bet those guys they just looked at you and wanted to fuck you. Who did you really want to fuck? Was it a big guy? Do you know how big those guys' cocks are? Did you want to fuck more than one of them?"

"Yeah. A couple of them."

"Yeah, ten of them," he said.

"All of them," I added, looking into Art's intense eyes and thinking of him, not them.

In the meantime we were trying everything, struggling against the old theater seat, clutching a wood beam trying to balance. Art built up his fantasy but was just too wasted to enjoy it. "Do you know why you did so well there?" he said. "Because they could all tell that you wanted to fuck them. You're really warm down there where a woman should be, and you're one of the hottest women, one of the most radical women that I've ever known."

40

"I find that hard to believe," I said.

"I had a dream that you really wanted to fuck this black guy in the prison . . . . Is that true?"

"Yes," I said.

"Is this guy still in prison?"

"No."

"Did you fuck him after he got out?"

"No. I didn't really want the Black Guerrilla Family to know my address, so it seemed better to let it go."

"Yeah, that's probably wise . . . . This is really a dirty place to fuck, isn't it? You're so out of place here, you're such a lady . . . . You're so out of place here."

He sounded intrigued. A tiny minority of strippers have postgraduate degrees. Many have some college, but some never finished high school. For a dancer at the O'Farrell, I had an exotic background.

Art's brown eyes were so warm and compelling. His half-aroused condition was a tease, but didn't deter him from pleasing me. After awhile he said, "The sex that I have with you, it's always really different and really neat and bizarre."

Since I tend to take flattery with a grain of salt, I thought he probably said that to a lot of other women—exotic, sophisticated women that I imagined were part of his life.

While I waited in the tech booth to go on, Ron talked to me. Ron was a friend of the Mitchells who hung out and watched the shows, and was part of the security. Like Jim and Art, he was in his late thirties. He looked a little like Elvis Presley.

"Hey, did you see Art? He told me I'm getting too old for this kind of thing." Ron told me about the Ultra Room S and M show going on this week, "They've got a coffin in there. Say—that's a bizarre thing, isn't it. Wouldn't that be a once-in-a-lifetime chance, to fuck in a coffin?"

"Oh, I don't know if I could handle that," I said.

"But think of it, though, that's an Artie Mitchell type of thing, you know, with the candlelight—that would really turn Artie on," Ron smiled. "The Old Master . . ." He pondered for a moment. "Maybe you could have a three-way in this coffin," Ron suggested. "Uh, you could borrow it."

"Borrow it? But aren't those things heavy?"

"Well, there's a whole bunch of handles on the side."

We laughed.

The more I thought about it later, the more I was aching to do it. It would just be so scandalous. I wanted to fuck Art in that coffin. It would be a true literary event. Something very few people would ever do. I would be terrified though, if the lid closed.

～

I went in early to ask Vince if Gail and I could do a Halloween theme in the Kopenhagen. He said yes. Later I asked the Ultra Room girls if I could borrow their coffin or rent it because we were going to do a Dracula show!

At that time, dancers who worked the lucrative Kopenhagen and Ultra Room shows were booked for one week or three-day stints as feature performers. Before being booked in these rooms, dancers had to have experience working the New York Live show and become comfortable interacting with the audience. A dancer who had worked the room shows already would break in someone who never had. Gail had needed a partner, and asked me to do the show with her.

A customer had just given me an album he was promoting, of the most beautiful electronic music, called "Vortex." I wanted to use it in our show.

Justine gave me a note from Harvey, "I know you're really disappointed that I wasn't here last night, I know every thought you have. Please call me tomorrow night, Harvey."

It was so irritating. I didn't know how to stop him.

Valentine said I should call him up a few times about 4:00 or 5:00 in the morning and say, "Hey, Motherfucker, I feel like busting a nut. You got your dick out?" That would do it.

Glynis said she's going to law school, taking nine units. One night a customer followed her all the way home. "This really isn't fair," she said to him. "You can watch me dancing. I have to keep my private life *separate!*" Then she told him a lie—that she was married and her husband was in their apartment waiting for her—and managed to get inside.

～

Mistress Sarah and Sonia Summers were in the Ultra Room for the last night of their weeklong booking. I wanted to take my first look at the room, and see how they used the coffin.

The Ultra Room's black leatherette walls were trimmed with chrome studs, and a chrome trapeze hung from the ceiling over the deep red carpeting. Customers were watching the show from individual booths surrounding the room, slipping money through the new tip slots if they wanted the dancers to come to their window. In the middle of the room, lay the coffin.

Sonia sat on the outside and opened it up. Sarah climbed out, wearing black leather chaps and a garter belt, a cape over a black leather jacket, looking more like a guy than any dancer I'd ever seen at Mitchell Brothers. Mistress Sarah had a hard, scary, intense expression. Sonia was pale, with jet-black hair, and looked sweet and adoring.

Sarah did all the ordering around, and Sonia all the obeying. Strapping Sonia into a heavy black leather bondage harness, Sarah swung her, holding a candle under her ass, not burning her, but close. Then she let her down. Sonia crawled around on her hands and knees with a lit candle up her ass, a rose in her teeth. Sarah rode her like a horse, hitting Sonia in the butt with a black leather paddle, not real vigorously. It slapped but left no red marks. Sarah pissed in a wineglass. Sonia drank the whole thing. Then they ate a little bit of pussy. A couple of Japanese put dollars through the slots. Never even once did Sarah and Sonia go up to the windows. They were totally into each other.

After seeing their show, I hated to go over and pick up a coffin from them. Gail didn't want to use it at all.

If I got it on with Art in the coffin at Mitchell Brothers and *anyone* found out, what would they think of me, I wondered. Would there be enough privacy to do it?

A coffin is so heavy and so obvious as to what it is, it would be impossible to quietly move it somewhere. What a wild idea! After that night I thought it would be better to abandon it, although I hated to.

If we did something so very outrageous together, I would get closer to Artie, I thought. Then I wondered if I was deluding myself.

Harvey the Nut sent me a letter, a card and a box of apricot roses with baby's breath. I told the house manager working that night, "Keep them in the lobby."

"Do you want to take one for your hair?"

"No." At the end of the night a couple of the dancers took some of the roses, beautiful roses really, home. I couldn't stand to look at them.

My friend Greg, a writer I'd known since before I was a dancer, came in to Mitchell Brothers sometimes to watch the shows. Greg was going to phone Harvey's mother and say he was my fiancé. Try to get together with mother for a cup of tea to explain the situation. Get Harvey out of our lives. Greg joked about going over to Harvey's house, getting into a 69 on Harvey's rag rug. We could also send him presents, like maybe shit.

Gail said everybody that goes to Mitchell Brothers is nuts, which I still think is carrying things a bit too far.

～

"Marilyn Chambers has the hottest show running," Ron said. "She gets a thousand dollars a day. Marilyn's very quiet and puts all her energy into her shows. Her boyfriend techs them, and there's a lot of touching that goes on. They never had one customer ask for their money back." Among many feats, Marilyn put seven golf balls on a string up her ass. "Marilyn is totally dependent on her manager/boyfriend Chuck Traynor," Ron added. "He is her total security blanket."

"What do you do when something happens to the Master?" I asked.

"You put an ad in the paper 'Master Wanted.'"

"I think that coffin idea is so hot, but I don't want to borrow it from Mistress Sarah."

Ron laughed.

"Can you imagine returning it with a little sperm inside?" I said.

"Yeah, what could you do. Could you take the coffin to Tijuana and get it reupholstered with roll and tuck?"

～

At home I finished off the props for the show. I trimmed a bridal bouquet of wine-colored flowers with black lace, sequins and

45

miniature bats and placed a spider on the center artificial red rose, which, oddly enough, was given to me by Harvey. It fit right into the middle, perfectly. I made my skeleton a necklace of garlic, and attached a great big pink cock between its legs.

Gail had a dildo that looked like an ice cream cone. She wanted to use it in our show. Very inappropriate—not the least bit Gothic!

I felt apprehensive. We'd be competing with Erica Boyer, Wicked Wanda, and Princess Bethany in the Ultra Room. It wouldn't be easy, but it would still be fun, and God, I hoped it would be a good show!

The music sounded good. There was a pause in one song. That's when I would give the skeleton a little bit of head and use Greg's line: "*Come* back and satisfy me. Come *back* and satisfy me. Come back and satisfy *me*!"

Named for the world-famous shows of Copenhagen, Denmark, the Kopenhagen Lounge was advertised as an intimate European setting. The undercover Vice cops would be there because it had just been reopened, and we would have to be real careful about asking for tips. If you gave a little show first, when they put the money down on the floor, it was supposedly cool to pick up the money and put it in a basket, or in your stocking. Otherwise, the guys tended to pick up the money again. How rotten!

Gail said she usually takes the first couple of songs to undress and, about the third song gets totally naked and starts working it for tips. During the last song, you have to get into the love act or whatever. I was just going to see how it worked out. When they're not tipping, Gail said she goes up to somebody she's sure isn't a Vice, either somebody Asian or a real old guy, and says, "Tipping is permitted."

∽

Gail and I were booked in the Kopenhagen for three days in a row. It was exhausting, each day we were at the theater for twelve hours and did ten half-hour shows. The Kopenhagen was a small mirrored room that got crowded with people, especially at night. It was impossible to dance as freely as on the stage.

To get to the backstage entrance of the Kopenhagen we went down a staircase. Curtains of heavy velvet hung over the doorway in the back, with a little square hole you could look through into the room, to see who's in there, and what's going on. The senior DJ who had hired me, Rob, was our tech the first show. He had on a silly witch's hat, carried a broom. We made our entrance—Gail dressed as Dracula; I wore a black lace bustier with a mini skirt, black ostrich boa, and carried my bouquet. Against the wall hung my skeleton with the garlic and its big pink plastic cock. I felt embarrassed when Greg came in for the first show and Gail and I hadn't worked out any dialogue.

When we first talked about the format, I said because I was going to be the victim, I should go in first and cower, then she could come in and surprise me. But Gail said, "I've got top billing, and the guys will expect me to come in first." Big deal.

"How're you doing, Slave?" Rob joked at the end of our first show. The newspaper ad called us "Mistress Gail and Her Slave Simone."

I laughed.

After the second show I ran into Vince, who asked, "How's the room going?"

"O.K."

He looked at me quizzically, with a certain amount of amusement, "Well, who are you, are you the aggressor, or the victim?"

"I'm the victim."

"We're all victims," Vince said.

When I was copying down my schedule in the hall, I heard Artie's seasoned, bright-toned wolf whistle, just as I had turned away.

Later, as I was walking down the hallway near the editing room, Art and this woman with long flowing brown hair past her hips, who must have been his wife, walked by in the opposite direction. She was carrying an infant. I said, "Hi," but I wasn't looking at him, so much as at her. She had this intense expression of anxiety, fear, love, hatred. In love with this impossible man. It must be tremendously difficult to be married to Artie, I thought. He had access to all these women who were loose, including myself. He was acting so lordly.

A little later they were standing in the hall. Gail went out and said, "Babies are great. I had one but she lives with her father. I just can't handle it." I could not bring myself to go out there and say "Hi," because I'd been fucking Artie. Gail hadn't since last year. I thought her remark was sad.

As the night went on we kept decreasing what we were doing, because we were getting less and less money each show. Gail leaned out the door and said, "Get us out of here as quick as you can." and they cut the music.

My beautiful Bride of Dracula bouquet was getting more and more flat. We stepped on it by accident occasionally in the dark, after the first part of the show. Some pushy new nineteen-year-old with ivory skin and a classic black panther tattoo on her ass had admired my skeleton's cock, "This thing would be really great in my act, you know."

Kenny, the DJ working that night, put on a tape of a woman screaming. Justine said it was some woman Kenny was kissing who couldn't stand it. We all laughed.

Walking around barefoot, in just a robe, when it was quiet upstairs over the weekend, I felt connected to the O'Farrell. It must have had something to do with having such bewitching sex with Art.

Both Gail and I were very tired. Just before sunset, I went out and got us two bacon cheeseburgers from Caesar's, a block and a half away into the Tenderloin, on Geary. I figured it was still early enough to be relatively safe. Later, from upstairs I watched a little of the film playing in the Cine Stage, *Dracula Exotica*, starring Jamie Gillis and two incredibly flexible brunettes.

Gail liked working out at the gym and watching Jane Fonda movies—because Jane Fonda always looked so good. She was in love with Rob, but unhappy because he dated other dancers, too. Gail said she wanted to do some porn movies and go on tour. She was waiting to see if this place was going to become a private club, where there would be more sexual things happening in the audience, like it used to be.

~

I told Greg I took the dildo off the skeleton both nights during our show and carried it home with me, because everything that was detachable got ripped off, at Mitchell Brothers. Even if you were friends with somebody, they still stole from you. Then I described Art coming in with his wife Friday. Greg said he bet Artie's wife wishes every time he goes to the O'Farrell she could take off his cock and keep it locked in her jewelry box.

I got indelible lipstick prints on the hard rubber cock I had on the skeleton; impossible to get it off. It was licorice color, dark red lipstick.

With a shy smile the Count throws open the door to Castle Dracula for the curious woman waiting outside, revealing hundreds of glittering candles, illuminating the depths of his world with the promise of sharing it passionately with his lover.

Vampires and witches romantically represent people who stand outside society, and the power they can possess, as outsiders. Gail said she was tired of doing Dracula. I wasn't. When our Kopenhagen ended, I knew I had found something I would always love doing: creating and performing shows. I was having the time of my life.

~

Valentine died in Japan last week, Rhonda told me. They called her last employer, Vince, and said Valentine ate some soy oil and went

49

into shock. She did have asthma and some allergies, but how awful. It was hard to imagine Valentine, of all people, gone. Rhonda thought she was knocked off. She heard it had happened before, over there.

Right before my second show, I looked down from the tech booth and Harvey the nut had come in. He was looking up. I knew he could see me, the bastard. I gave him the finger, but I didn't know if he could see because I had a black glove on and was standing in the dark. Then I mouthed, "Fuck you, fuck you."

I went down and danced, knowing Harvey was out there, staring straight at me. I tried to avoid looking at him directly. When I went in the audience, I sat on the opposite side from Harvey. Gail sat with him, he was quivering. Finally he split.

"This is the feudal system," Glynis observed. "There is such a hierarchy at Mitchell Brothers. The girls are the slaves, the peons, the surfs. Paulie is the overseer. Jim and Art are the kings. If someone gets yelled at, they have to yell at whoever is below them."

Gail went into the toilet stall and yelled out really loud, "WHO LEFT THEIR COCAINE IN HERE?" Everyone laughed. Drugs were part of their scene—not mine.

I haven't smoked marijuana since the 70's—but I loved it in college. Of course, an essential part of the "new" countercultural lifestyle was the search for a fresh, sensual, mystical revelation. In grad school, I took a special interest in the eighteenth century poet William Blake, who wrote, "If the doors of perception were cleansed, every thing would appear to man as it is, infinite." Jim Morrison's band called themselves the Doors, and captured the spirit of the time in songs like "Break on Through (To the Other Side)." Drugs were considered a catalyst. Moderately, I smoked marijuana, hashish, and tried opium. As a result, my creativity increased and I became more perceptive and open-minded. But after the real nightmare of my marriage, getting high made me too paranoid. Acid I had by mistake when it was dropped into punch at a party, angel dust on a joint before anybody realized how weird it was. I haven't tried alcohol since I began getting sick from low blood sugar when I was twenty-five. Sex became precious, my only passionate indulgence.

When I was thirteen my mother told me a dark family secret. In the 1890s someone from the French/Cherokee branch of my father's family committed suicide. One of my father's brothers inherited the pistol. In 1938, after a military ball he attended with his wife, he went home alone and used it to blow his brains out. He was thirty-two. My father's other brother inherited the gun. One year later, he used it to kill himself. Before long my mother found my father polishing the weapon, admiring it. She convinced him to go with her to a bridge, and throw it into the Sacramento River. "Don't talk about this to your father," she warned me.

This story was so somber and mysterious I knew it was best to keep it secret, except from friends who became very close to me. To me, it meant there was something vulnerable about my family, some tendency towards malcontent, and brave but impulsive action. I came to believe that drinking and getting high could only open me up to misfortune.

My reasons for not doing drugs or drinking were so unique and personal, I never chose friends because they didn't drink or get high. Anyone in my generation who never had gotten high would have been too alien for me to relate to.

CHAPTER 3:
Why Fools Fall in Love

NOVEMBER 16, 1982

As I went through the door to go upstairs Paulie was hovering around by the safe, singing to himself, tongue-in-cheek, "Why Do Fools Fall in Love." It was playing close by, in the Ultra Room.

Vince gave me three more letters from Harvey and said, "Have you sent that guy anything yet? You ought to send him something, like a picture cut out of a magazine or a pair of panties. Tell him, 'Thanks a lot but you're moving to Florida.'"

When I got to the dressing room, Art grabbed me. Nick, his friend who was a doctor, stood nearby. Art asked, "You don't have to go on for awhile yet, do you?"

"No." It was 5:25 p.m.

"Well, come on down, we want to interview you. We have a special interview room for the star."

I laughed. "Let me put this stuff away."

I had become pretty uninhibited and had experimented a bit with sex before I became a dancer. I wasn't uncomfortable being with Art in this situation. I walked out with them down the steps past the tech booth where the DJ was. They seemed pleasantly high and were joking, "Let's take her to Puerto Vallerta." And, "Yeah, we want to do a special UPI interview with you." I laughed. We went down the staircase. "You know, I don't usually like jeans, but look at her ass in those," Art said. "Doesn't she look nice?" The green and amber beaded rattlesnake pattern belt I had just made gleamed against the denim.

Nick wasn't saying a lot. He was not that interested.

"We got a cushion for your ass," Art said. We walked towards the back and there was a big foam mattress. He threw it down. "We gotta close the door first," he added, and blocked the space off with a big piece of board.

"The only thing I'm gonna have on is my boots." Art had knee-high rubber boots on. "We'll double-cock you before your show."

I slipped off my clothes and sat down on the mat. Nick removed his jacket. Art took off everything but his shirt, but it took him awhile to pull his boots back on. Nick said, "Art has to get his boots on first."

I lay back on the mat, Nick was up by my head and Art facing me. In knee-high rubber he looked charming. Art directed, "Give him a little head," and went down on me. In a couple of minutes he moved next to Nick and said to me, "Put both cocks in your mouth. Suck on both cocks." Nick wasn't into it. Art was, and in a moment he was on top of me on the mat. "Look, look at how she's already used to me," he said. It felt so good. Then he turned me over onto my knees, and I was dizzy from the movement. In a few minutes Art was yelling loudly.

When I looked up, Nick, who was Art's sidekick and our audience, seemed vaguely hostile. Over our heads all this time we could hear loud pounding and music, somebody was dancing hard, like it was their last dance ever. Artie laughed.

He loved performing, even for an audience of one, and it was obvious how much I liked him; he needed that to be satisfied. Getting dressed he said to Nick, "God, I haven't seen you for awhile, old buddy. You must have been pissed."

"I was just really busy," Nick answered.

"No, you must have been pissed, because you didn't even call."

Art looked at me. "If I'm a witch . . ." he paused. "No, I mean, if I'm a warlock, you're a witch," and he drew me over to him and kissed me, so warmly. As we were getting ready to go he said, "Hey, if I get a divorce, would you marry me?"

I looked back at him and said, "You don't really want to get a divorce, do you?"

"Whether I want to get a divorce, that isn't the question," Art replied. "The question is do I want another marriage."

Now, this encounter seems like a test of my openness. Then, I was focused on the sexual energy between Art and me, and I wanted more of him, not a wedding ring.

On the way upstairs we passed the gazebo. Belladonna came out and teased, "I'm really tight, you know."

Art laughed, "Don't come on to me with that, after what I've just had!"

I walked back into the dressing room happy, but thinking all the women knew and might feel funny about me, but I guess none of them had noticed. Later, Belladonna gave me a smile, like maybe she knew, but it didn't matter.

∼

In recent years, it has been fashionable—especially for women—to express disapproval of the free, experimental attitude toward sex that was prevalent before AIDS. This experimentation was made possible when reliable birth control became widely available, for the first time ever. The sexual revolution was part of the colorful ferment of the era when I was a young adult, and it played a major role in liberating women from traditional stereotypes. Of course, it is unrealistic to claim that women never experienced inequities and abuses when they experimented with sex. Sometimes, even I did. But my being highly sexual was part of what brought me to the charged atmosphere of the O'Farrell to begin with. It attracted me to Artie, and linked us together. It also had a beneficial effect on my becoming an independent woman. I live in a different century and place now, but to say I regret my experience during this turbulent time would be false to who I am, and to the spirit of this book.

~

Driving in to work, I felt quite turned on but afraid. When I got ready to walk in I thought, What if Vince or the other guys in the office heard about the other night?

I felt that wouldn't be good, and I started to worry. In spite of what they may say, most men are afraid of women who are sexually uninhibited. I wondered if Art was.

How did he feel about me, I asked myself. I didn't want to flaunt my affair with him since I knew he was married.

Art was in the dressing room trying to hug Justine, and she was trying to keep away from him. He picked up Rhonda and was carrying her on his back. She said, "Take me to heaven."

He put his arms around Gail and me at the same time. Then he walked over to my side and said, "How are you today, are you on fire, like usual?" and moved towards me, like he was going to kiss me. Because the dressing room was filled with people, I felt funny about kissing him in there. I gave him a hug instead. "Or is that just for show?" Art asked.

"No," I said, meaning it wasn't just for show. But I think he took it as no, I didn't want him. So Art turned around and left and I felt just awful.

I hoped he would come back and he didn't. I even looked out the door near the offices a couple of times and his office was all locked up. I wondered what he thought. I kept wishing I had kissed him, even if everyone had been watching.

I had to go onstage to do the chorus line and as I was doing it, I fucked up. At the very end when we were supposed to back into the line and start kicking, I turned around instead. I'm in love, I kept thinking. I'm in love with Art Mitchell. I felt totally powerless. He was in control of my whole surroundings and everything. I was in love with somebody that I probably couldn't have. Anyway, we finished our number and I fell down the steps backstage.

At work that night I thought only of Art, and when I got home I sat in my car thinking, I would give anything for a real crack at this guy. I wanted him so terribly.

Yet it seemed crazy. Artie was a trickster. I would have fucked him in Times Square, there was something so hot about him. And yet I knew, that even if you *really* want something, that doesn't mean you're going to get it.

~

"Well, this is the big day for the boys, they were getting their toothbrushes ready," Ron said while I waited to go on. "The judge had to rule on the case today."

"Jesus, was that today. I didn't know."

"Yeah, they haven't been to jail for thirteen years. They're biting their fingernails."

Art and Jim were nervous about the court ruling for good reason. In an effort to close the O'Farrell, late in 1980 the District Attorney had charged the brothers with violating the state Red Light Abatement Law, and they were ordered to prohibit lewdness and prostitution at the theater. The judge had just ruled that Art and Jim were in contempt of this order, sentencing them to six months in jail and fining them $62,000 each.

I had forgotten my shoes and had to borrow Gail's too-large white pumps. It was terrible dancing in them. The audience felt different. A lot of people came in because of the article in the newspaper—thrill-seeker types who had never been in before, who weren't tipping that much.

Frank the security guard said, "It's too bad the brothers have to suffer because of the mistakes some of the girls made."

A regular who was always friendly, never grabby, was there that night. I told him what Frank had said. "Oh, no, he must be very servile, a real company man. He's flashlighting you much more than anyone else, he must have something against you," he said. "Around him, only say the most subservient stuff."

I've never been able to say anything I don't believe. Because of Harvey the nut I couldn't completely get on Frank's bad side, though, because I needed his protection.

"Dancers, even if they're not politically sophisticated, are basically radical people," the regular continued. In his snazzy hat and coat with a slight film of Tenderloin dust, he looked like an urban hipster from the Beat Generation. "Dancers know the world is governed by assholes, trying to make it better for other assholes, and they can see beyond it."

Some customers told me they really believed in the theater and that it wasn't hurting anybody. A lot of people felt that way. It was fascinating. I wanted to be there for whatever happened. Since now I cared about Art, I cared about the O'Farrell.

The dancers and theater staff took up a collection for a wreath for Valentine. It was a heart, made out of purple carnations with yellow roses. The ribbon had silver glittery lettering, "In Memory of Valentine, Gone But Not Forgotten, Eternal Friends."

Frank tried to deliver the wreath to her father, who was doubly in shock—he hadn't known his daughter was a stripper. He wouldn't accept it because it came from notorious Mitchell Brothers, so it had ended up in the O'Farrell's TV room. "This is where the wreath belongs," someone said, "if it's in her memory."

The first dancer on stage was dressed the way she came to work, in a motorcycle jacket, leather pants, bizarre sunglasses, snakeskin cowboy boots, looking a little like a guy. For her next set she wore a body suit that must have been funky, because she tore it off herself. During her last song they dimmed the lights, she put matches on her nipples and set them on fire. Afterwards, I asked, "Did you have to blow them out or did they go out?"

"They went out."

It looked great. Somebody else used to do it, but it didn't look that good, because she weighed one hundred-fifty.

～

When I first walked in, Chelsea said a lot of really boring things have been happening.

"Oh, what?"

"Power trips."

The dominatrix who did the S/M show in the Ultra Room recently was out in the hall, lipstick kiss on her cheek, dressed from head to toe in black leather.

"It's Mistress Sarah. She is just practically swaggering around, on some kind of incredible power trip. It is just fucking absurd. She's also wearing a whip. It's ridiculous to have somebody who's watching us wearing a whip!"

Mistress Sarah had been hired as a tech—there were always three or four on the staff—so she was learning to do the lights and music for all the shows, and to be a security person. The other techs were pretty mellow, but not Sarah. She was after me a lot, to go downstairs into the audience, when in five minutes I'd have to come back up to the dressing room to get ready in time for my show. When I was trying to relax right before I went on she was really bugging me, and saying over the microphone while Gail was dancing, "Do it baby, I wish I was down there with you." in this odd country voice she had. I was joking with the guys in the audience about it, "Imagine, hire a sadist."

Art walked up to me and said, "How's your personal life?"

58

"I'm taking some art classes, I almost have enough classes to get a real job. Not that I'm going to do that."

"I understand that. I think you should always keep learning new things. Last year I learned to drive eighteen wheel vehicles, and this year I learned to tie fishnets. I like working with my hands."

"I do, too."

"And with my tongue. And with my mouth."

"Yeah," I leaned forward, wanting to kiss him and he moved back a little.

"Why don't you come back to my office?"

Some big friend of the Mitchells wearing a rain slicker came up and said, "How are you doing, killer?" Art pulled him aside. After talking to him, Art disappeared.

It was really a slow night. Harvey the nut was there. It made me nervous.

"Maybe it would help if I said something more to Harvey," I said to Glynis. "He's still writing tons, even though I'm mailing the letters back." I had gotten an official looking rubber stamp to mark them with "Return to Sender."

"You ought to threaten him with a restraining order."

I mentioned this idea to Frank the security guard.

"No, that wouldn't be good, that would put him on the defensive. You've got to bullshit a little. Say something like you're married, and you enjoy his attention but your husband sees all these letters coming, and you don't want it to disturb your personal life. Be polite, but tell him like that. But don't go over to him right now, right after you talk to me, wait."

I moved around the audience, talking to different guys. Then for the first time in months, I approached Harvey, "I really wish you'd stop coming in here and bothering me so much. I'm in love with someone.

I'm involved with somebody. I'm not interested in you at all. I wish you would stop. You've *gotta stop this.*"

"You love me," Harvey said.

"No, I don't. I HATE YOU."

"How long do you want me to stop for, forever?"

"YEAH."

"Why do you read the letters?"

"I DON'T. I mail them back to you."

I was so mad. I turned away from Harvey and went upstairs. The Christmas party was that night.

"Are you getting ready to go on?" Art asked.

We went into a room on the way to the New York stage called "The Gates to Paree," past the gazebo with the mannequins dressed as strippers on its roof, near the palm trees. A Christmas tree was half set-up in the corner.

"You like to get down, don't you," Art said, starting to fondle me. As soon as the next endless Pink Floyd song was over, I had to face the audience. I leaned forward on my hands, dressed in a strapless black velvet bodice with a shocking pink taffeta skirt.

"You turn me on so goddamn much," I said.

The girl on stage finished her set, came backstage and looked appalled at us on the floor, me with my skirt pulled up, Art in back of me on his knees.

"Go ahead and dance and I'll stay upstairs for the first two songs, then I'll come down and fuck you," Art gave me a playful slap.

From the stage I could see the guy from San Jose I sat with sometimes, out in the audience, and I blew him a kiss. Thinking, I'm having sex with Art right after my set.

After my show, there was no sign of Art. Upstairs he was talking to some new girl that was in playing pool with him earlier. She was wearing a costume that looked like tails, and a top hat—a sleazy

Frederick's of Hollywood type tuxedo. He was saying, "There's this party going on . . .." I was jealous. But as soon as I had my audience clothes on, he led me back to the office.

Paulie was in Vince's office with a big tray of money and asked, "What's up?"

"Nothing," Art said, and locked his office door behind us. A cage with a couple of birds now stood against one wall.

"Sit down, tell me about yourself," he said.

I sat down in one chair, he sat in the other across the poker table. I told him where I got my Masters in English, that I liked to try things that are different, and that I had had some straight jobs and didn't like them. He wanted to know my father's rank in the military.

"You seem really independent," Art said. "And this is a Marinism, or whatever, but you seem so well-centered. You are one of the hottest women in this building. You're the hottest woman here. Have you always been on fire like this?"

"Well, I think as I've gotten older . . ."

"You're more accepting of it?"

"Yeah."

"Did you always like hard fucking so much?"

I smiled.

. . . "Blot your lipstick."

I looked around. The only thing I saw to use to do that was a piece of torn envelope. When I picked it up it already had *another* lipstick imprint on it. Some other girl had been told this before she gave him head earlier. I used the envelope anyway, and went down on him.

Art radiated a confident heat and a charming recklessness that made his touch electric. For a precious half-hour, he made love to me high above O'Farrell Street.

"I really like you," he said.

"I really like you, too. I think I want to give you my phone number."

"Write it right in here," Art opened his phone directory to the "S's." "Put it there, right on top."

I was practically the last dancer upstairs. Justine was dressed, ready to go. I threw my clothes on. "Are you going to the party?" I asked her.

"Yeah, it would be good to go and be social with people in a different setting." We drove a couple of blocks away to a bar the dancers went to often, the Brick House.

The place was crowded. Art was sitting at a table with someone with really long hair. The room was too dim for me to tell who she was. Maybe I shouldn't say anything more to him, I thought. At the bar I sat next to the stunning redhead that was dancing the night I was hired. She said Vince told her she looked so bad, like a truck ran over her and he wouldn't have her back in the theater.

"Jesus Christ, what a horrible thing to say."

I looked over. Paulie, on the other side of her, was now talking to Art.

"I'm intimidated by Vince," I told her. "I just try to stay out of his way."

"I did, too. But I couldn't."

She asked Vince if she could come back in a couple of months. He said no.

"I don't think there's anything wrong with the way you look."

"Well, I can think of at least one chick who's still working, who has a pretty face but a really big body. I know I look better than that."

"I think you do, too."

Vince wouldn't let her work anymore. She felt so bad about it she stayed inside her house for two months.

Art left the bar and moved into the shadows of the next room. It seemed strange that now he was ignoring me. At the party, it was almost like nothing had happened between us before, when it had. This disturbed me. I walked out of there alone. Past Art, who was once again talking to Paulie. I couldn't imagine what they could have been talking about for like, fucking hours. How many other women does he have in his life? I thought, why should I be anything other than *completely independent?*

∾

One thing intriguing about Mitchell Brothers was that an incident would happen, then it would just disappear. It was truly episodic.

Suddenly they decided to tear out that entire backstage room they called "The Gates to Paree." They tore up everything in there. Carpeting and all. Just a few nights before I had been in that room with Art. Strange there should be an incident like that and then, bam, the whole room vanished.

Lisa said the brothers build and tear down rooms in the theater so much because they do too many drugs. They enjoyed feeling like they're God, seeing their hand on things. Saying, "Put this over here," and seeing it happen. Lisa said they must have a lot of money stuck away somewhere.

As I left the building this fireman that I had talked to in the audience was in his car out in front. He called out, "Hey." I kept on walking.

That was so like Mitchell Brothers. I talked to that guy for awhile near the end of the night when it was slow, even though he hadn't tipped me much. But the next step was his trying to be friendly outside the theater, and my walking away from it. It was feeling close and then having that taken away from you. Similar to what happened to me at the Christmas party, with Art. With the customers, I knew everything was superficial because it was tainted by money.

Glynis had one regular customer from Canada. She told him she was born there, so every time he came in he greeted her with, "Oh, the little girl from Canada." She had to keep her story straight. He would say, "How long have you been down here?" She had to pretend, not very long. He would ask, "Do you know what the Fourth of July is?"

Justine said working this kind of a job you get so used to acting artificial, saying the same things. And when someone boring calls up you feel like they ought to be paying you for listening to them, I said. Talking to a lot of different men every evening, you become a bit fickle. After awhile you feel there will always be someone else, in the next seat. And the very next one might be better. Art could have felt like that, too.

DECEMBER 17, 1982

Friday morning at 10 a.m., there was a staff meeting all the dancers were supposed to attend. Just before it started, Glynis and I went into the downstairs bathroom to talk. "I got so nervous coming down here because I thought maybe they were going to close—but I don't think they would tell us and close," she said. "When they closed before they didn't even tell us, because they knew we would all be out looking for other jobs."

Soon thirty or so of us dancers filed into the Cine Stage and sat in the theater seats. Art was there, wearing a red plaid flannel shirt, rubber boots over jeans, and a beret. Gail spotted him and said, "Artie, are you going to dance a jig for us, you look like it." He laughed. Somebody said, "It's Artie's birthday today." A few people ran up to him and gave him a kiss, saying Happy Birthday. "Are you going to get up onstage, Artie?" someone asked. "Yeah, how about taking it off."

"Hell, yeah, I'm going to get onstage." There was a single chair up there and some Christmas tinsel draped near the footlights. He climbed up and sat in the chair relaxed with his legs spread, looking over his harem. As I looked around most of the guys on the staff were there too, including Vince, seated way in the back.

Art began, "Well, to start things off, do you know how many cops it takes to screw in a light bulb? One to screw it in, and fifty others to pull his dick out of the socket." He said they were going to appeal their six months jail sentence, but it was still up in the air as to whether they were going to have to go or not. They would put their appeal in on January 3. Right now there were a lot of undercover cops and they come in with these cameras, sort of Gestapo-like tactics, or more like the KGB, and they take pictures. And we're going to have to be really tight about not letting the guys touch our tits or our crotch. Because once they get out of the slammer in six months, he really hoped that they don't have any more pictures to say, "Well, you're going to have to go back in for another six months." That would be really a drag. So we're going to have to police ourselves, and that means if you see somebody doing something, first talk to them, and then come to us. We are going to have to layoff or fire people that let things like this happen.

Originally, when the New York Live show started out, it was really hot. People were down in the audience nude partying. Art thought that was fine. But now an act of prostitution is considered by the DA as touching your tit, it doesn't matter if there are clothes on, through your shirt, or whatever. Exchanging money, getting a dollar, having someone touch your tit, that's an act of prostitution. We can't have that. Everybody was going to have to sacrifice. There would be less money, but he thought that the laws would be changed. It would take maybe about a year. There is a question as to how hot the show can be. "Jeez, we use to have more fun in the back seats of cars," he said. "You really have to keep the guys' hands off of you."

"What if the guy's grabbing you and you pull his hand away?" Sonia asked.

"You've got to let them know they can't touch you because a picture can make it look like he's been touching you forever," Art said. "These cops lie a lot."

Frank the security guard said, "Remember a picture is worth more than one thousand words."

One of the guys said, "Yeah, a picture is worth more than $1000," referring to the $62,000 each fine that Art and Jim got.

Art said the more theatrical the performance, the more freedom you have under the First Amendment. The judge is trying to say that using a dildo onstage is an act of prostitution. But he felt that those laws wouldn't stand up if it was part of an act, as long as it wasn't in exchange for money.

Someone raised her hand and said, "What if they put money on the stage?"

"Well, go ahead and do your show. Don't touch the money or pick it up until the end of the set."

Justine asked, "Is it O.K. for us to make love to each other?"

Art said that as far as he was concerned, it was. That was part of the same thing.

"Hey, nobody likes to party more than I do. But you've got to separate that from your job. You're going to have to be a lot more like geisha girls, be a lot more entertaining, without letting them touch you. You're going to have to talk a lot more. Hey, in the old days, some girls would just go down and sit down on the guys—Art spread his legs on the chair—and hey, the guys loved it. And I thought it was fine. And my brother didn't have a problem with it. But we're not in that situation right now."

Somebody asked about rocking on laps and Art said, "Well, you know it's one thing if you strap the guy on—he gestured—and the

guy's getting into it, having an orgasm, he's coming, that's not cool.
Use your good judgment, you know, if the guy is real cool, that's one
thing. But you have to be really careful because it doesn't look good to
have somebody getting off like that."

Gail said, "Well, who's going to run this place if you guys go to jail?
This place is going to fall apart."

Everyone laughed. Art joked that Paulie would probably be in
charge if that happened. He said he didn't want a bust in the next few
weeks. It would be really bad press to have a bust before they went
to jail. He said it's a tough job, but he thought the laws would be
changed and within a year things would be different again. He ended
the meeting with "I guess that's all there is to say, Merry Christmas,
Happy New Year." Gail rushed in loud and bubbly, with a birthday
cake. More people went up to him, including me. "Happy birthday," I
said.

"Thanks, beautiful," he answered with a warm kiss.

That evening, when Lisa was sitting with this Japanese guy who
gave back massages, Paulie called her into the back and talked to her.
She said she wasn't doing anything. "It's very unlike Art to say that
we should police each other," Lisa said. "I guess he must be pretty
paranoid himself or he wouldn't have said that."

Our situation was unsettling, but a bit of a turn-on, too. The
O'Farrell had been busted a couple of times, a year or two before I
worked there, when the dancers were nude in the audience. Many
of the women who had been there were still working, so I'd heard
the stories. Customers lined up around the block to get in when
the O'Farrell was wide-open, in 1979-80. Some women were
averaging $1000 a day. When the bust came, three of the dancers
joined hands and skipped out to the paddy wagon. The dancer who
had been onstage accepting a dollar when the cops jumped up had
terrible luck—she was the only O'Farrell dancer ever convicted of

prostitution. If a bust happened it would go down during the daytime, I heard, when the Vice Squad had more available personnel.

Just after Christmas, Gail said two girls were caught fucking in the audience Sunday night, and they were both here working today. That after the meeting we had, where they warned us against touching because of the court case, nobody seemed to mean what they said.

I figured Art and Jim were showing some Christmas season compassion.

CHAPTER 4:
Mardi Gras

JANUARY 7, 1983

Art and Jim with six lawyers had just filed the appeal. I didn't know what the result had been, but as soon as I got to work, Gail told me the brothers didn't have to go to jail. I was happy. But when I was getting ready, the dancers were talking about something else.

Glynis told me Art was there last night, really fucked up, and was coming on to a lot of the dancers. Art waited for her after her show, with Nick. She said no, and Art said, "We'll get rid of Nick, and it'll just be you and me."

She kept saying no. On the steps backstage Art grabbed onto her and wouldn't let go, and Glynis was still saying no. Taking off one of her shoes, she hit him with it, kept hitting him with her shoe. She was afraid of getting fired, if she'd hurt him too much.

"Five years ago, when I was eighteen and just started working here, I used to fuck Art, when he was young and we were young. We all did," Glynis said. "It was different then. I haven't for a long time. He's come on to me since, but always friendly. Most of the time he acts like a big brother, giving me advice, and he's met my boyfriend . . . .. Jim demanded that I give him head, years ago, and I refused and I was fired. Then after a year I could come back."

Rhonda came in and presented Glynis with a small white paper bag. "She brought me some candies," said Glynis, looking inside. "She felt sorry for me."

"I'm sorry," I said to Glynis.

"Well, don't be. He didn't do anything to me. It's really stupid. It's really bad for his reputation. And for his going to jail and everything."

Well, Art didn't go to jail. But that night the stress about the court decision would have been at its peak. He had to have felt terrible about what happened. He must have been plastered.

Glynis said she kept telling him, "I have to do my shows."

"Don't tell me that," Art had said. "I own this fucking place. You don't have to do any shows at all!"

"If only I had been there," I thought, "I would have made love to him."

For a long time Glynis stood in front of the mirror over the sink and hacked away at her beautiful long hair, like she was trying to become less tempting.

"She might not have been fucking him here," said Belladonna. "But she has this weird thing with him where he goes over to her house."

A couple of weeks later Ron said, "This one night Art wanted to just plank Glynis. In that case, it would have just been easier to lay down and take it. If you're *not hot*, just what are you doing here?"

Ron said it was a cliff-hanging situation where up to the last minute it looked like the brothers might have to go to jail. Art's wife, Karen, and Mary Jane, Jim's wife, had been asking, "Where's the *money* stashed?"

Jim is pretty solid, Ron said, but Art will crack under pressure; he particularly can't stand confinement.

Paulie looked quite relieved, since he realized the brothers weren't going to have to go to jail. "Gee, I was looking forward to being in charge," he grinned, "playing pool all day, and being back there."

~

I took an expensive new white costume to the cleaners. The hot pink ostrich boa I got at a garage sale got wet and bled dye onto it. A tall old man that worked at the cleaners asked if I would put a little strip show on for him, in the back of his place. When he was a kid he ran errands for the strippers in a theater, and he loved it. When he said they turned tricks, too, his eyes glowed. "If you know me, you wouldn't be embarrassed, would you?"

"I don't mind if somebody I know comes into the theater, but otherwise, I don't do it. It's a job." Why did I ever tell *him* I was a stripper? I learned not to let ordinary people know. Once I got the costume back I stopped going there.

~

January through March was our slow season—and we were in the thick of it. When I was making a lot of money in the audience, and somebody said, "You're beautiful," or they gave me a decent tip, then I felt completely on top of it. But when it was a slow night, I felt unsure of myself, anxious about what I was going to do next. A new girl started working Wednesday night. She was nice, but it was debilitating when it was slow and there was a new dancer working on my shift. To the customers, brand new dancers seem more attainable—so they usually make more of the money.

"By the way, he really appreciated that thing you did with him and that other girl," Paulie said to some dancer out in the hall. "You ought to get another girl and do it on the stage down there."

"What, on the STAGE?" she asked.

"Yeah, well, we'll close up early and put the spotlight on him," Paulie teased. "He'll love it."

I only heard this smattering, but the only "he" Paulie could have been referring to, was Art.

71

I felt a little sad, hearing Paulie's rave review of that three-way. Maybe Art's gone through his run on me, I thought. What a selection of women he had. In the early 80's, he bedded nearly everyone in the dressing room at least once, and some had a lingering attraction to him. "When I hear his voice I just want to jump on top of him and fuck him to death," said one nineteen-year-old. All the dancers appealed to Artie, even if they were illiterate and immature. I wasn't so sure my being educated, tolerant, or well meaning gave me any advantage.

"It would drive me mad, changing partners all the time," Glynis said. "Even the people at work, who should understand more about sex, seem more fascinated by it than anyone else."

I made good money. It had become so easy for me in the audience, to turn off my feelings. I could charm the guys, talking to them or flirting, but it was not hard at all to just slide off their laps, and say "Bye."

After I got home, I looked at the day's letters from Harvey. He went on and on about his plans for our getting married. It made me sick. Quite a lot of it was completely demented, but occasionally Harvey threw in some tidbit I naively told him about myself ages ago. I hated that guy.

In one letter Harvey actually included the name of his psychiatrist and her phone number, even though I could barely make it out. In the morning, I gave her a call about Harvey's ten-month campaign of letters and presents—the volumes of Proust, the grandmotherly nightgowns, the musical valentines. She agreed to try to convince Harvey you can't do this type of thing to people. Although she would succeed in stopping his visits to the O'Farrell and the onslaught of mail, Harvey's obsession was chilling, and made me far more guarded with men I talked to in those innocent-looking theater seats.

~

"In about a week and a half they plan to have everybody naked in the audience again," one of the techs said.

"Really?" I wondered. "Are we going to get busted? What's going to happen?"

"I'm planning my own little escape route myself. But as long as you don't give head, you're O.K.," he answered. "Happy days are here again. There's gonna be cum all over the seats!"

They needed to do something. It had been incredibly slow lately.

～

I was going out a bit with Derek, who I met in the audience. He was in his early thirties, attractive, successful, intelligent, moderate in bed. The first time I went to dinner with him, he told me he lived with his girlfriend, and they spent two nights a week apart. I knew he was dating me just as a lark. Most guys, even if they seemed genuine in the theater, wanted to take out at least once, and score with a Mitchell Brothers stripper.

Derek and I figured out that after eighteen months at Mitchell Brothers, I might have sat on thirty thousand laps. He asked how many guys a night asked me out. I said oh, maybe five to ten. But most of them I would never want to go out with anyway.

One customer said he wanted to take me away some weekend. "We'll have to talk about it," I said. I couldn't lead them on. Jesus Christ, I would rather have died than go away with him. Then he said he would like to take me out to lunch. I couldn't have handled that either. With a lot of customers, eventually their fantasy attachment builds until they think they want some connection with you on the outside. It was tiresome.

Glynis told me seeing customers outside the theater destroys the glamorous illusion for them. Then they stopped coming in.

～

73

Artie was pretty drunk, and high. I couldn't understand all he said. I could make out, "Hey, are you going to marry a doctor?" teasing the young dancer Nick was dating, who looked like the singer from Blondie. She just gave him a look, like, "Are you out of your mind!"

Then Glynis said, "My mother wants me to marry you. Is that all right?"

"You know, I'm really sorry. I hope I apologized enough about that."

"Oh, yes, you did. You did."

I felt especially mellow, since I spent the afternoon with Derek. Art was flirting with all of us simultaneously, I thought. As he came up to me I tried to play it really cool so Glynis wouldn't feel funny about me.

"I want to fuck you," he said. "My dick is so hard."

As we were going down the stairs Art asked, "What have you been doing?"

"For my class, I've been dying some silk."

He said something I couldn't quite hear about hot pussy.

"What have you been up to?"

"Nothing much. I did get three white sharks, though," he said. "It's going to be my first G-rated feature."

"Really. What are you going to call them?"

"Jaws, Jaws II . . ."

"You ought to name them after some of the characters in Moby Dick. Let's see, the captain's name was Ahab and then there was Ishmael."

By then, we were in the basement. They had added a big box full of Christmas tinsel, and a long piece of metal pipe. Cartons of stuff.

Art peeled off his clothes and we lay on the mat. "You drive me crazy. I want you to be my next wife, after I divorce my wife."

I laughed.

"I don't know why I get so hot for you," he said.

I was so radically turned on, as he bent down over me I found myself shaking.

His timing was impeccable. At just the right moment he held back for a long time until I said, "I want you so bad." Just then he rammed into me, so perfect, saying, "You're going to get just as much of that as you want." It felt so, so exquisite. In the shadows, I could almost imagine we were in a bedroom somewhere, with no time limits.

"Welcome to work." he teased as he got up, leaning against the pipes, " . . . Sex—it's cosmic!"

I wanted to keep making love, again and again and again, I stayed so aroused from being with him. It was so hot.

Half an hour later I was in the audience, sitting with a talkative guy around thirty. "You seem to be more at peace with this place than anyone else," he flattered me. "You look like somebody at an MDA party."

"MDA? What's that?"

He said it's a drug that makes you—not sexual, but sensual. He'd taken it once and highly recommended it; he ended up in a pile of people where men and women were holding each other, sucking toes and stuff and it didn't matter if it was a man or a woman's toes you were sucking. "Just the way you were walking around this place seems very different than the way everybody else is," he said. "Why are you working at Mitchell Brothers?"

"I really like men. I'm comfortable with the sexuality of it, and I like people, I like talking to people. And it's surreal."

The guy said he wasn't a cop, but he worked for some people that had fucked this place over. He was a reporter. The guy sitting in back of him wrote the series of articles in the *San Francisco Examiner* that came out last summer. I glanced back. A new girl with huge tits was sitting with the guy, in a bra with red fringe and rhinestones.

"Women that work at Mitchell Brothers are entertainers and therapists," he said. "People don't recognize, because of the Puritan ethic, that you are performing an actual service for people . . .. I spent an evening with Chelsea last year. We ended up taking some qualludes and rolling around her apartment for awhile."

The next time I went into work Paulie gave me a broad wink, a warm hello, an appreciative smile. Art must have said how good it was the other day. I was happy.

~

Finally we were allowed to go back in the audience wearing lingerie, after being encased in tights and body suits for months! The security person was told to stand back, and not watch us. Suddenly it seemed like it was wide-open, even if it was ambiguous as to what was O.K. and what wasn't. They were giving the dancers the feeling that if the management didn't have knowledge of what we were doing, they weren't liable. I felt paranoid, but elated. The audience was happy. Gail said she had forgotten how sneaky the guys could be, like trying to put their hands down her panties. That didn't happen to me, but I was watching their hands, expecting security or a cop to run over and grab me.

Ron said they threw all the security people out, because if nobody sees you do anything wrong, then you haven't done anything wrong. Typical Mitchell Brothers theory!

I noticed Frank the security guard was gone. Glynis told me he got laid off, "Doesn't that seem a bit strange, because he's been here for years and years?"

The brothers made some cutbacks: Frank, and Mistress Sarah. They wanted to cultivate a lighter weight atmosphere to increase business. I certainly wasn't sad to see Frank go. He really had it in for me, because I was fucking Artie.

"Frank? He's gone down the tubes. He was sucked into the bay," the tech made a sucking noise. We both laughed.

~

Friday night a list of nine dancers who had been fired was posted on the bulletin board next to the dressing room. The notice said they weren't supposed to be let in to get any of their belongings unless they were escorted by the security. I was shocked.

"Just look around," Glynis said. "All the dopers are gone."

Well—the most flagrant dopers were gone. Officially the management was trying to cut back on the dancers using drugs and drinking, when there was fear of another bust. But guests, dancers, and staff continued getting high. Art's close friend Nick, who dropped by the theater often, was just one example.

"The first time I saw Dr. Nick I couldn't believe how high he was. He's always loaded on pills or something. Have you ever noticed that twitch he gets?" the tech said. "I call him Doc Holliday."

APRIL 1, 1983

It was Good Friday and pretty slow. Rhonda did her Easter show where she came out in a white bunny outfit and fucked some carrots.

"Carrots—feel them—they actually feel better than a dildo, it's sort of more human, a carrot."

I touched one. They still had their leafy green tops.

"After one day using a dildo in all your shows you're just raw, but this is better!"

Sonia Summers stepped into the spotlight in a baseball jersey, number "69." On her knees Sonia inserted the handle end of an adult size plastic baseball bat into her shaved pussy, then asked me to pitch a white whiffle ball, as Sonia swayed her hips to swing the bat. To my amazement, it was a hit!

Our star for the week, Edy Williams, came out on the New York stage to plug her show in her white Indian costume with the warbonnet. She had abandoned the bra that went with it, that used to fall down. Two young guys who had been to see Edy in the Kopenhagen told me she was outrageous. Edy was an ex-wife of film director Russ Meyer, and had starred in his cult film *Beyond the Valley of the Dolls*. "Edy is getting on," one customer said, "and she's only an R-rated star, trying to look X."

When I came up to dance around 11:30 p.m., Artie was standing there with the woman I'd seen him with the previous fall. He had a black suit on, and she looked very pretty. "Simone," he said, "I want you to meet my wife, Karen."

"Oh, hi. Nice to meet you."

"Simone's a school teacher turned dancer," Art said.

She looked so smart and warm. They walked away towards the tech booth. It looked like they were in love. *Damn*, I thought, this woman must be incredibly accepting.

I was getting it on with Artie, and the whole building full of women had had sex with him. I wondered how much she knew about it. She must have known. I almost wanted to say more to her, but felt I really couldn't.

With warped DJ humor, Kenny picked out "The Other Woman" for my first song. It made me a little nervous, but Artie and his wife weren't out there watching.

Late, around 12:30 p.m., when I walked into the little dressing room, a steak knife was sticking out of the wall. I touched the handle and it was in solid, like it had been thrown. Was this a sign, an offbeat omen? It was late, we all left. Still wedged in the wall was a shiny serrated blade, pointed straight into the heart of the O'Farrell.

78

~

The next week Jody Maxwell was the star. She was friendly, not standoffish like Edy Williams. Kenny announced Jody's show, "The Singing Cocksucker from Kansas City, Missouri!"

Soon a bright young dancer from Berkeley, Nina Hartley, would sit with the New York Live customers and focus on starting her own porn career.

Sarah sounded melancholy, "I'm not cut out to be a stripper. I'd rather stay home and make my honey happy. I want to grow old with grace, whoever Grace is."

A gorgeous, wild nineteen-year-old blonde was jokingly tagging along behind Jim Mitchell. I thought to myself it looks like she's just about to fuck him—she will think she's one up on me, she's made it with Jim . . . as well as Art.

Justine said she fucked a famous film director last night, but she didn't know who he was at the time. A new girl was telling everyone she was a semi-finalist in the Ultimate Showgirl Contest in Las Vegas. It was to be on TV in a month. "I get a trip, and I get to take someone. This is the biggest thing that's ever happened to Vegas!" Such typical dressing room chatter. It sounded so mainstream.

Since I had worked at Mitchell Brothers for nearly two years, the other dancers and their points of view now seemed less exotic. Although I still loved dancing and the freedom it gave me, life at the O'Farrell had become somewhat predictable. I was beginning to want a more serious relationship—that allowed me space. It was a natural progression: Rhonda was engaged to a man from her hometown, Atlanta, and planned to marry him in the fall and return to college; Rita had set her sights on a director she met on a movie set.

By this time, I knew I would find little understanding or acceptance from men who were not in the sex industry. Working as a house dancer, the only men I met who *were* in the sex business were the half-dozen guys on the theater staff, and all the attractive ones had serious partners. Since I had a hot thing going with Artie, and—as I would soon discover—his union with Karen wasn't ideal, it isn't surprising how things developed.

Belladonna got fired. She was on drugs again.

"You know, sometimes you sense that something's wrong, but you just can't do anything about it," Justine said. "I miss Belladonna, too."

Kenny said she was at the Market Street Cinema. A lot of women were dancing there by then, and sitting in the audience like at Mitchell Brothers. In the paper they ran an ad for a show a couple of ex-Mitchell Brothers dancers were doing there, "Valley Girls in Bondage."

Upstairs an edgy voice came over the intercom, "O.K. This is Paulie. *Red Alert.* Jim Mitchell just walked in. So if you're *not legal,* get downstairs!" To keep the customers happy, the management had started limiting the dancers' time upstairs in the dressing room. Everyone but the two "legal" girls getting ready for their shows rushed to go back down in the audience.

In the evening, when I normally worked, Jim was rarely around. "He's been paranoid ever since Larry Flynt was shot;" I heard from a manager, "he doesn't like to be recognized in the lobby." "Try to stay away from Jim—he has a cruel side," one of the dancers warned. She said he locked a porn star in the dressing room late one night and demanded that another girl fist-fuck her, even though she was crying out for him to stop. That story was enough for me to give Jim plenty of room.

Jim stood in the back of the tech booth alone, smoking a cigarette, looking over the crowd. Serious and removed from it all, cool and calculating. Such a contrast from Artie. Then he was gone.

Ron told me Art and Jim's father was a professional card player, and "Jim is a fool, but Art is real good. He could make a living playing cards. Artie can be real fucked up—you would think his mind is totally gone—but he will know who has every card. Art has a keen sense. If you only have ninety-nine dollars, he will raise you a hundred!"

In the early days of the live shows, Ron said, the entire U.S.C. football team came to the theater one night and got so drunk and unruly, they started grabbing framed awards right off the walls to take with them. Art chased the team out of the O'Farrell with a rifle, firing over their heads, and scarring the building across the street with bullet holes.

Night after night, Ron watched the show and gossiped with the dancers, with occasional news of Art and Jim. But about everyone who ranked lower in the Mitchell Brothers hierarchy Ron was condescending. "All the new manager can do is to keep the doors open," Ron remarked, and, "Those girls, all they think about is where they're going to get their next line of cocaine!"

"You're definitely the artiste of the group here," Ron said to me. I wasn't sure he meant it as a compliment.

A little later Ron was coming on to a tall friendly redhead with huge breasts, "I told them to put you back on the schedule." followed closely with, "You ought to come over and sunbathe on my yacht!"

～

They let Mistress Sarah come back to work as a tech. She wasn't wearing a whip anymore, and was acting mellower with everyone. Belladonna was back dancing, too. She wasn't getting quite so high.

After work, Rita and I stopped to get something to eat. She told me last fall one of the dancers and a security guy she was dating did a live male-female sex show in the Kopenhagen. Right after that, the brothers took their cousin out as one of the house managers and sent him to their Bijou movie theater on Market Street, because he had arranged it. Some guys came in and offered a lot of money. I hadn't heard that story before. Everyone involved kept quiet.

~

By this time, I wanted to know more about Artie's history and the O'Farrell's. I got to know a woman who had worked at the theater for years, but whose perspective on everything was quite different from the dancers'. Laura was modest, quiet, and forthright, lost in a pleasant daze much of the time. Contented with clocking into a low-key job in an outrageous place.

"Art's playing the Boys' Game," she told me. "What's important is who you can have." She said Vince and Jim and Art were into it and Dan O'Neill. "You don't have to fuck Art, you know," she looked at me, irritated. "Just tell him 'No.'" I mostly listened. Laura couldn't comprehend how much I wanted him.

Art's wife Karen worked in the Ultra Room when it was new and had been very enthusiastic, Laura said. Karen had wanted to marry someone with money, who was attractive—and she *had* wanted to be rich. Karen got Art because no one tried harder, she added. He didn't marry her until their baby was a year old. I had seen some photos of Karen in the Ultra Room, but they were taken years before I started at the O'Farrell. I didn't have first-hand knowledge of the history of Art's wives. Karen would later deny she ever worked as a dancer, and say the pictures were publicity shots.

Art kept his first wife, Meredith, pregnant and secluded, all the way over in the East Bay. Meredith seemed to handle Art's fucking everyone, so well, Laura said. She suspected they split up because Meredith wanted more independence and Art couldn't handle it.

What a double standard! This was just second-hand information and theory, of course, but in time I would learn that outrageous Artie had many traditional expectations of women he was serious about.

Ron told me, around 1977 he didn't think Artie would live very long—because he had such a heavy coke habit and went two or three days without eating. When he did eat, he threw up. Art's wife Karen was a vegetarian. She got him to eat better, Ron said, and since then he had minimized his cocaine habit and bought a farm between Moraga and Oakland. It's beautiful out there and he had lots of animals. When they pulled us out of the audience in July, the brothers were losing four thousand dollars a day. Art couldn't have cared less. He was ecstatic because his vegetable crop was coming in. Jim was concerned about the money.

~

Chelsea was acting so crazed the last few days before she left for vacation. The very last night she was running around slamming doors, even before she got real drunk. Later she sat in the dressing room, cutting up a one-dollar bill.

She cut out the figure of a woman with tits and nipples and a little triangular slot for a cunt and pinned it up on the mirror with those sticky things from juice cans. She said, "It only costs a dollar."

I laughed. Then a new dancer walked up and Chelsea kicked her in the stomach.

"Gee," Chelsea said, "I hope you're not pregnant."

"Well, I am, as a matter of fact."

"Well, I hope you're not going to keep it."

"No, I'm not."

~

Belladonna's lover died on July 3. He drank a whole pint of vodka. They went to bed together, and when she woke up in the morning he was dead. It was a horrible shock. She went to work the same night. Glynis and Justine looked after her. Belladonna was alienated from her family. Her father was a doctor.

83

A week or so later Rhonda asked her, "Did you make love to him that night, the night before it happened?"

"Yes. We made good love."

Belladonna sounded brave, "My husband died. But other than that, everything's O.K."

"That guy gave her a pretty hard time," Rita said to me later. "Maybe now that he's gone she'll be able to get it together."

Belladonna said the worst time is when you go to sleep because when you're asleep you forget about it, and when you wake up you realize, yes, it's true. That person is gone.

∽

In June and July, Art started calling me at home, at more extreme times. I began to wonder what this was leading up to, and if something was going to change and we would get closer.

Late Sunday night he called, and had me talk him through a fantasy. He was so seductive, even on the phone I felt close to him.

The next night he was at the theater. "Hi, beautiful. So how do you want me to fuck you first?" He grabbed me and I kissed him.

"Oh, what first?" I let my hand glide over the slick blue nylon of his jogging pants.

Art was wandering around, talking to everyone. A new girl was in the little dressing room with me, dressed for stage in a white-fringed dress studded with rhinestones, under a cloud of long blonde hair. Art teased her, "My brother's been looking for you."

As soon as he left she asked, "Do you think that's true? . . . Artie's real easy, but Jim's hard," she looked serious. "I want Jim."

Why be interested in somebody who is so remote, I thought.

Not knowing where Art was, I put on my black satin dress slowly. When I looked up, he stood in the doorway. "You know, dressed up like that with diamonds and everything you look just like a lady. But I know that all you think about is hard sex."

From the office windows, I could see out onto the early evening street. People walked by below on O'Farrell, unaware of the one-way glass above them. I unzipped my dress, and turned to Art, my eyes gleaming. Then he asked me how I wanted it.

Each time he made love to me was shaded with fresh nuance. And he had the stamina of an athlete, and a reckless outlaw beauty.

"I love you, Simone," he said. "You drive me crazy."

"I love you, too, Art." It was exciting for him to say I love you. Even though I thought I knew exactly what the extent of it was.

In the darkened office near the glowing jukebox, Art pulled me into position in the most unforgettable, seductive way, and took my hand as his partner, to dance.

When I finally left the office, the new manager stood at the coffee machine. Showing no recognition, just pouring out the coffee like, "I'm kind of shocked it's you."

CHAPTER 5:
Changes, and the Arrival of Dr. Hunter S. Thompson

JANUARY 6, 1984

"Well, it looks like I may be getting a divorce," Art told me in my living room. "My wife Karen has all the papers together, but she hasn't filed them. She's out of the country right now. And usually in this kind of a deal, the wife loses out, and I hate to see it. When you have three children, your money gets used up pretty fast. On the other hand, I already had the job when she was still in high school; I was going to court. What happened to Karen is she tried to look inside Pandora's box. You just can't do that . . . .." He looked thoughtful, "Of course, this will open up some other possibilities for me."

I was thrilled. And because he was getting a divorce, no longer would I feel guilty or need to keep seeing him a secret, ever again.

∼

Within days, Art told me that Karen kicked him out of the farm they had shared in Canyon, spitting on him in front of their three young children. In February, he came to stay with me for six delicious weeks. I was smitten.

For the next year and a half, I saw things through a haze of warm emotion. I was enjoying living in the moment, instead of focusing on the details. Some events are razor-sharp, but most of what I remember of it now is glowing, muted, and evasive. It was the last time I truly felt young. I wasn't aware that serious heartbreak or loss would touch me, ever.

Art took me to dinner at a romantic restaurant on an antique schooner (that used to be near Pier 40) on the Embarcadero; on another evening we held hands at Enrico's in North Beach. He had a vasectomy and asked me to have my IUD taken out, which I gladly did.

I knew Art was far from settling down—freedom was too important to him, and too new. Quite worried about the custody of his children and his divorce, he threw himself into the first movie projects the Mitchells had worked on for years. Sometimes he had me set the alarm for 4:30 a.m. for a salmon-fishing trip with Jim—commercial fishing was their latest venture. Tolerating Art's angling for other women was crucial to loving him.

I enjoyed being independent and having time for creative projects of my own. I had been fortunate to find a one-bedroom apartment on mellow Potrero Hill. It was a flat in a two-unit building, built long enough ago to have gas light fixtures left in the ceiling and a claw-foot bathtub. When my neighbor left, Rita moved into the upstairs flat with her children, and we grew closer. My other close friend, Rhonda, had a storybook wedding that many of the dancers went to. She and her new husband had moved away in the fall.

To decorate my apartment, I added an elegant black iron and brass bed I shared with Art when he stayed with me, and hung pictures everywhere. I filled my place with books and art supplies, sewing equipment, mannequins, music, and a sleek black cat. My flat took on a starving-artist decor I loved. Late at night when lights sparkled over Twin Peaks from the windows and I was alone, was my most clear, focused time. Much of my energy I poured into my shows.

From 1983 through 1989, I put together and performed about thirty different theme shows, many of them comic. I loved designing costumes and props, choosing music, and playing to an audience. For one show, I dressed as a fencer in white with a foil. In another, I was a prom queen who died during the second song, to return as a teen angel in the third. As a shark, I slinked in a green lamé gown to "Mac the Knife." Creating these shows was very fulfilling.

My gorilla show started out as an innocent idea—I had thought a gorilla in a pith helmet running through the audience to wild drumbeat music would liven things up when we had the larger-than-usual O'Farrell crowds during the 1984 Democratic convention. Once on stage in the gorilla costume, I chased, then seduced my "startled" glamorous partner. As a surprise I unzipped, then ravished my partner with a strap-on dildo worn under the fur suit. Then I quickly stripped out of the suit offstage, to lingerie worn with the mask only. For the finale I did a brief girl-girl show with my partner, as a feminine ape in heels, before taking off the mask. It was fun to blend comedy with the audience's hard-core expectations.

In November of 1984, preeminent gonzo journalist Hunter S. Thompson and his girlfriend Maria came to the O'Farrell to do research for an article for *Playboy* magazine. I had fallen in love with Hunter's books for their ultra-wild humor, unique style and their insights years earlier, but I had no idea that the tall, angular man watching the shows was their brilliant author. After bringing a few friends to the O'Farrell, he commented that no one could stand to watch more than a couple of hours of dancers performing in the New York Live show—because their shows were so similar. One evening after Hunter had seen my gorilla show, I met him and Maria at a bar to talk. When I said I had taught in a prison, Hunter said, "Yes, you could pass." I told him how much I loved his books. Hunter said he had met his match in my gorilla show.

Later that fall Hunter told me he thought of that show as "the rape of innocence by pornography." According to Harold Conrad's

May 1987 article in *Spin,* in December of 1984, Hunter received half a
million dollars as an advance to write a novel on Mitchell Brothers.
In a few months, he was writing weekly columns for the *San Francisco
Examiner.* Over the next three years Hunter spent a lot of time in the
San Francisco bay area, much of it at the O'Farrell or hanging out with
Art and Jim or Jeff Armstrong, who managed their video business, to
get material for his columns and for his book on Mitchell Brothers,
which was to be called *The Night Manager.* Art and Jim connected
the dream of having a gonzo novel by Thompson written about them
to his praise of my shows. Hunter referred to the O'Farrell as the
"Carnegie Hall of public sex in America," a quote the brothers proudly
displayed on the theater's marquee.

Spurred on by San Francisco Mayor Dianne Feinstein, Prosecutor
Bernard Walter and the Vice Squad had pressured the theater for years,
trying to close the O'Farrell down permanently and put Art and Jim
in jail. Mitchell Brothers had the perfect stage for a dancer dressed
as the prim Dianne to appear, I thought. It was irreverent fun to
perform as the Mayor, an appropriate way to poke fun at the intolerant
establishment. Art and Jim understood this and loved my show. Then
Art asked me to mimic her in one of their movies.

For *The Grafenberg Spot,* I tied a silk bow over a conservative
blouse under a modest navy blue suit. During a crowd scene, I sat
next to an actor dressed like the Chief of Police, turned-on by the stage
show. It was one of the brothers' little bad taste anti-establishment
jokes.

Months before *Grafenberg Spot* was filmed, Art and I were lying
in bed talking. The controversial book *The G Spot* by Alice Ladas,
Beverly Whipple and John Perry was published in 1982—I had a
copy, and Art asked to borrow it. Over the summer he took *The G
Spot* to heart. Soon the dancers got to view a grainy black and white
documentary on the G spot (first described by Ernst Grafenberg in

the 1940's), loaned to the brothers by San Francisco's Institute for the Advanced Study of Human Sexuality. Art and Jim sent out for a case of rubber gloves, a case of K-Y jelly, two lab coats, and cleared off the pool table for research. After experimenting, they developed a trick: shooting a douche bottle of water into a woman, having her count to ten and then push resulted in a dramatic gush. This effect was used again and again in the movie to simulate female ejaculation, as Jim Mitchell hovered in the background with a nozzle-ready blue plastic bottle, and Artie directed. The men in the cast were drenched.

Grafenberg Spot, which was filmed in 35mm during the last week of October 1984 with a budget of $140,000, had problems which surfaced later. The cast of porn stars included veteran performers Harry Reems, Annette Haven, John Holmes, Lily Marlene, and Rick Savage; and newcomers Ginger Lynn, Amber Lynn, Nina Hartley, and Traci Lords.

Traci did the wildest scene in Grafenberg Spot with Harry Reems and Rick Savage—and she was sixteen and a half years old at the time. Her scene had to be cut in 1986, when it was discovered that Traci had been underage when she made about one hundred films and won four adult film awards. She had shown a fake passport and California driver's license to her film producers. The sex industry eliminated Traci from their films immediately, and banned sales of videotapes she appeared in, costing producers and distributors millions. The story broke just when the Meese Commission was pressuring prosecutors to get tough on porn.

At the premiere of *Grafenberg Spot*, Art introduced me to *San Francisco Chronicle* columnist Herb Caen, who complimented my Mayor Feinstein show. Hunter attended, too. He made a great impression on one of my old friends by saying, "This woman is very special to me."

～

During the last week of January 1985, Marilyn Chambers appeared at the theater's Cine Stage in a show called "Feel the Magic." She was the lovely model who starred in the Mitchells' huge hit *Behind the Green Door* in 1971, who became one of the most famous porn actresses of all-time. Marilyn was blonde, athletic and spirited, yet not as slender and striking as in her early films. After she danced on stage, the spotlight followed her as she walked through each row in the audience naked, and the customers briefly fondled her. When I saw her show from upstairs—at the same time the brothers' attorney Tom Steel was watching—I was shocked. Marilyn was doing everything that all of us house dancers had been warned not to do, with the spotlight pointed directly at her. The theater was packed with customers all week. The vice cops waited until Friday night to stop her show, arresting Marilyn and her bodyguard/boyfriend, but not busting any customers, staff or dancers. The highlight of the week, for me, was being able to perform my comic shows in front of a packed house, and enjoy their laughter. When I did my TV dinners show, Art, Jim, and Hunter were upstairs watching. A drunk in the first row stood up to shake hands with me on stage and say, "You're the best, you're the best, you're the best."

Ironically, the Marilyn Chambers' bust was a coup for the theater. Marilyn's arrest was a reminder of the previous year's Rathskeller scandal, when a handcuffed police recruit was given a blowjob at a San Francisco Police Academy graduation party. After writing some articles in the *San Francisco Chronicle* criticizing the Police Department's actions in Marilyn's bust, the brothers' friend, journalist Warren Hinckle, was arrested for walking his dog without a license. This led to a rush of more bad publicity for the cops. Marilyn wasn't prosecuted for prostitution by the DA. Within weeks, the San Francisco Board of Supervisors ruled that the Police Department would no longer have the authority to regulate adult theaters.

In April 1985, when the San Francisco DA got a court order to padlock the doors of the O'Farrell, ten dancers and I went down to the steps of City Hall carrying picket signs. I dressed like Mayor Dianne and carried a sign with a cartoon figure of her, that read, "Let them eat cake!" Hunter arrived at City Hall, cocktail glass in hand, to attend the Red Light Abatement hearings. They weren't able to close the O'Farrell that time, either.

That same month, Al Goldstein, the editor of Screw magazine, made a trip to San Francisco. He arrived at the O'Farrell in a stretch limo with two slender young blondes. Goldstein asked Art and Jim to put on an orgy to celebrate his divorce. Hunter Thompson was put in charge of this and called me, "By the way, Artie says you're on tonight for the Goldstein Show."

Oh, no. I thought for a moment. "O.K. Has Al seen the gorilla suit yet?"

"No."

"I'll come in and surprise him after the other girls warm him up. I'll wear my strap-on. Tell Goldstein 'Bend over, I'll drive.'"

We talked the plan over at the Waterfront Restaurant. Hunter never seemed comfortable with public sex, but he loved to pull off inventive jokes, and would enjoy Goldstein's reaction.

Wearing a complete gorilla costume would be the best protection from doing anything sexual at Goldstein's orgy, and I didn't want to be photographed doing anything unsavory dressed as the Mayor of San Francisco, which could have been the next thing suggested.

Art directed the orgy, staged in the Ultra Room, as Goldstein's friends watched from the booths. Hunter wasn't there—he was too savvy to be on the spot when he had a hand in the production.

"Goldstein's so nervous," Art told me as I put on the fur costume in the dressing room that evening. "Tonight at dinner he says to me 'Art, you can't tell me you never had any anxiety about dick size.' I laughed. 'Al, I guess you're right,' I said. 'I've had some women leave me because it was too big!'"

"First get Al to suck your dick," Art said. "Then fuck him in the ass, dry, then take the gorilla costume and the strap-on off leaving the mask on, and just as Al thinks he's going to get to eat some pussy, piss in his face!"

My jaw dropped. Was Art *serious?* He sounded like a coach delivering a pep talk just before the big game. Before show time he introduced me to actor Buck Henry, there to watch the fun.

Before I was to come in as a surprise two dancers cuffed Goldstein, who was naked, and got him excited. Another girl took a can of hairspray along and used it to flare her Bic lighter. Goldstein freaked and bit her ankle. As soon as he saw a gorilla coming for him, he began rolling away from me, even though he was cuffed. All of us orgy participants stood up civilly and left the Ultra Room. Goldstein kept asking me, "Who is that in there?"

After Art and Jim bought matching white Mercedes sedans, Art had his wood-grain Jeep wagoneer driven to Mexico, where it was tricked out with a chrome bulldog on the hood, red ball fringe around the inside of its top. For a short time Art loaned Hunter this car, which he drove until he was in an accident with another vehicle early in May. Hunter was arrested for drunk driving, his passengers Art and Jim were unhurt, the car was totaled. Later Art complained that car insurance for the theater skyrocketed as a result. Hunter loved to drive fast. On our way to a dinner, he sped along in a rented convertible, making some slick lane changes, impressing his passengers, one of whom was thinking about filming a program on porn for PBS.

Hunter's presence always intensified the mood at the theater. He experimented to get reactions from people. One night Hunter was clowning around in the dressing room, looking for just the right red lipstick, then he applied it to his lips in front of the mirror, to outrageous—but still macho—effect.

When Hunter took an interest in the O'Farrell, there was a sense of hope that the sex business could become acknowledged as a viable part of American culture. Porn hadn't been chic since the early 70's, during the heyday of the original *Behind the Green Door.* The mood Hunter brought to the theater was a bit like the excitement, goodwill, and iconoclasm of the late 60's.

Hunter was always kind to me. He did seem suspicious of porn, and the way Art and Jim played with people. Hunter genuinely hated to witness any abuse of power.

Michael Nichols / National Geographic Image Collection

The Night Manager, Hunter S. Thompson, with Simone Corday (right) and another dancer, in a dressing room at the O'Farrell Theater in July, 1985.

~

In June 1985 I went on a trip to Europe, and Art and I had a wonderful reunion when I got back. "I want you to be my woman, Simone," he said. All night long he held me. I wanted time to stop, to hold every sensation in my mind forever, to always be in his arms. Art told me, "You should be glad I've chosen you."

I laughed, "But isn't that what God said to Christ right before they started pounding the nails in?"

∼

Although I had a need for independence, I did want my relationship with Art to progress where we would grow closer. Art was so sexual he craved variation. A few weeks after I was back from Europe, he was asking me to do a three-way. I'll just think of it as a show I'm doing with another dancer at the theater, I thought warily. Since every day Art was getting high to some extent, I didn't always notice when he was slipping into the outer limits. And I had been at the O'Farrell so long, I didn't perceive that it was a lush fantasy island, isolated from many of the reality checks of the outside world.

∼

Early in August, he brought someone over. Sliding his tongue lasciviously into my mouth at the door, he said, "I've brought you a girl." I thought he had picked somebody up in a bar. A blonde stood on my porch, grinning a little too widely for someone I had never seen before.

She waited in my living room, while I gave Art some oral sex. "You have to be tough to be my woman," he said to me. He was doing so much cocaine he wanted an outrageous twist: what would it be like to do a three-way with a gorilla, he must have been thinking, and to be right in the middle of Hunter Thompson's favorite O'Farrell show—having GONZO SEX! To please him, for a couple of minutes I slipped into the fur costume and fucked her with a dildo. That satisfied his fantasy, and he wanted us naked.

Art was playing the role of a dead serious, impossible-to-please Master. The blonde, who he introduced as Missy, seemed stiff and uncomfortable. We both put on a show for him rather than having sex with abandon. Art was too coked up to come, and she started to whimper. In half an hour he told her to get dressed and went down to his car, leaving her and me alone for a couple of minutes. She asked if I worked at the theater, and said she did, once in awhile. I told her, "I'm in love with Art. I've been involved with him for three years." I was angry, and said I wasn't sure he was capable of love.

The whole coke-driven episode was *unreal*. What a bastard he was to leave with someone he barely knew, when I'd done all I could to please him. I couldn't understand his cruel behavior.

Months later, I would find out that our three-way was one of a series of many sexual adventures Art encouraged to prepare Missy to deliver an uninhibited performance as the star of the sequel to *Behind the Green Door*. For me, that night began a difficult time when I would be tested by Art's cocaine-fueled destructive behavior. Never again would I feel quite the same about the gorilla show, about any of my shows, really. Just as my relationship with him was becoming comfortable, he had put me down tyrannically. I could hardly believe it. It seemed like I was been punished for being too open and trusting with Artie, and for my shows having interested Hunter.

Next to my bed, I found a pearl choker, after Art brought her over. I summoned the high-mindedness to return the necklace the next time I saw Missy. "Oh, thank you so much," she bubbled confidently, ready to dance in a white angora dress. I let the pearls click sadly onto the counter and left. Later I could hear the Saturday night cheers of the crowd. She was on stage with three other women as Art beamed down encouragingly from the darkness of the tech booth.

A couple of weeks later, after Missy entered but lost the Miss Nude America contest, I heard she called the theater to say, "I'm not going to work for you any more. It's not a good idea because I'm dating one of the owners." Then she stepped up her campaign to get rid of her competition for Art, me.

Like a mischievous sorority girl on spring break at Fort Lauderdale, Missy romped around the theater. She taunted me at the O'Farrell, and began crank-calling me at home. Art was doing more cocaine, seeing me less, and appeared to be giving her the run of the club. It was intolerable. Even the pleasure I had taken in creating new shows seemed empty. But passion is rooted in emotion, not in reason—it's not convenient or safe. I was furious with Art, but I still loved him. And since Missy had begun a major campaign to get rid of me, at the time it was easier for me to place most of the blame for Art's bad behavior on her.

I heard that Missy was the rebellious daughter of a Mexican-American who had been successful in Republican politics. She had grown up in conservative Utah. With the attitude of a tourist, Missy had been experimenting. The dancers said she had been running an ad in the local adult paper as an escort. She was captivated by Art, and becoming a film star and marrying him were powerful fantasies that at that time she would stop at nothing to achieve. At twenty-three, she had no idea how realistic these dreams were, no sense of her own limitations, or of what she was getting herself into.

∽

On a Sunday evening in October, Missy brought a couple of her friends to the theater. She spotted me in the audience in the New York Live show and ran down to sit nearby until they announced my Ultra Room. In the dressing room I slipped on a crimson negligee and fire and ice rhinestones, over black lingerie and stockings, blood red stilettos, and grabbed my paraphernalia for the show, including a whip. Even though it was show time, I was downcast.

Surrounded by booths and a gallery fronted by glass windows with slots for tips from the audience of voyeurs, the notorious Ultra Room had been the first O'Farrell live show, and the scene of numerous other escapades. *Never a Tender Moment* was shot there, capturing one of Marilyn Chambers' more extreme performances. I enjoyed dancing in the theater's other rooms more, but the Ultra Room was the O'Farrell's heart. The dramatic tension and S/M mood of the room was palpable. Since I'd been doing shows within its black leatherette and glass walls for three years, it seemed as familiar as my living room. That night the Ultra Room was shadowy and still, as my tall raven-haired partner and I waited for our music and the show to begin. Missy stood in the open gallery at the back of the room close to our entrance doorway where I couldn't miss her, her voluptuous size-twelve body poured into a tight gray mini dress. Her smooth blond pageboy hair reminded me of a young Republican from some safe suburb.

"We went over to her house, and we both fucked Art and she had on a monkey suit!" Missy gloated to one of her friends. I didn't relish performing in this fish bowl setting while she made snide remarks. The tension between us had been building for three months. Rarely have I felt such anger.

"Are you down here to torture me, Missy? Get out of my show, you whore!" I struck the glass with my black leather whip. It made a lovely sharp crack, a typical S/M gesture. Although I was a true denizen of the place, Missy didn't move an inch. She gave me a smug smile.

"Don't do this," my partner murmured to me, and then went closer to plead through a tip slot, "Missy, honey, please don't watch my show. I'm really shy."

"You've already got the man I love. Leave me alone! Get out of here!" I demanded with a crackle of black leather. Missy fled, followed by her friends. The lights came up and the pure, hypnotic beat of the music started our performance. In a few minutes, Art appeared in the doorway and I went over. "Do you have a problem with her?" he asked, looking mellow and amused, a cool green bottle of Heineken in his hand.

"You don't love me anymore," I found myself saying.

"Yes, I do," Art said. "I'll come back to you."

"You brought her over to my house and you used me to impress her. That really hurt me," I protested. "It wouldn't have hurt so much if you'd picked somebody who didn't care about you, but you did."

"I'm sorry. I'm coming back to you, I will," he said.

"I find it hard to believe you meant everything you said when I got back from Europe," I added, remembering his loving promises made weeks earlier.

Missy crept up to stand behind Art in the narrow hall to the doorway, to aggravate me further and hear what we were saying. "What are you doing here? Get lost!" he said to her in feigned irritation. "Go on, do the show," he told me. After a few minutes I noticed Missy standing in the doorway alone, arms crossed staunchly. "I need to talk to you," she insisted over the music.

"The show must go on. On with the show," I answered, half-remembering our small Sunday evening audience.

She shook her head vigorously, so on impulse I went back there. Although I was fifteen pounds lighter, and at 5' 5 1/2" a couple of inches taller, in my three-inch heels I towered above Missy in her sandals. "I just wanted to get to know you and find out what kind of person you are," she whined. It hardly sounded sincere.

"Don't you realize how superficial that is? I've had a relationship with Art for years. I care about him. I don't want to get to know you. You and I aren't going to be friends. That's impossible. If you had any sense, you would leave me alone."

"You are a very sick person," said Missy.

Instinctively I reached out with my right hand and for an instant dug my fingernails into her fleshy forearm. Missy's lips tightened into self-absorbed purpose as she turned away and left. Although the whole incident left me feeling uneasy, the show continued uneventfully. When it was over, I went back to sitting in the audience, and Missy and Art were gone. But I soon found out Art and Jim were catering to her demands.

A week later I got an official phone call from Vince, "Art wants to cool your jets for awhile, Simone. You can call it a layoff. Go down and apply for unemployment." That gray afternoon my security crumbled. I was banished from the inconstant O'Farrell and from Art's life.

CHAPTER 6:
Hunter's Defiant Note, and Double Trouble: The Mayor vs. the Senate Page

JANUARY 18, 1986

Three months after being laid off, I got a message on my machine from the O'Farrell. I called Vince in the morning. He said, "Jim asked me last week, 'Whatever happened to Simone?' So he'd like to have you back, and I don't think Art would object too much. What you should do is come down here and catch the two of them together. Call me this afternoon and maybe they'll be back by then."

I talked to my two best friends for strategy and dressed with care—as hot as I could but with a serious conservative edge befitting an accused—black suede Yves St. Laurent heels, marquisette pin, black jacket, short red dress to show off my legs. Spraying on a discreet amount of "Paris," I tried to summon up a smile in the mirror. With long dark hair and green eyes, I still looked too serious and idealistic, for a stripper. Clearly reflected in the glass was an ex-schoolteacher with an addiction to the outrageous. Unmistakably, I was a woman who was old enough to know she was deeply in love.

I felt a sea of mixed emotions. Being away from the place for awhile had given me a clearer perspective. Now I knew that walking into the O'Farrell was like crossing a border into a principality as foreign as Shangri-La, with its own unique customs, and a constantly changing party-line point of view that necessitated denial. Jim and Art Mitchell were kings there, and games were played for power. Women were encouraged to prove how hot and uninhibited they were, while the men measured their sexuality by their number of conquests. Once

101

I stepped back through those doors, I had to deal with life on their terms, no matter how fanciful, harsh, or strange it might seem. Once I was within Mitchell territory, I'd be living on X-rated time.

I was going back. There was no question about it. I drove shivering with fear, keeping a sudden sense of nausea in check. Dealing with a pair of countercultural entrepreneurs bent on a pornographic crusade wasn't easy. Would I get to tell my side of what led to the argument? I wondered. What would they do to try to make me crawl? Everyone had to do some penance to come back to the O'Farrell—it's a ritual, and part of the game. Thinking, they're not going to break me, and thinking, what more could happen, what do I have to lose? And thinking, I haven't been this broke in the last five years, I pushed open a mirrored glass door and felt the slightest chill.

Inside the plush lobby, past the box office and the king-size fish tanks, was the staircase to the executive offices of Mitchell Brothers. Moving past the photo of a sleek Marilyn Chambers used to promote *Behind the Green Door*, I ventured in on the thick green carpet of the inner sanctum. Vince, tall with wavy brown hair, sat behind the roll-top desk from which he cleverly administered the entire operation. He was Machiavellian, yet at times, benevolent; feared yet cultivated by the dancers; implicitly loyal to the brothers and adept at defending them. "Simone, you came at a good time," Vince greeted me. "They're in there."

"Simone, it's good to see you," said Dan O'Neill, notorious since the 60's as an underground cartoonist, and longtime O'Farrell groupie. A disreputable hat, irreverent overgrown mustache, and long hair heightened his whimsical expression. Just beyond him was Rocky, Art and Jim's bearded cousin, a tough-looking, quiet good old boy, who worked there as a janitor.

Three dancers in lacy lingerie, rhinestones and heels, perched on the edge of the pool table. The pretty California girl-next-door types, whose clean-cut image and sexy magnetism have been so essential to the success of all Mitchell Brothers productions.

Jim Mitchell was just inside the door. They were having a drunken spaghetti feed and had already half-eaten a dried-up, out-of-season game bird they shot early that morning, to destroy the evidence. A faint odor of marijuana hung in the air.

"Simone, you're back," Jim turned toward me, steel-eyed. Ralph Lauren casual, he was bald with a trim mustache, slightly overweight but powerful, a man who clearly savored the accouterments of success, and his position of authority. Half-drunk at the moment, Jim was seductively forceful in his touch. Referring to my argument with Missy, Jim stated, "In these cat fights, the rule of thumb is, both kitties have to go because it disrupts things for the other kitties. It doesn't matter who started it." Jim sounded typically sarcastic, but was relishing the King Solomon aspects of his role that day, having been able to banish, being able to pardon, "But you have friends in high places. And since Christianity, we believe in giving a guy a second chance, so we'd like to have you back. Art, Simone's here."

"Party Artie," devastating, bearded and slender, walked over with the assured style of an outlaw, and gave me a kiss. It was polite. I didn't want it polite—I wanted it passionate. Art kept love intense and compelling, he was a flawless player in control of an ever-changing, unfolding game. A game I had to win. I followed him longingly with my eyes down to the other end of the pool table. Art stretched out on the floor like an animal, on top of one of those padded cloths used to cover packing crates.

"Help yourself . . . ." Jim suggested. "Have some spaghetti."

Vince came in. "Yeah, you can have some of that," he snickered, pointing to a paper plate of parsley.

O'Neill helped me to a serving of this horrible white spaghetti, red sauce with bird gizzard cooked into it, which I felt I had to taste as some kind of sacramental gesture. The girls were looking through the new *Playboy* and pointed out a small photo. "Oh, there's Missy. Miss Congeniality." Missy—the kitty who had me fired.

The office looked the same—it was dominated by the pool table, fishing relics, mementos, and a poker table reminiscent of Art and Jim's Depression-era, Okie gambler father, J.R. Mitchell, who schooled them well in living outside the law.

Art got up off the floor, came over to me, and said, "I want some of that pussy," in his rich Oklahoma drawl, lawless, always melted me completely. I put my plate down and followed him down the hall, into a scene from one of his movies.

He closed the door softly, then pulled me onto his lap, and I told him, "I really missed you."

"No," Art said, as I looked into his sultry indecent brown eyes, "you mean you love me."

He pulled my red dress up and slipped into me, while pressing his head to my breast, "Keep your mouth shut and I'll fuck you in secret," he said. Fat chance. "Be the slave to love that you are, Simone," he said, stealing a line from the dreamlike Bryan Ferry hit song.

"I still love you, Art," I said as he was coming. "I'll always love you."

"Is whoever's fucking you fucking you right?" he asked.

"I'm not seeing anybody," I hugged him.

Art said, "Enjoy your spaghetti."

I went right out to the manager, Vince, who asked, "What happened?"

"I think I can come back," I replied.

Vince told me to call Monday and O'Neill kept offering me his chair. But I didn't want to sit down, I wanted to leave. Vince said, "By the way, did you ever see Hunter's note?" Hanging down over the window were six sheets of yellow lined paper all taped together, penned in a large defiant scrawl by Hunter Thompson. I tried to lean over Vince to read it.

The first part deplored the evils of the business and then over and over he was asking whatever happened to his friend Simone, the spirit of the O'Farrell, the most creative girl act, what evil bastard was responsible for this hatchet job on his good friend Simone. All this really heartwarming stuff.

Vince said, "You know, there're probably five or six versions of that story, one of them's over there, I'm saving that for the archives."

"I never told anyone my story," I said. "But I don't care, if I can come back."

And as I turned and walked away I heard O'Neill say softly, "And now we have a gorilla."

～

The weekend floated by. I had the confidence that I was getting my job back at Mitchell Brothers, the money tied to it, and hopefully even Art. Maybe everything would be the way it was before—before some of Missy's lies led to my being laid off. I had no idea at the time what crazy stories she had concocted. Someone thought it was advisable to separate us during the preparations for the new movie epic.

I was nervous going back to work that first night. You never knew what they might have in mind. As soon as I got upstairs Vince, in a Yale sweater, asked me snidely, "What shows are you doing tonight, Simone, are you doing the gorilla show?"

I told him no, I was doing Mayor Feinstein and my TV dinners show.

Art was there, over in the side dressing room flirting with some dancers, but I ignored him. Because I didn't have to dance for awhile, I put on some black satin lingerie and went downstairs into the audience to make some tip money.

At the bottom of the stairs I ran into the Ultra Room girls—Lisa, wearing just a glistening gold chain belt and black patent heels, and her partner, in thigh-high boots of black leather.

"This is just like the Twilight Zone, you know, how suddenly you're out and then you're back in here again," I joked.

They laughed.

After the local dives I had been exiled to briefly, the O'Farrell audience seemed like heaven. No great cloud of smoke. Nobody visibly drinking or passing out. No one doing handjobs in the back. Nobody grabbing me so hard I had to physically struggle with them to get away. A clean-cut, well-heeled bunch of customers, with a tad more intellect and sophistication. Finally, it was time to go upstairs and get ready.

For my first show that evening; I chose my imitation of then mayor, now California Senator Dianne Feinstein. I played her as a wide-eyed innocent discovering her wild side. Having done this show hundreds of times, it didn't take me very long to get ready. I got my props together, including a white plastic dildo with a red valentine sticker, which I would brandish for a few moments at the beginning of Tony Bennett's "I Left My Heart in San Francisco," my last song. I made sure the toy cable car I would play with—that would be the Mayor's ultimate turn-on—fit snugly with my "Mayor's Office" sign and everything else inside the briefcase. With black fishnets under the suit, new highway patrol sunglasses, a negligee over my arm and my music cued, I was ready to go on.

Art appeared all of a sudden with three male visitors who were going to watch my show from the tech booth above the stage. He introduced me as Dianne Feinstein. I smiled and said hello, then Art pulled me away. Grabbing my briefcase first, I went down the stairs to the deserted side of the stage and found him, jeans already unzipped.

"That was fun the other day," he said. "I might want to do that all the time having you back here. But maybe I shouldn't bother you anymore. You're a part of the team. You were never actually fired, you know. Missy might be here tonight."

Rats! Why was she still around? I wondered silently.

"You better stay away from her," he warned. "You better keep your emotions under control."

"Art," I said, "you really pushed me beyond human endurance talking me into fucking her wearing that costume and then walking out on me. How could you do a thing like that to me?"

"I'm sorry. I don't know how I could do such a shitty thing like that to you," he said arrogantly. It sounded like he was still doing tons of cocaine. Whenever Art was doing drugs or drinking a lot, he spent less time with me—I hated it. It was cyclical. Coke put him in a mean mood and gave his imagination a grandiose bent.

"And," I continued on in an irritated tone, "You never even listened to my side of the story."

"Well," he said, "it doesn't matter. I don't care what actually happened. The only thing that matters to me is what I think happened."

"Well, I care what really happens," I said. "It's important."

"Maybe I should just leave you alone," he taunted. "It might be better for you anyway. I'm headed for the slammer." The slammer! He'd been using that one for years.

"No. I still love you," I heard myself say.

Meanwhile, my music was starting and I had to go on right away. Art was zipping up his Levi's as I adjusted my mayoral bow and walked toward the stage. "I don't think you can get on that way," he said. "It might be locked!"

Luckily it opened, and I stepped onto the stage just in time. As the spotlight hit me, I felt so much anguish I almost turned around and walked off and away from Mitchell Brothers forever.

"I'm coming back to you, Simone," Art promised three months before. I knew he would—no matter what he was saying at the moment.

The music began playing, and I did my set like an automaton. Afterwards I changed quickly and went back to the audience, figuring that if I could last the night I'd make the money I needed. My controlled anguish came across as seductive determination, and I made my tips.

I dressed for my second show in a white satin apron over a black sequined dress, to look like a glamorous 50's housewife preparing dinner. I rinsed a big aluminum pan of plastic and real food, and dusted off my rubber chicken. Then I spotted underground cartoonist Dan O'Neill. A Mitchell buddy, he was one of the muralists decorating the set for the new movie.

"Are you ready for a joint?" he asked.

"No," I glared. "Art did something really horrid to me! He got me downstairs with him for some sex, then he told me, 'Stay away from Missy.'" I can't believe he's still seeing her! He made me so angry I felt like leaving here forever. If it's going to be like this, I'm not going to be able to stay."

"So stay away from her. Besides, Missy might wear out her welcome. Who knows what may happen next?"

My eyes burned back at him.

"You look so sorrowful. You don't have to feel that way, you know. If you want to feel sorrow all you have to do is turn on the TV."

"I never watch television," I snapped back.

"Besides, there is no good or bad behavior, there's just behavior."

"But you could say that of Caligula. Did you know he had me fuck her in the gorilla costume?"

"Yeah, I heard that. I bet she'd have a different version. Anyway, you can't go, we've written you into the movie."

"As what, a gorilla or somebody being ravished by a gorilla?"

I guess I wasn't supposed to have known that much yet, because O'Neill just glared with hostility and coldness. He backed away from me, the figure of a deranged housewife, a figure out of time that should be in a tidy kitchen somewhere baking apple pies, not on stage at the O'Farrell.

After I locked the door of my apartment that night, I screamed.

I couldn't help thinking about Missy. Missy, who had plopped her ass down in the middle of the lobby announcing, "I'm not leaving 'til somebody fucks me," until Art ripped the crotch out of her black lace body stocking and hustled her out the door. Her mindless grin, her drunken enthusiasm, her limitless, crazed energy. Missy, who walked in one day in a pair of those glittery red fuck-me shoes, flaunting her twenty-year-old tits, and walked out with a coked-up Art.

Rita suggested and I understood, that if Missy ever came after me again, that I should beat the living fuck out of her—and be punished for a real attack instead of for something that never took place, like I had been the previous fall.

I had no trouble imagining an even more satisfying showdown: " . . . Prepare to meet your maker, Missy." . . . I stand before her, a loaded German field-marshal's pistol pointed at her heart, wearing iridescent turquoise cowgirl leathers, a machine-gun bullet bandolier glistening against my tanned breasts. The tip of every fifth tracer bullet gleams red, my thighs are bare and pussy wet under the fringed skirt, spurs shining against soft, tan boot leather. I can feel the grit of hot red Texas dirt under my feet. Behind us, looms the Alamo. Missy begins to whimper as I look at her with the coldest of steel gray, relentless eyes.

Unexpectedly I hear the voice of John Wayne: "And if you're right in your heart, you're right. And if you're in the wrong, you're deader than a beaver hat." Just before squeezing the trigger, I pause . . ..

The first time Art came over to my house he was wearing one of those Davy Crockett hats, raccoon tail hanging down to his shoulders. Art lived his life like scenes from movies he was directing. How I missed him. I was eager for our next scene to start.

Friends tried to console me or to tell me I was better off without him, "I'd give it at the most, two, maybe three months more. Maybe he's fantasizing he's a pimp."

"If he doesn't realize he's a pimp by now, he's in trouble."

Sometimes Art would just peer down at me from the darkness in the tech booth, letting me know he was there.

"If you don't fucking want me, just stop," I told him.

"Admit it, you really loved it last week," he said.

"You could come over. Call me and come over."

"If I wanted to come over I still have your key."

"It doesn't work anymore . . .. You'd have to call me."

Just as soon as I unlocked my door that night, my phone rang. But when I answered, no one was there. This began to happen regularly.

In a couple of weeks, I stood over the schedule for March in the hallway. I was almost shaking. They gave me twenty-two shifts—a phenomenal number—and the Ultra Room and Kopenhagen shows by myself. I would earn the best money of my life if I could keep up the pace, and it would be fun to carry the room shows alone. Maybe they were paying me back for laying me off unjustly in the first place—or trying to bribe me to be in the film. The general craziness surrounding this movie intrigued me. Maybe by being inventive I could turn the situation around. What would happen then? Since I had developed an understanding of Art's nature, I could triumph over any woman.

I always loved a challenge, and my competitive drive propelled me through the next months, and sustained me throughout my affair with Art. Maybe the military fervor I grew up with—of ignoring adversity and keeping your mind on victory—came into play. Come hell or high water—I was determined to win in the end. Why not fight for what you desire?

Although it may sound crazy now, during these years my sexual attraction to Artie was so strong that I tended to overlook his insensitive behavior towards me. And I felt so embedded in life at the O'Farrell, I never thought seriously about leaving the place. Art was skilled at using his sexual flair as a lure to keep women captivated.

Up the stairs from my flat, past her collection of posters from our trip to Europe, in her warm kitchen with Canadian mementos, I spent the afternoon sharing ideas and strategizing with Rita. Five years earlier, we had each started dancing at Mitchell Brothers. Once a teacher and a bookkeeper for Revenue Canada Taxation, Rita had moved to the States with her two children, and was now a single mom. She was a practical inventive survivor, and a solid supportive friend.

"You can store the gorilla costume up here, if you like," Rita said. I packed it into her closet, inside a suitcase near the carefully constructed dummy of a man she used in a show. Now it had a little fake Christmas tree leaning against its stomach.

After three weeks, I was in good financial shape again, at least compared to recently. It was hard to beat the money you could make dancing at the O'Farrell. Vince sought me out one afternoon, "Did you see this?" he asked, pointing to the casting call notice they put in the paper for the movie. "Make sure you go to that. Don't worry, if we have you do something in the movie we'll make sure it's weird." Great.

≈

"Would you step into the light, please," a disembodied voice asked, from a tiny window high above the darkened auditorium. They were videotaping auditions for the new movie for Art and Jim and the crew to review later, while projecting a gigantic live camera image of each person being auditioned on the movie screen at the back of the stage. Despite all this pretension, Kenny, the DJ I had worked with for five years, was running the equipment and asking the questions. In his white-bread Florida accent he said, "State your name."

"Jerri Fallwell," I joked, standing alone in the spotlight on the stage.

"No, state your name."

"It's Simone," I gave my stage name.

"And would you tell us why you would like to be in a Mitchell Brothers movie."

Softly, "I want to be a gorilla."

"What?"

"I really think they want me to be a gorilla."

"Why else would you like to be in the movie?"

"It might be interesting." (It might be horrible.)

"And could you tell us if you have any sexual fantasies that you would like to act out in the movie."

"Well, I'm certain they have something in mind." (IN MIND, IN MIND, IN MIND, reverberating down a canyon.) I can't think of anything."

"Oh, but can't you think of some sexual fantasy you would like to take part in?"

"No. They have something in mind. I can't think of anything." I was afraid to think of anything, afraid they might make me do it. At that moment, I never wanted to have sex again, on or off camera. I said, "I guess I could try almost anything."

"All right. Would you step off the stage now and take off all your clothes, and then step back into the light."

I stepped back into the light bare-ass naked, feeling doomed.

"Will you turn slowly, please." I did, wondering who would scrutinize the tape.

"Moon the camera."

"Do I have to?" I couldn't. This reminded me of strip searches, draconian prisons.

"No. That's all. Thank you."

I said to the next two dancers, "These people have seen enough of my body in the last five years."

After Rita had her interview and left the stage to strip, I ran back into the light in a black bustier and tights and the infamous fur mask that caused all the trouble. Behind me on the huge movie screen at the back of the stage, my gorilla head loomed eight feet wide, and I began to sing:

"It's very clear, our love is here to stay.

Not for a year, but forever and a day."

Louder, "In time the Rockies may crumble,"

Still louder, "Gibraltar may tumble,

They're only made of clay, but . . ."

And stretching my arms out wide I leaned forward, an ape once more, towards the camera, and sang . . . with feeling or its illusion, "Our love is here to stay."

I had heard the rumor before, but seeing it in print was still awful. Looking down at me from the bulletin board was a photograph of my rival. "Cover Model Missy! The Next Marilyn Chambers?" the adult paper *Spectator* asked in red letters. Inside was an article scooping her debut in the coming movie.

What an unlikely adult film actress she was. Missy's father was a wealthy Washington politician she would call from time to time to say, "Daddy, I'm going to be a porn star!" Art would have eaten this right up. And I heard she was doing things like crawling under the tablecloth to titillate him in restaurants.

Since movie sales of *Behind the Green Door* skyrocketed in the early 70's when the press discovered that Marilyn Chambers' wholesome, girl-next-door face appeared on Ivory Snow flakes boxes, the Mitchells hoped to cash in on Missy's equally unusual background. She had served as a page for conservative Republican Senator Orrin Hatch.

Months before, a timely issue, which affected the adult industry, had been engendered by the AIDS epidemic: safe sex. By making a safe sex film, Art and Jim could market their production as educational and socially redeeming.

The brothers wanted another big hit. Sales figures for films released by the Mitchell Brothers Film Group were never disclosed by them. But in his October 1991 Penthouse article, Al Goldstein estimated that world-wide box office and tape sales for their most popular movie, *Behind the Green Door* starring Marilyn Chambers, has grossed $50 million. With two clever publicity angles, Art and Jim thought the sequel to *Green Door* should make them a fortune.

No wonder Missy had been able to get me out of the O'Farrell for awhile, since the brothers were serious about starring her in *Behind the Green Door, II.* How awful it could be for me to be on the set, with her the center of attention—for Art and everyone else.

A week went by and my restlessness grew. I dreaded the movie getting nearer. It was creepy no one had yet told me what I would be expected to do in it. Did they still want me to be a gorilla? No one mentioned my singing in the gorilla mask at the audition.

Sunday evening I noticed that the cover photo of Missy, still posted, had been vandalized. Now matted lashes framed her eyes, a pirate-like scar marred her cheek, and oddly misshapen lips announced in a cartoon bubble: "I want you to cum on my face." I relished looking at this each trip I made upstairs, but toward the end of the night I began to wonder in paranoia if they would think I had done it.

It was natural that other dancers, too, would feel jealous of the extraordinary piece of luck that had fallen into Missy's hands.

～

A few nights later Jim came into the side dressing room and said to a group of us women, "In Roman times you would have been called . . ." and he said some weird word, like "danaeids."

"Oh, not vestal virgins?" I asked.

"These are like the Roman times," Jim continued. "Before Guilt."

"Before Shame," I said.

"You know, for the movie we're having a guy from the San Francisco Opera make up a costume for the guy that comes through the green door. He'll be made up as the god Pan. He'll have cloven hooves that will clatter across the tile."

"That's brilliant," I said. What had they been ingesting?

"Yeah, this guy, he'll look really like a mythological creature. His balls and his face and everything will be red, and he'll have these cloven hooves. And everybody that sees him will know all he wants is—pussy."

What a scream.

"Oh, I like it!" I enthused. The other dancers were silent.

"You like it," Jim said. "You'd volunteer to practice with the guy?"

"Yeah," I laughed softly.

Jim gave me a cool smile and left our dressing room.

~

Friday I was called to the office. Jim said, "Stand up straight so I can see your posture . . .. Good. Now we need to know what you are willing to do in the movie. We have four different categories: people who don't want to have sex, people who will do girl-girl, those who want to do boy-girl only, and those we call B & D, those who will do anything!"

Art walked past me into the office and leered warmly, "You should have an extra special category for Simone."

"What do *you* want me to do?" I asked him.

"Oh, I want *you* to do *everything*." Art stared intently.

"O.K." I agreed. "I don't have to make it with a dwarf, do I?"

They both laughed. In addition to the general casting call, they had run an ad for midgets, fat ladies, and geeks for the shoot.

I was told to change into an evening dress for approval and Art said, "I'll cast her." In a quiet upstairs room he stared into my eyes icily, slipped his hand under my dress and started to finger me. "You better go ahead and get a nut against my finger and show me how hot you are, and how much you want to be in this movie," he murmured. What a parody—was he really testing me for the film? After a couple of minutes, he asked me to go show my dress to their co-director, Sharon McKnight.

I turned for Sharon's approval of a glittery royal blue dress, as Artie eyed me from the doorway. "She has really nice thighs," he said of me.

Back we went into the same room for some sex. This time Art reached for a Polaroid and snapped a picture unexpectedly. Next to the open window over the street he pulled up my blue dress and put me over a chair to finish it off, finally hitting my g-spot perfectly with his cock, to orgasm. Then he took a photo of my face for the movie and I burst into laughter. "Here's a little souvenir for you to take home," he handed me the first explicit picture—I was glad to get it, not wanting it floating around for other eyes to see. Relieved that they seemed to have abandoned the gorilla concept, I went back into the dressing room elated.

My friend Suzanne called me at 1:00 a.m. Her truck was towed from behind the theater and she wanted to do shows with me the next day to earn the money to get it out. I told her sure. Like schoolgirls, we talked most of the night in bed, wearing the two pink and white lace Dior nightgowns I splurged on the previous fall. Suzanne had been dancing only a few months. They had been after her to do the film. Art had offered her the leading role in front of Missy, saying there were two leads. Polite as pie, he took her back to the office alone and offered her five thousand dollars to do it. I couldn't tell her how serious he was. Rita had told me that it was customary for some porn directors to talk about the lead to a lot of women to get into their pants. Then the star would be some established actress from LA.

"You might have to fuck Art if you want a major role in the movie," I told her.

"You're kidding."

"No. They wouldn't let you be the star without you having sex with somebody to see what you were like, probably Art. Remember, this is a sex film."

Suzanne hesitated, believing everyone would know her secrets if she was in the movie. There would be no more mystery. Everyone in her hometown would see it.

Until that year I hadn't considered doing a sex scene in a film, either. By the 80's, porn movie work was highly competitive. For women, it was crazy to expect much success if you weren't very photogenic, uninhibited, and under twenty-five. I knew my limitation would be doing live shows. Still, taking part in *Behind the Green Door, the Sequel* had the intoxicating appeal of all things taboo. If I had to re-enter the straight work world in the future and someone said they recognized me from a Mitchell Brothers film, I thought, maybe I could just say, No, that wasn't me.

In the morning I brought in the Western stuff I'd had made to use in shows for the first time: a cowgirl costume; a horse mask with a sprig of hay in its teeth, that I would hang on the side of the Ultra Room that day as a prop. The strap-on dildo harness with a horsetail would only be used if someone was tipping well, and wanted to see it at the end of the show. I had a branding iron with the letters "M B," for Mitchell Brothers, made in a metal shop. A sound technician had added a real sizzle to a couple of pauses on my last song to sound like branding. It was the perfect day to do a new show. Art, Jim and Vince were all there, getting ready for the movie. As I pressed the branding iron into some black theatrical makeup and onto Suzanne's ass, I could see by the expression in Vince's experienced eyes I'd come up with another novel idea. There were so many beautiful women at Mitchell Brothers, being hot wasn't enough. I had fun being hot and inventive.

One of the songs I chose for that show was so ironic it made me smile:

"Movin', movin', movin', 'though they're disapprovin', keep them doggies movin', Rawhide . . .

"Don't try to understand 'em, just rope and throw and brand 'em ..."

After all, hadn't that been Art's doctrine for years?

My buying an expensive costume right then would be taken as a show of good faith on my part. It was an indication I believed I would be around for awhile and was capable of dealing with Missy's expanded role in things. Art, Jim, and Vince liked to feel you trusted them. If they were about to fuck you over it was much more fun if you didn't expect it. O'Farrell dancers learned to look over their shoulders, knowing at any moment the blade could fall.

Jeff Armstrong said, "I'm really glad to see you around here again. Your friend Hunter Thompson called the other day and asked how you were. Now I can tell him you're back in the saddle again."

Sharon McKnight told me I was to wear my cowgirl costume in the movie with my gun belt. This was comforting. Somehow, I felt this would depict my being angry, Western style, at the turn things had taken.

Jim walked into the dressing room a little later to say, "Well, Tex, we've found out after considerable research about a substance that kills AIDS. And we have plenty of it back in the office if you ever want to clean your sex toys. It basically boils down to—alcohol. So when in doubt, add vodka and stir."

"Ah, just like a swizzle stick," I answered. Jim was being cordial to me—the movie was only a week away. There were so many lesbians, and followers of the Bhagwan Shree Rajneesh dancing at the theater, they wouldn't have too many women willing to do heterosexual stuff on film.

There had always been a few gay women dancing at the O'Farrell, but after the early 80's, the Mitchells recognized the positive political aspects of hiring more of them.

The late cult leader Bhagwan Shree Rajneesh's popularity brought a steady stream of young women from all over the world through San Francisco, on their way to visit his 64,000-acre communal Oregon ranch. Many of them were hired at Mitchell Brothers, as well. Wealthy enough to keep a fleet of ninety-three Rolls-Royces paid for by his supporters' contributions, the Bhagwan was a strong advocate of sensuality and sexuality. But since AIDS, he had issued specific warnings so his followers wouldn't get the disease.

On Monday Rita called the O'Farrell and got Art on the phone. "I'd like to be in your movie. What are you paying?" she asked.

"A hundred dollars a day to suck and fuck."

119

"Oh, I can't do *that.*"

Art hung up. At her boyfriend's North Beach apartment, she agonized. Rita wanted to do the movie. She hadn't been allowed to work at the O'Farrell for a year—ever since she starred at the Market Street Cinema, and Vince noticed her name on the marquee. Since then, she had been working in a club on Broadway in North Beach. But what if Rita needed to return to Mitchell Brothers? Doing the movie would help her to come back, give her another club to work while she spent time in San Francisco with her children.

Late in the afternoon, Rita called the theater again, "I think I was a little hasty this morning when I talked to you. I would like to be in your movie," she managed. "I was just surprised at what you're paying." Art, considerably drunker, softened right up.

Rita was asked to come in the next day for approval of the costume she planned to wear, a red-beaded stripper gown she had paid twelve-hundred dollars to have custom-made for her feature bookings on the road. She asked Art if we would be paid for the Saturday rehearsal and he answered, "It's a labor of love."

"I think somehow I blew it today the first time I talked to Art," Rita told me that night.

"No, you didn't. You're in the movie," I said. "They know they're paying ridiculously low money for this. And if you're willing to accept that just to appear in a Mitchell Brothers film, they want you to be fully aware of it."

Her boyfriend Charles De Santos, also a film producer, told her it didn't hurt to kiss ass sometimes. "Never mind about kissing ass," Rita said to me, "I don't want to have to suck dick to be in this thing! The only way you can win in this situation is to do something outrageous. Everyone will see this film because it's the sequel to *Behind the Green Door.* Nobody will know what I'm getting paid. If they have a dwarf, I'll do a scene with a dwarf . . . .. They're kind of cute, anyway."

120

"They do have a dwarf," I told her. "His name is Bernie. He's from Chicago. Forty-one inches tall."

"I think we should both go completely crazy and fuck every guy there and steal the scene from that bitch!"

The brothers wrote "Dwarf" across the bottom of Rita's Polaroid. Lucky Bernie!

A few days later both Rita and I got the flu, but I would not phone in sick. This was *my March*. I was determined to work every last shift they had given me. And no way would I miss the movie. Missy, Art, Jim, and everyone else would interpret my absence from the movie as a lack of guts. I had to hang tough.

By Thursday night, I was pretty sick but still working. As I walked by Vince, I gave him a smile. He was asking Jim, "Has Missy been able to lose any weight?"

One of the gay women said, "No dude is even going to touch me." Her possessive girlfriend didn't approve of her being in the movie at all. She had already told Art and Jim she would have sex with a guy as long as she was wearing a mask. But she wouldn't suck anybody's dick with one of those *things* on (The brothers would provide condoms and rubber gloves.), because she thought it would make her throw up. I told her about Rita's plan to get it on with the dwarf. "Oh, no. I can just see it," she said. "I'll get there and it'll be six in the morning and they'll tell me to suck a dwarf's weenie."

Friday was my last day off before the movie and my last opportunity to see a doctor. Not only did I have a particularly bad cough (How could I possibly give head without starting to cough crazily?), but suddenly I had a yeast infection—I was hardly in the best shape for a sex film.

If I couldn't perform in the movie they would be damned disappointed and probably retaliate by cutting my work schedule. Art and Jim applied the motto they used for their Ultra Kore productions to everyone but themselves; it was "There are no excuses."

Just as I got ready to leave for the clinic the phone rang. It was Vince asking me to work, "Pick up some cough syrup and come down here, it'll be warm."

He must have been desperate. All those bitches were phoning in sick, getting their hair done, nails done, out of general exhilaration and worry. We're going to be in a movie, they were thinking. A MOVIE! The O'Farrell bubbled and pulsed with excitement that March, caught up in the American dream.

I told Vince I needed to go to a doctor—not why—but was not anything major, so he would know I wasn't trying to dodge being in the film.

Although the doctor was concerned I might have pneumonia, the x-ray showed I didn't. That night I was still feverish and coughing. I forced myself to lie horizontal for hours letting the Monistat seep into me, remembering when everything about the sex business seemed glamorous.

Chapter 7:

Problems Behind the Scenes at the Filming of **Behind the Green Door, the Sequel**, and the Quarrel at Hunter's Hotel

MARCH 7, 1986

At 8:00 in the morning I got up and made myself drink some chicken soup, and Robitussin. Thinner from being sick and from tension, I put on an "Alcatraz Swimming Team" sweatshirt, jeans, and high-heeled boots. Rita and I took a cab down to the theater feeling like hell.

Everybody dressed in costume and sat down in the cine-stage. Sharon McKnight, a former fiancée of Jim's, now a stocky cabaret singer, was co-directing. Spiked with hair spray, her short asexual blonde hair kept her look current, and harsh. A tough-as-nails attitude hardened her expression as she began speaking officially from the stage. "This is a movie, not a fuck film," she barked. "If at any time tomorrow any of you think you're not having safe sex, we want you to raise your hands and report it to us." Like so many grade school children, I thought. The whole concept of a safe sex orgy seemed ludicrous. I never saw Art in a condom, much less in rubber gloves. There was nothing safe about him. Sex and love can be ever so dangerous.

"And now I want to introduce Missy, the woman we all believe is going to be hotter than Marilyn Chambers." Wearing a long Laura Ashley dress of blue and white pinstripes with a high neck and an enormous white lace collar, Missy stood like a Hollywood star of the silent screen, holding a little pint-size dog. She pointed to the dog, indicating *it* was Missy. "Missy has such a *great* sense of humor!" Sharon enthused, "For her audition tape she pulled some streamers out of her pussy when she had an orgasm." I cringed.

Art made a brief appearance to welcome everyone. Next, we were introduced to the only member of the cast from the original *Behind the Green Door*, a gray-haired man, about sixty. The only reminder that day of the pornographic rush of time through our hands.

We were asked to sign a release. One of the dancers listed her name for the credits as "Anita Rubber." As I had been doing a little reading for a French Revolution guillotine show, I added "Corday" as a last name to my stage name "Simone," after stoic Charlotte Corday, who murdered the Jacobin deputy Jean-Paul Marat in 1793. The French called her the "Angel of the Assassination," and pronounced, "She has ruined us, but she has taught us how to die." At the guillotine, her severed head was said to have blushed with indignation when held up to the jeers of the crowd.

I was keeping my own head, still. We were told to change back to street clothes and go into the room where the scene would be shot the next day.

The newly christened "Green Door Room" had become exquisite. Dan O'Neill and a few of his artist friends had done some huge faux mythological paintings, Rubenesque goddesses embraced by satyrs, on the two-story high walls. The painters joked that Jim's art student wife Mary Jane had sketched some of the heads on backwards, creating extra work for them. Furnished with padded tables and chairs, the large split-level room was decked out as a nightclub, heavy on Greco-Roman statuary, verdigris, and grapevines. The rear section of the room was higher and a long mahogany bar had been installed at its back. A shiny brass railing ran along the edge of this upper-level, opening for three steps, which led to the larger lower front of the room. A curved stage had been built at the head of the room, where three electrically retractable trapezes were suspended. Deep blue curtains hung at the sides of the stage, while along its back wall an 18-foot wide green door was decorated with a head of Medusa.

Years before I had painted my own bedroom door green, after someone told me the first *Behind the Green Door* was a special and very erotic film. That was long before I saw the movie or came to the O'Farrell. Perhaps I was supposed to be here.

Rita and I were lucky. We had been placed opposite one another like older brunette chess queens, in the inner corners of the elevated back part of the room facing blonde Missy, who had surprisingly left a couple of inches of dark hair roots unretouched. Getting domestic? I wondered. Or was this a sign of how much booze she'd been indulging in?

Missy looked over at me and tittered, either at my Alcatraz shirt or at the man I had been paired with. He was large, tall, gray-haired, balding, and vaguely straight-looking, sort of a cross between an insurance man and a Buddhist. What did she know about this guy that I didn't?

Was I expected to fuck this guy, or would some other form of merciful musical chairs intervene? The thought she might have selected him for me was too much to ponder. I glanced at Missy, a nervous, matronly-looking twenty-four-year old, then at Rita, self-possessed and still beautiful, infinitely grateful that Rita was there.

The cast was briefed on the sequence of the first thirty of the two hundred scenes to be shot tomorrow. This took forever and I began to feel as though I was about to pass out, not having eaten much the day before. My mind wandered and I mulled over how many times I had had sex with Art in this room, in its earlier incarnations. How many times in the basement under the stage while some dancer like Gail jumped around heavily over our heads, performing for the crowd. It wasn't just the fucking that was hot, it was the excitement of the situation, the pressure of time ("You're not next, are you?" Art would tease, seductively.) and his power. How many other dancers had I watched improve and grow stronger as performers . . . after they were singled out for attention by Artie? I remembered the ending of William Butler Yeats's poem Leda and the Swan:

". . . Being so caught up,
So mastered by the brute blood of the air,
Did she put on his knowledge with his power
Before the indifferent beak could let her drop?"

Artie was the spirit of the O'Farrell. It was Artie who kept the shows hot for years. How many women in this room had been infatuated with him? How many had he been with? Probably most of them, at least once. Blossoming under his attention, warming to his touch, bewitched by the steamy conviction in his words, "You're the hottest woman here!"

During a short break in our briefing by Sharon, Art walked up to me and said, "Rita's gonna fuck the dwarf. Do you want a piece of that?"

I said, "You want me to do *that?*" incredulously.

With a cocaine leer, he walked off in Rita's direction. She had begun talking to the dwarf, who was calling himself "Squirt." Later she told me when she first saw the dwarf, her heart sank. Art came up to her and said, outside my range of hearing, "Getting acquainted? Hey, how would you feel about Simone doing a three-way with you two tomorrow?"

"Art, go easy on Simone," Rita said protectively. "She's not well, you know. The doctor thought she had pneumonia."

As soon as he suggested this, I worried even more. Wasn't this already ordeal enough? Art was trying to come up with something I would not want to do. And with something he and Missy could laugh about forcing me into. Maybe this was even her suggestion. The evil bastard!

I could see myself as Charlotte Corday, racing around the stage to avoid the guillotine and the evil executioner, trailing wine colored velvet and throwing off my gold slippers, in a futile attempt to escape. Prince would intone "Head" from the orchestra pit. Then Jim Morrison would join in to eloquently roar, "Blood in the streets it's up to my ankles; blood in the streets it's up to my knees. . ." I would cry out in protest: "No, no, anything but that."

Anything but that. I had told the brothers from the beginning that I didn't want to fuck the dwarf. Now I felt like a pawn in chess, not a queen. Perhaps we all were, all except for Art and Jim.

I had wondered about Artie's intentions concerning Missy, much as I hated and despised her. What, exactly was going through his diabolical mind. Wouldn't it be some kind of triumph for Artie to be able to say in film, "Hey, there, Mr. Washington Politician . . . I've got your little girl. Wanna watch while I have her gang-banged by my handpicked, multi-ethnic studs? Ever see this before? Ever think about it? Now you can watch your own daughter do it, preserved forever on film, for the entire world to watch for the next hundred years."

Art hated the political establishment. It made me smile to remember his using the California Democratic Convention flag as a towel, after the '84 convention failed to bring free-spending crowds to the O'Farrell.

I would have to protect myself during the movie. If I was going to have sex, I would stay away at all costs from the dwarf, from the fat black-bearded transsexual, from her enormous lover Voluptuous Venus, and from the too friendly gigantic man named Rex Havoc seated near me. I would leave my mask on in case something unexpected came in my direction. All this for a lousy hundred and twenty-five bucks.

We took a lunch break, and all that was left was parsley. Paulie, perpetually struggling to stay on top of things, was gleefully throwing sprig after sprig into his mouth as I asked him, "Is that it for the food?"

Much later in the afternoon, I found Sharon McKnight and said, "Art came up to me this morning and suggested I get it on with the dwarf. I don't want to. My friend Rita said she would do that."

"Don't worry about it," Sharon said. "You don't have to."

That reassured me a little. But it was still a dastardly long night. Once again, I lay sleepless. I kept thinking, That cold hearted son of a bitch never did love me. How could he and want *me* to fuck a dwarf in one of his movies. And after Rita's outmaneuvering and never once having sex with anyone connected with the O'Farrell, I would be damned if he would have us in a three-way on film with some freak. It seemed like the last straw, somehow. Art was trying to force me into something I hated, and humiliate my best friend and I, together. Goebbels could have thought of something this clever.

Since I had come back, I felt almost like a street urchin in a Dickens novel, my cold nose and fingertips pressed longingly against the glass window of the parlor of the big house, as Christmas dinner was served and Art, Missy, and all the others sat around an elegant table. The darkness outside without him was profound.

My being pleased with him days earlier now seemed laughable. Set in the heady world of the O'Farrell, playing and winning at love with Art Mitchell was no tranquil endeavor. The game required total concentration, perseverance, and an infinite capacity to forgive. For me, playing well was imperative. There was no way out.

My father had to be tough—he survived three wars, and even a stint at the Nevada Testing Grounds in the 50's. When he got a letter from the government years ago inquiring if he had cancer, I asked, "Gee, wasn't it awful scary out in those trenches in Nevada, Dad, when they were exploding those atom bombs out there?"

"Oh, no," he said. "You just put your arm up across your eyes, like this." He demonstrated.

That night I thought of the cowboy riding the warhead home in director Stanley Kubrick's *Dr. Strangelove, or How I Learned to Stop Worrying and Love the Bomb.* I would dress like him in the morning, very nearly the last straight dancer at Mitchell Brothers, a Western survivor of a fading heterosexual world, where men were men and women still loved them. I was an inflexible survivor of a previous era, when passion was still empowering and loyalty wasn't just drawn out of you and then laughed at with contempt as the rules were changed. Against the most menacing of odds, I was still ruled by my heart.

At 6:00 a.m. the next morning, Rita and I took a cab down to the O'Farrell in the rain. The place was alive with a hundred people, slated for the most atypical mainstream porn film of the 80's.

BEHIND THE GREEN DOOR, THE SEQUEL — TAKE 1

Jim Mitchell in a starched white formal shirt, black tie, stood in front of my tuxedoed partner and me. I was dressed as a cowgirl. "You don't want to have sex today, do you?" Jim joked. He looked perturbed, because so few of the women on the set were willing to actually have sex. Only a few women came to the advertised audition, although nearly three hundred men showed up, so the brothers drafted the O'Farrell dancers, offering $100 for the day ($125 if you supplied your own costume). Even with condoms, in the dawning age of AIDS, few of the dancers wanted to be there at all, let alone indulge in filmed group sex, although most of the men wanted to—this produced a hostile undercurrent. "What if they threw an orgy and nobody wanted to fuck?" was the joke of the day. Of course, I had different priorities.

"What do you want me to do?" I asked Jim.

"Reach around and start playing with his dick, get it out, put a condom on it. When he's hard, raise your hand, and we'll come over with the cameras."

Missy stood facing me, on the stage twenty-five feet away, professionally made-up and coifed, watching my every move. Hoping I would fail or do something worthy of being fired again. I could see her smirking, even through my cheap gold Halloween mask.

Thrilled to be in his only sex film ever, my guy was up right away. I raised my hand and the cameras arrived. "O.K. He's hard."

"I'm afraid I'm gonna come too fast," my partner worried.

"You can't come too fast. We don't want to be here all night!" Jim said. "Drop his pants down around his ankles."

I eased the pants down and the guy peeled off his shirt, revealing more appalling dark body hair over his back and shoulders, than anyone I've ever seen. Prior knowledge of this hair was probably why Missy was tittering earlier.

"We want you to give this guy a blowjob," Jim leadenly directed. "Do you have any problem with that?"

"No." Almost none of the other women in the room would be willing. I had to upstage the amateur star.

If it was the opening day of the World Series, the stadium would be jammed with fans, and I would be playing Mayor Dianne throwing out the very first ball. And he's up!

Missy was surrounded by six sultry brunettes in yellow mini-togas, bearing vibrators (plugged in) to heat her up for the action. Too heavy to appear naked like Marilyn Chambers in the original Green Door, her tits protruded out of a white bra, she had on a garter belt attached to white fishnets, and wore low heeled dowager pumps. She looked stoned and afraid, and complained the other girls were hurting her. "These people are taking advantage of my good nature," she said.

I took some lubricant from one of the many bottles standing about and put some on my partner, then slipped on a sheer green condom. As soon as I went down on him the lubricant seeped its toxic taste through the latex and numbed my mouth—it was Non-Oxynol 9. The turpentine-like flavor made me want to throw up but I couldn't stop, the cameras were on me. I went at it with the intense anger and anxiety of the last six months, determined to get this stranger off and off fast, and my cowboy hat fell onto the floor. Rats!

I could feel my partner getting close and I started to vocally cry as he was in my throat, louder and louder in encouragement as he got close to orgasm. Lose it, go ahead and lose it . . .. It sounded ancient . . .. You bastard, you're ending this in my mouth, when I want so much more. Come, goddamn you. It was too difficult. As soon as he did, I tore off my rubber gloves with the condom and cast them onto the floor in victory.

Framed in the window high above the Green Door Room was Vince, grinning, placing his hand first over his eyes, then above his head. Like—Oh, my God, you did it, after all, Simone. How embarrassing! Then a video person walked to the window and gestured, "O.K."

I rushed out to look for water to rinse the Non-Oxynol 9 taste away.

On my way back Art walked by and gave me a fast appreciative glance. "Hi, Simone," he said.

Rita was trying to inspire the dwarf, while keeping a too large condom on him, as he stood on a barstool wearing boxer shorts printed with red hearts. Later he told Rita, "All those other guys standing around watching me made me nervous."

In the next scene, three men made up in body paint to look like fauns were lowered on trapezes for Missy to condom, then fellate. Missy kept gagging on the latex, and on them.

When the men were hoisted out of sight, she balanced on tiptoe gazing up after them. Art directed, as she sat down on the edge of the platform, pouting, because they disappeared. Art advised, "Do it with your eyes . . .. Don't just drop your mouth!"

Even though she was getting off to such a bad start, *Green Door II*'s success depended on Missy's performance, a burden as much as an opportunity for any unknown.

One man looked and sounded mad. He'd been assigned the role of walking back and forth through the nightclub carrying a cocktail glass, wearing only a top hat, bow tie, and condom. He'd been watching what action there was and wanted to fuck, not play some role out of Samuel Beckett. "I don't need this!" he glowered, red-faced and Irish.

We broke for dinner—the Kopenhagen was set up with a table and cold cuts. I began talking to Gary, an educated and compassionate-sounding amateur actor.

Earlier that afternoon Gary was paired with Erika Idol as her bridegroom. An enormous white 50's formal had been cut down to Erika's size. Erika, who had done porno before, climbed on top of Gary, enveloping him almost completely with the voluminous skirt and rode him, twirling her bouquet. Erika yelled to almost everyone's amusement, "I didn't think you had it in you!"

Gary had pictures in his head of being immortalized on film, his dick in Marilyn Chambers—or at least, in some actress. I told him I wanted to have sex that day too, and we agreed to fuck on camera. Considering some of the very strange people present, it was a comforting pact.

The only actors that went back onto the set after dinner were those who intended to be filmed having sex. I was the only Mitchell Brothers dancer to walk back in there.

Three other actresses went with me: my friend Rita Ricardo, who had starred in a dozen hard-core films; a beautiful Asian woman; and three-hundred-forty-pound Voluptuous Venus—who said, No, she would not roll on top of the dwarf and "kill" him! Maybe Art wasn't the only coked-up director that Sunday.

Accompanying the scant group of women were a larger group of enthusiastic amateur male actors. Jim Mitchell began explaining to a guy dressed as the god Pan, who looked like half a goat, brown yak hair stuck to his legs, how to amble over on his cloven hooves and ravish Missy on one of the tables.

"She robbed me of everything I care about," I told Gary, dryly. "I hate her guts." He gave me a kiss as the action started.

Soon I was going down on first my original partner, then Gary. One of the guys made up in gray paint to look like a statue came over. Having posed artistically all afternoon in a recessed hole in the wall he was eager, "People tell me I give good head."

"I want to fuck," I replied, ripping off my leather heart-shaped g-string.

Gary rammed into me hard, as I held onto the railing, and I began to yell. Banshee screams, seasoned by the Ultra Room, empowering. I ripped off my skirt; Gary put on my cowboy hat and grabbed onto me by the gun belt.

The Statue, looking soft, tried to talk me into a double insertion. I wanted to stick with Gary. We were acting so wild we got all the cameras.

Missy, on a table, mildly copulating the god Pan, looked very upset. She kept calling for Artie.

The camera people told us to turn sideways. "You don't mind if we show some penetration, do you?"

"No," I answered.

"This is something we haven't had very much of."

I was yelling, loud, every encouragement I normally said to Art, ending with, "I want you to get me so goddamn WET." This penetrated the entire room, and petrified Missy.

I looked up. In the window high above us several dancers who wore mini-togas earlier kibitzed, Sharon McKnight behind them.

"How are we doing now," asked John Fontana, the tall expert cinematographer who shot the original *Green Door* and the brothers' earlier movies.

"Fine," I said.

"Now, we want you to come," Fontana directed. I moaned. The cameras left. Gary picked me up by the waist, and sat me down on the railing.

Artie walked up as Gary and I were lost, looking at each other. We had been good. "Nice hard dick," Art told the photographer. "Take some stills."

"You were great!" Dan O'Neill said. "It was so Western! We were watching upstairs on the monitors. Ride 'em cowgirl!"

It was 10:00 p.m. After the sixteen-hour day, everyone was ready to leave. "Now don't go away without saying goodbye," Gary sweetly said to me, heard by O'Neill, who smiled.

Out in the lobby a downcast Missy said to Art, "Just call a cab. Call a cab. Can't we just go!" By then, she knew she didn't like porn, and couldn't do it.

～

Even though it was an ordeal, the day gave me hope. No one on the set could have failed to see that Missy was no Marilyn Chambers.

Art was entertaining himself, playing out some fantasy that had to end in failure.

Kenny told me when they viewed the footage the next day, Missy was indignant. "It's gross!" she shrieked, each time I appeared on the screen. She demanded I be eliminated from the movie.

"It's good," Artie countered, refusing to cut me out. She said that on the set I was screaming "Fuck me, Artie," which I wasn't.

The longtime Mitchell Brothers carpenter spotted me upstairs. "There's our star. I saw your act," he said. "You saved our ass." Draping my red silk dressing gown around me, I walked back to the projector near the office, curious what he was talking about. Since on the day of the shoot I had been focused on what I was doing and the action close to me, I didn't know what the entire orgy had looked like. Jim and Sharon stared grimly through the little window toward the screen in the Cine-Stage where footage from the expensive new movie was running. They said nothing.

From a sixteen-hour day, a cast of eighty amateurs, a costly set, costumes and professional crew, the brothers had filmed almost no sex. At considerable expense, the scene would have to be reshot. (Like *Grafenberg Spot*, *Green Door II* had a budget of $140,000, astounding in comparison to the minimal $3,000 or $4,000 budgets that became common in the 90's.) Among numerous disappointments, the handsome blond male lead never got a hard-on.

⌁

Over the next four months, filming proceeded with difficulty, at a snail's pace. I sensed Missy never wanted the project to end, fearing her role in Artie's life would be over the moment the fuss about the movie ended.

My life was low-key. I took more classes at San Francisco State, and tutored handicapped kids at a high school in the city. Once in awhile I went out casually, with a couple of men. I chose more themes, made costumes, found music for my shows, and became a professional, cool performer.

For a few days in April, Art took Missy to the Cayman Islands, to get some sun and hopefully slim down a little for the reshooting of the orgy scene. On his return, he came to the theater alone, opening a bottle of champagne to celebrate, to announce he was splitting up with her. Then he watched the Ultra Room show I was doing by myself, in scarlet tulle and rhinestones. He smiled from the doorway, while I danced and pulled in money through the tip slots. It was like we were doing the show together.

The next day they reshot the orgy. I was doing shows, warned to stay away from the delicate proceedings on the movie set over in the Green Door Room. The dancers who acted in the scene filled me in.

Unlike other porn stars, Missy refused to have much actual sex on camera. With partner after partner, she balked. During Missy's scene with a black actor made up as a statue, they used a body double. Toni Brooks, a dancer whose build was similar to Missy's, who had done porno, put on Missy's garter belt and white fishnets. They filmed the close-ups with Toni, to intercut later with footage of Missy simulating intercourse in the long shots. Still, by the end of the day Missy was complaining her shoulder was injured, and that she was exhausted. Not surprisingly, the next morning Art came looking for me.

The blond male lead never could maintain an erection, so a fairly realistic looking silicon dildo was covered with a condom and stuck out of his tuxedo.

In the tradition of Alfred Hitchcock, Art and Jim made a walk-through appearance early in *Green Door II* in the wide corridor of the Oakland airport. In the original *Behind the Green Door*, they played the leather-jacketed men who abduct Marilyn Chambers from the Alta Mira Hotel. By making a walk-through appearance in their own porn film the Mitchells were making a statement of another sort—of acknowledgment and pride in being part of the X-rated industry. They were the first porn producers to put their real names on their movies—something most people in today's sex industry are still afraid to do.

Art loved directing and playing in his films, and directing and playing in his life. And as flawed as *Green Door II* was proving to be, Art and Jim seemed to savor every minute of its creation.

In May, while *Green Door II* was still in progress and the craziness surrounding the movie was in full swing, Art held a twenty-fifth birthday party for a friend of his who was a fisherman. Art did some of the crank someone had brought in, which they were all sharing. During the party Art pulled me aside alone, and said he wanted me to go with them to their boat. I was angry, and told him I didn't want to go. Then I decided the better choice was to go and be so wild Art would hear about it.

I knew his favorite fantasy woman was the heroine in Pauline Réage's *Story of O*. As she takes part in an evolving sexual initiation, O becomes more attached to her lover. O's sexuality unfolds to become as spectacular as Marilyn Chambers in *Behind the Green Door*. Art sent me on this adventure not only as a test of my love for him, but as a sensual gift for me. I also knew he was so possessive that my doing this would stir up his jealousy. On the *Maelstrom* the good-natured young partier recovered from the crank, and led me up to the captain's chair for quite a marathon night.

Two weeks later, when Art wasn't at the theater, Jim called me back to the office. There sat the fishermen, returned from the sea. They must have given me rave reviews. In a matter-of-fact tone, Jim told me I was to replay the experience with them that night. It wasn't a request; if I wanted things to go well for me I had to do it. It was obvious Jim was relishing my discomfort. As a result of that evening,

Jim would not only have something on me, but would also put these guests in his debt. And in the process, he was asserting dominance over someone who had a longtime relationship with his brother. "Do your stage shows first," Jim said. "Then they'll meet you and take you out to the boat." It was terrible anticipating this. The fishermen didn't really want it; all but two of them left by the end of the night. I had gone out to the *Maelstrom* on one occasion for Art, but I had no reason to do something like that for Jim, other than wanting to keep my job. Feeling insecure about my position, and not confident about what would happen with Art if I left the O'Farrell a second time, I hated it, but I followed Jim Mitchell's order.

I regret being outmaneuvered by Jim. Other women in the sex industry, who I knew well, experienced at least one similar incident. I didn't dwell on it, but I learned. During the rest of my time at the O'Farrell, I didn't allow myself to be manipulated in this way.

Sometimes I heard about other O'Farrell dancers being asked to have sex with visiting VIPs, and friends of the Mitchell brothers. Many dancers who felt pressured quit or were fired. Still, the continual influx of dancers who prized their jobs and the money it was possible to make at the O'Farrell, led to some dancers being quietly persuaded or outmaneuvered. Other VIPs weren't into the sex. They frequently received financial contributions or other assistance. How valuable this special history of incriminating interaction would prove to be for Jim Mitchell.

∽

On a sultry June night, I was doing the Ultra Room with a partner. We were dressed as harem girls, in glittering bras and flowing cerise veils. Art showed up about 9:00 p.m., coming into the room for a minute during our performance and toying with me in front of the window, surprising the packed house of customers watching our show

138

from their booth windows. A moment later, back in the doorway he was taking off his pants. What a delicious situation.

After the show, Art and I stayed in the room together. The house manager shut the outer doors so the customers couldn't watch, and canceled the Ultra Room show. In the darkened heart of Artie's club, surrounded by infamous black leatherette walls, oblivious to business, to the movie and to everyone else, we made love. I was thrilled. Art did this so freely. It was an open acknowledgment of his relationship with me, when the movie wasn't yet completed and Missy was likely to hear about it.

When I came to work the next day, Vince gave me a swat on the ass with his clipboard. "Who're you doing the room with today, Simone, Art?"

I blushed. When I saw Jim, I avoided his eyes. I knew Jim would blame Art for risking aborting the movie and getting the place busted, but would know I had encouraged him in this delectable coup.

Art looked sheepish, totally different from the night before. "Hello, Simone," he said.

∼

A couple of nights later in the dressing room, Lisa told me Hunter Thompson was in town. Soon Hunter pulled me up off the ground to give me a friendly kiss. "If there's ever anything I can do for you," I said, "let me know."

"I'm writing a column on the Meese Commission," he said. Edwin Meese, under the auspices of the Reagan administration, had just released a report on pornography that had been feared by everyone in the X-rated industry. "Do you have any plans for tomorrow? Maybe you could come up and I could interview you."

At the Cathedral Hill Hotel I went up to the room Hunter was sharing with Maria, his sleekly beautiful, twenty-four-year old girlfriend/assistant. Over lunch, I explained what led to my being fired. Hunter, who hadn't been at the theater for months, said he just knew there was an argument.

I told Hunter about the places I danced while I was gone from the theater, and that since I came back they had given me a lot of work and I had made good money.

Wildly imaginative and insightful, Hunter was feeling bogged down by having to meet weekly deadlines for his column in the *San Francisco Examiner*. As he struggled to find good points for the column, he consumed a lot of Chivas and plummeted ice cubes into the pool from their eleventh story balcony.

Not knowing I was there, Artie called the room a couple of times, insisting that Hunter and Maria go out with him and Missy that night. He said Missy's father, from Utah, was going after Ed Meese; this could be part of Hunter's column. Missy had been a Senate page, Art added, she could do anything career-wise she wants, but has chosen to do porn.

Hunter and Maria told him they were working and had to get the article done, they couldn't go out. "I'd like to see the new movie," Hunter said, but understandably, Art didn't want to show it to him.

Around 7:30 p.m. Maria answered the phone—Missy was in the lobby with Art, wanting to come up.

"I'm busy working. Hunter will meet you downstairs in a few minutes. He doesn't have too much time, though. He has to meet his deadline tonight," Maria said.

Lost in thought, it took Hunter some time to decide what would be appropriate to wear for this.

The phone rang again; Maria was occupied and asked me to pick it up. It was Art, surprised to hear my voice.

"Oh. No problem," he said, but I sensed something was terribly wrong.

I handed the phone to Maria, "Hunter is just going down, wait for him," she said. Hunter, typically dressed in shorts and a sport coat, left.

In a few minutes, the phone rang again. Maria answered and handed the receiver to me. Art was livid, "You have five minutes. I'm at the O'Farrell in my office. Come over here and get your ass whipped. Then I'm sending you back to show Hunter . . .. If you want."

I was startled. Art had to have thought Hunter and I were having sex.

Maria and I were wondering how Art could be at the O'Farrell already, but the hotel was only a couple of blocks away. When Maria called the theater asking for Art, Missy grabbed the phone. "I haven't met you, but you seem like a nice person, but now I don't want to meet you or be in Hunter Thompson's company if he prefers the company of kennel sluts," Missy said to Maria. "*You'll* find out who *really* wields the power behind this place!"

I never heard anything as nasty as "kennel sluts" in a strip club. Maybe Missy refined her vocabulary on Capitol Hill.

Hunter returned from his search of the lobby. "What happened?" he asked. "You're both white as ghosts. Did somebody die?"

Maria and I explained.

"I've been in love with Art for a long time," I said.

"I'm in love with him too, but he ought to be shot!" Hunter said. "Don't be in love with him. And you shouldn't fuck him while this bitch is still around, because she'll know you are, she'll sense it. I can't save you if there's another incident."

"I've been involved with Art for years. She's temporary—sooner or later she'll be gone. She's no reason to stop seeing him!"

"I can recognize a mean bitch on a roll," Hunter added, "and she seems like a strong-willed woman."

"Missy's been working in the business for awhile," I explained. "Her making this film isn't the overnight transformation the brothers are claiming."

It was impossible for Hunter to finish the column. We were all upset. Hunter took a bath, making horrible warbling sounds in the tub that echoed through the bathroom door into the room.

Maria sounded depressed, "I'm leading Hunter's life. Hunter and Art are much the same, they are self-made men. I feel trapped, like you do."

I didn't go the theater that night. After I got home, Rita and I went out to get something to eat and talk. In the Sunday paper was an article on safe sex that included a few quotes from local people in the adult industry. While publicizing the *Sequel*, Jim tried to sound politically correct, yet superior: "We've never been dictated to by the market—if we were, we'd be like all the other scumbags in the industry." Missy sermonized, "You have to have a social conscience when it comes to having sex." In her photo she was dressed primly; the brothers had just begun promoting her as "Missy Manners"—what a spin.

Later Kenny called to say Ms. Manners had blustered into Mitchell Brothers last night, poured into a transparent garish gold lace dress, nothing underneath. She'd been looking around the dressing room to borrow a whip, but none of the dancers would lend her one.

Cautiously, I went to work that evening. My Ultra Room partner was crying. She was drunk, probably did some qualludes. I still wanted her with me. If she went home, I would be alone in the Ultra Room. I kept watching the door, anyway. For Art and/or Missy, with or without a whip. I didn't take a whip into the room for a long time.

In the morning, even though I worried about the consequences of Art's anger, the episode made me smile. Art was never violent with me, and I sensed his outburst was hotheaded bluster, brought on by the unrealistic hopes for this movie. How ironic such an incident would take place at the very time the brothers were trying to promote such a goody-goody view of porn. So ironic that Hunter's anti-Meese theme was "Pornography is Unrelated to Violence." Art, jealous of my friendship with Hunter, plunged into a scene right out of *The Story of O*, when he threatened to whip me. It was rare, and embarrassing for a VIP the brothers were cultivating to glimpse an inside scandal at the O'Farrell. "Fuck Art," Hunter said. "What is so sacred about that blue building, after all? It should burn down!"

Monday morning I began getting crank calls again. I was nervous about Hunter's column, what he might have said about me, and whether there would be anything unsavory about Mitchell Brothers or Art, in it. But when I picked up the *Examiner* his column, "Dealing with Pigs," was fairly mild. At the end of the piece, Hunter included what I told him then and still believe, that porn and violence are not connected. This column would later appear in Hunter's book *Generation of Swine*, along with "A Clean, Ill-Lighted Place," his other perceptive piece about the sex business.

When I got home there was a message to call Jim Mitchell at the theater, and I did. He asked, "Is there any truth to the story that you and Rita are planning to slit Missy's throat?"

"Would you repeat that?" I said. He did.

I was astonished. "Who said that?"

"Missy. Art and Missy."

"No." I told Jim what took place at Hunter's hotel; about Missy's "kennel sluts" faux pas, and "You'll find out who wields the most power." Then I explained the gorilla incident. "I've been in love with Art for a long time, Jim. He's still seeing me," I said. "I've always tried to stay away from Missy. The night we got into that argument last fall I was trying to avoid her. She has kept provoking me, to get me out of Art's life."

143

"Art's really far gone, as a result of too much fuel and octane consumption, psychedelics, anxiety about hitting forty, and too much life in the fast lane," Jim said.

"I'll be there tonight if you want me in the scene," I said. They would be shooting the last scheduled scene for *Green Door II* at the Oakland Airport.

"O.K.," said Jim. "We'll be expecting you, then."

I was shocked that anyone would invent such a serious accusation. But since Jim and Hunter had heard the essentials of what had happened, it was clear why I had been scapegoated.

On the long day we all spent at the theater when the orgy scene was shot, it had been obvious that Rita and I were friends. It wasn't surprising that she was included in Missy's accusation.

I put on my outfit for the scene, a white cotton blouse with jeans, a belt with a silver Western buckle, and boots. It was a horrible hot day. Feeling a bit edgy, Rita and I drove down to the theater. Once there, we stuck together.

In the dressing room, Jim put his arm around my back and I put mine around him, patting gingerly. "Safe hugs," Jim said.

Vince looked at me with restrained glee, as though he was thinking, You are hot, and in this impossible situation, you have been tough and patient. You're seeing your enemy vanquished. There is karma!

"Congratulations on all this," Vince told Rita, referring to her succeeding Carol Doda as the headliner at San Francisco's Condor Nightclub. I had pinned Herb Caen's column mentioning it on the bulletin board.

There was no sign of Missy, but I was dreading her arrival. Jim was making a point: that he wielded the most power behind the Mitchell Brothers Film Group, not Art and hardly Missy. To make that point,

Jim confirmed my role in the movie. Since Hunter was in town and aware of the incident, most likely Jim wanted to impress him, too.

Hunter had said they wanted him in the scene, but he didn't show. At 5:00 p.m. we left in vans for the Oakland Airport, for the filming of the long non-sex sequence on an airplane that would open the movie. The crew and cast were cordial, but tense. At the airport, there was space to spread out and talk. "Last week on the trip over here Missy was complaining," said Justine. "She wanted her own personal van to drive here, she was saying she should have one, she was the star!"

Sharon McKnight gave me my one-word script. To my partner's question "What's a seven-letter antonym for recklessness?" I was to answer "Caution."

I didn't know until we were milling about the airport that the star wasn't coming. Sharon McKnight wore a stewardess blouse and skirt over a tee shirt. She was to be Missy's hands and feet. The eyes of Missy would be the camera. Sharon commented, "This will be the best piece of acting Missy ever did."

For the first scene, all of us sat on the twenty-seat plane, got up, grabbed our luggage, and left the plane, saying our good-byes to the camera. While the crew filmed the dialogue, the cast stood around waiting for their individual scenes forever.

I told a couple of the actors about Missy's refusing to show if I was present, even though I knew Jim and others from the theater were watching me. They were afraid of the story getting out to tarnish the Pollyanna image of the production. My saying too much to outsiders would have been viewed as an indiscretion.

"You should consider this a victory, Simone," Rita said. "Jim listened to you, believed you, and you're here—in the scene—instead of the star."

What had been a very ugly situation had become fortunate. My friendship with Hunter would prevent Art from doing anything too weird. Jim and Art would assume Hunter would find out and could write about it. I knew Missy must have been in a state and Art was baby-sitting her.

She would be considered unprofessional for not showing up, considered crazy for making such a delightfully wild accusation—that Rita and I intended to slit her throat.

By this time, I thought, Art had to be sick of the whole movie, and her.

～

The next night Hunter and Maria came to the theater. Hunter looked around, and took some Mitchell Brothers personal stationary, joking that it's really hard to get out of cocaine treatment if you commit yourself and Art was going, for a couple of years. I could visit him.

"Art will be hit by a truck soon," Hunter predicted, "and Missy will be out in the street claiming she never knew him." Hunter referred to her as "That bitch who called me a pig."

When the house manager looked in, Hunter told him he had a fight with Art, then he left with a bottle of the brothers' booze, for the hotel.

～

I was slated for an Ultra Room show at the premiere of *Green Door II*, and I was dreading it. Art scheduled the opening of the movie for August 7, precisely one year after he first brought Missy over to my house for that star-crossed three-way. It felt strange knowing only Art and I, and possibly Missy, would recognize the date as significant. Two days before the opening I began getting crank calls from her, so frequent I had to pull out my phone. Not content to be the center of all the media attention, Ms. Manners had to nettle her rival, still hoping I would do something rash and lose Art.

Vince made it quite clear I had to be at the opening anyway. The Mitchells were promoting *Green Door II* extensively. Initial sales were good, although the content was so unarousing that later it was voted "1986's Most Disappointing Film or Video" by the editors of Hustler. The local mainstream press would pan it, in reviews with titles like "Safe and Sorry Behind the Blue Door." The premiere was to be a politically correct benefit for AIDS. The brothers expected it to be well attended.

～

Rita and I arrived at the premiere together—she was in a red beaded dress with deep décolletage; I wore a black suede mini-dress. "Hello, ladies. Two of the hot ones," Art greeted us. He grabbed me, but I pulled away from him and went upstairs. After my stint in the Ultra Room, I took a seat briefly in the New York Live audience, next to Rita and her date. On stage, a starkly beautiful blonde danced a tribute to safe sex, wrapped in Saran. Up in the tech booth, elegant in a tuxedo and black tie, stood Artie Mitchell, leering impishly over the crowd of 3,000, and smiling at me, like Zeus from the heavens.

～

Even though no one knew it that night, this was the last lavish porn movie premiere—the days when porn was shot on film, had big budgets, and was shown in theaters was ending. The era of porn chic in the early 70's, when couples had attended premieres, seemed to be a fad of the past, a culmination of the sexual revolution. Video had made low-budget porn possible, and new directors would flood the market with films people could watch at home. Directors who were used to working with bigger budgets, including Art and Jim, would find porn hardly worthwhile to shoot.

Green Door II failed, and showed how the times were becoming more conservative. The original *Behind the Green Door* succeeded

147

largely because of the charged performance of its alluring, lovely star, Marilyn Chambers. Only after the movie was released, did the press discover that she had modeled for the Ivory Snow flakes ad, which became a marketing coup. Art and Jim had placed more value on marketing the safe sex novelty of the *Sequel* and its Republican porn star, Missy —with interviews on *Oprah*, CNN, in *Playboy*, *Atlantic Monthly* and in the local press—than they had on their artistic product. Missy's brash enthusiasm for experimenting with sex and having a lot of it on film peaked the summer she met Artie, but had burned out six months later when the cameras started to roll. The brothers' reliance on an amateur cast—whom they were barely paying—had produced mostly lukewarm sex.

People who worked in porn and adult theaters were worried about how AIDS would affect their lives and their business. Many were wondering why the sexual revolution seemed to be coming to such an alarming end.

CHAPTER 8: Celluloid Heroes

Behind the Scenes at the Filming of **Grafenberg Girls Go Fishing***, and Documenting Hunter Thompson in* **The Crazy Never Die**

NOVEMBER 1986

Soon after the movie premiere, the mood at the O'Farrell shifted, and I began to relax. Art gave Missy three thousand dollars to finance a trip to Hollywood to audition for some television roles, they were saying at the theater; he's fed up with her and trying to get rid of her that way.

Art was a master at turning up the heat, building my level of anticipation to an erotic burn. Saturday he came into the theater early in an upbeat mood and lured me into the office. "Jim and I are moving today. We bought a place out in the country, in Moraga," he explained. At 5:30 p.m., he found me and said, "I need you tonight, on the mast."

It was the fiftieth birthday celebration of the San Francisco-Oakland Bay Bridge and there was to be a huge fireworks display over the water that night. Jim took his camera, and Rocky, Ron, Kenny, Art and I boarded their fishing boat, the *Graciosa*, on the wharf. "After we get out there I want you to climb up a couple of steps," Jim said to me. "Art will have his nose up your ass. You'll be trying to escape from the deranged captain!"

It was a big boat, and Art and I crept away for some privacy. The low-pitched boom of gunpowder was in rhythm with the explosion of cascading pastel light over our heads. The bay was very crowded with boats, and one of them hit us. "We're a big guy," said Jim. "We'll just slide on through." It got too crazy, though, water splashing, people from other boats yelling at us. They filmed the fireworks but never did the scene with me, which was O.K. I was terrified of climbing around out there.

The next time I saw Jim he gave me a hug and danced around in a circle with me, sharing the joy he knew I felt. He referred to me as the "star" that night. Maybe he was trying to partially atone for the ordeal of *Green Door II*, and curious what I might say. What had happened in the past didn't seem important—to me what counted was being with Art in the present and future.

~

The fireworks filmed on the bay were being included in a new porn movie Art and Jim would shoot at the end of November. Since *Green Door II*'s amateur cast had produced such lukewarm content, the brothers wanted to redeem their reputation quickly by coming out with a hot film they would call *Grafenberg Girls Go Fishing*. This time they hired professionals—five established actors and seven beautiful actresses they would fly in from L.A: Sharon Mitchell, Tracy Adams, Elle Rio, Tanya Fox, Shari Sloan, and the Melendez sisters.

Art asked me to do a costume for one of the actors, and I found a couple of vintage advertisements with the look he wanted—a Phillip Morris messenger. The jacket would have been perfect for a member of *Sergeant Pepper's Lonely Hearts Club Band*: bright red with gold-fringed epaulettes and thirty brass buttons. They needed it in two days.

When I brought the costume down the morning of the shoot, Art and Jim were pleased. Art and I stole away for awhile. Later Paulie drove me down to the boat in Art's white Mercedes with several of the actors: John Leslie, Tom Byron, Joey Silvera, and Jon Martin. "It went great this morning," Paulie said. "Art was yelling. It was like the old days!"

I climbed on the *Graciosa* with Art, Jim; a small crew made up
of Mitchell Brothers staff and a couple of technical people hired for
the day; and the cast. Only one sex scene was shot while the boat was
moving from San Francisco to Sausalito. Dressed as a chef, one of the
O'Farrell techs barbecued steak and underdone chicken for everyone.
A friendly actor, Buddy Love, asked if I would go down below and
rehearse with him; I said I couldn't. Everyone else was quite serious.
Soon they began shooting in the hold, which had been furnished with
mattresses covered with peach sheets. Unlike *Green Door II*, there
wasn't a condom in sight, although some bottles of Non-Oxynol 9
were placed around the set for the last scene.

A Chinese basket, covered with silver duct tape, was suspended
from a winch with chains, to lower the actresses one-by-one down
to the hold. The bottom of the basket was open, so after each girl
descended, an actor's cock was inserted and she was slowly spun. This
was an idea Artie had wanted to film for years. Fanciful but not very
comfortable—for the actors or the spinning starlets.

In a few days, Art and Jim were proudly showing footage from
the new movie in the poolroom. "Art and I bought a house together,"
Jim said to me. "In fact you'll have to come over and visit sometime.
Together, we have ten children there on the weekend."

They had no sound for the new movie, so groups of dancers were
recruited to sit around the pool table and moan into a microphone,
keep the moaning up for half an hour, say sexy things. Kenny had a
dishpan of water he splashed for bay and bathtub sounds and a can
of Crisco to plunge a vibrator into. He thought it would sound like
pussy.

Tuesday Art seemed very loaded on something. He wanted to finish off as much of the sound as possible, and use the vocal capacity of every dancer on the day shift. He wanted realism, and sent for me.

Art sat commanding and cool in his leather office chair, wearing a black sweater and jeans. On the floor lay a green blanket. "I need you to do sound, Simone, but you have to be willing to do everything I ask." When the tech set up the equipment, I went down on Art and got some deep throat sounds. Vince wandered in for a moment, his jaw dropped, and he left. "First you need a real hot slut, if you're going to do this," Art bragged to the new sound tech.

The film projector was on, so we could keep half an eye on the portion of the movie we were supposed to be doing sound for as we did stuff. Art grabbed me, made a fast deep move and I squealed in surprise. Art and I got into it for forty-five minutes of recording. I did a lot of yelling and moaning, and followed his lead in the dialogue. Finally, he said, "You just want to fuck, now, don't you." For a while he obliged, then I went back to doing my shows. Some other dancers did sound that day—considerably less motivated.

The following week Sharon Mitchell, Jon Martin and Buddy Love recorded some badly needed professional dialogue that was intercut with the rest.

～

Jim asked me to design a costume for a new movie they were planning called "Bride of Big Foot" or "The Big Foot Brothers." They envisioned shooting it in the snow-covered Sierras. So that Big Foot's cock would be silhouetted against a pelt suitable for an Abominable Snowman, Jim wanted something furry, yet form-fitting. He thought maybe I could glue sheepskin onto a scuba diving suit.

The Big Foot movie was never shot. Months later underground cartoonist R. Crumb, who had created the Bride of Big Foot character, and Terry Zwigoff, who later directed the independent film hits

Crumb, Ghost World, and *Art School Confidential,* spent time at the
O'Farrell. They planned to film their version of "Bride of Big Foot"
with dancers at the theater, but that didn't materialize either.

JANUARY 8, 1987

Art got really fucked up waiting for Hunter, who the brothers
casually called the "Night Manager," to come in to the theater. Art said
to me, "*Hunter* only loves you for the money."

Hunter had gotten his sizable advance to write a novel about the
O'Farrell two years earlier. Although he hadn't done the book yet, the
brothers were still hopeful.

Jim looked disgusted at Art's coked-out statements and left. I
wanted to be with Art and see Hunter, who hadn't been in town since
June when I was up in the hotel with him and Maria, and Art had
become so angry.

Around 11:30 Hunter showed up, alone. By then, Artie was
playing pool with three young innocent Japanese tourists that he had
befriended, and invited up to the office. Hunter began lamenting how
difficult Maria's father had been about her living with him.

Soon we went to Cafe Tosca, in North Beach—the neighborhood
was famous as the gathering place of Beat writers like Jack Kerouac.
Hunter spent half an hour on the phone with Maria, and seemed head
over heels in love. The proprietor, Jeannette, was warm to Hunter but
critical of Art, telling about a recent evening when her mother had
been there and Art was quite drunk, "How come your brother's such a
gentleman and you're such a swine?"

Art was edgy. I remembered how jealous he'd acted when he'd
been so coked up the previous summer. But it was hard for me to
believe he really thought anything had happened between Hunter and
me in the hotel when Maria had been there. We drove Jeannette to her

apartment. While Hunter was walking her to her door, Art teased me mercilessly through my jeans.

After Hunter returned to the car, he asked if I wanted to get something to eat and talk, but I wanted to be with Art. We dropped Hunter off at a restaurant and drove back to the theater.

"I really want to make love to you," I told Art. "When are you going to come over and spend the night?"

"Oh, I don't know."

"You have never given *me* even a chance!"

"I don't want to talk about it," he said.

I pulled my bag out of the back seat of the Mercedes and slammed the door as hard as I could. I didn't look back as I stalked around the corner to my car, furious. Art drove off.

A few days later Hunter was up in the tech booth, watching Lisa pose in a negligee on stage. She always looked bored, but immaculate and sensual as a model in a Victoria Secret's catalogue.

"Your shows are so different from what she's doing. From what everyone else is," Hunter said. "Why?"

"I got bored doing normal shows," I said. "I have to get over in different ways."

Hunter put his arm across my back, friendly, and I put mine around him. I was wearing a white nurse's costume and hat. Hunter stared down at the show and audience, curious about the whole weird phenomena.

The door in back of us opened and Art looked out to see us standing together, arms linked, jointly peering down into the O'Farrell. "YOU," Artie pointed at me furiously, "BACK!"

We dropped arms and I stepped away from Hunter. "What's wrong with him?" Hunter asked. "Oh, I know what he's thinking," sounding irritated.

Art had to be jealous. "You—Back!" sounded like what you might say to a Doberman.

Hunter's notoriety eclipsed porn. He was one of the very few men Artie respected as an equal. He was a notorious partier, a famous and highly successful writer, a countercultural celebrity, and was sharp enough to see through the games he observed Art and Jim playing with people. Although Art and I never spoke about it, I am sure he resented the admiration I felt for Hunter. Art liked competing with Hunter, while Jim cultivated him, determined to take advantage of this special opportunity.

∾

In a couple of weeks, Jim told me they were making a movie with Hunter beginning Sunday and Monday. He wanted me to be a gorilla throughout the entire thing. "Is the suit in good condition?" Jim inquired. Although it sounded strange and uncomfortable to dress like that for a couple of days, I agreed. Because my feet would show beneath the black fur pants, I bought the most feminine gold heels I could find.

∾

Late Saturday night Hunter was at the theater. Not only did he have a deadline to meet for his weekly *San Francisco Examiner* column, he was supposed to write three pages, to begin the book on Mitchell Brothers, before Maria would bring down the Chivas. An IBM typewriter was set up in the office and Hunter bent over it, teetering on a barstool. On the pool table lay a set of videotapes from the Survival Research Laboratories, and Hunter put one on. Huge destructive machines and flame-throwers battled each other. Then animal-like shapes, like sides of beef, were ripped to bits.

As Hunter typed, Jim summarized the plan for the film. They would shoot Hunter getting a medical exam by Dr. Nick. I smiled, thinking of the combination. "He doesn't know about this," Jim gestured to me covertly with his middle finger, indicating Nick was to probe up Hunter's ass. " . . . The doctor will tell him he's on his last legs and that he has to come here—to the O'Farrell. Everyone comes here to drop their last tusks—tusk. Then we'll follow him around. You'll drive a golf cart as a gorilla—as Hunter's caddy. Late at night, we'll hit Tosca and just you and Hunter will sit at the bar. Then we'll make a stop at the Goethe Institute where you and Hunter will discuss German philosophy."

Hunter interrupted, "I argued with the guy at the Goethe Institute, and I can't go back there in the middle of the night, not even in the afternoon!"

"O.K.," Jim said. "We'll end up here, Hunter will line up all the girls and he'll ask them, 'Are you eighteen?' or whatever he wants to ask them."

Hunter wanted me to stay, but it was now 3:00 a.m., and Jim wanted me back at the theater at 2:00 the next afternoon. "Trust me on this one," Hunter said to me. "Don't go." Hunter must have been ill at ease with Jim's scenario and would want to plot something viciously provocative. While Hunter was absorbed at the typewriter, Jim pulled me out in the hall to say, "Make a run for it."

The next afternoon I took my costume and some props down to the theater. Art and Jim drove up in a battered white van. "Where are you parked?" Jim asked, "Come on, we'll help you carry your shit."

Showing Jim what I had brought along, I had second thoughts about the horse head and branding iron.

"Oh, let's take it," Jim said. "This is show biz."

"I also have a pith helmet and a bandolier."

"I don't think we'll need the helmet, but Hunter works pretty good with hats. This may be nothing else but a call to arms!"

Jim tried to reach Hunter, who was watching the Super Bowl in Pacifica and wouldn't be ready to begin filming for several hours.

"I missed you, Simone," Art said. He led me back to the brightly-lit deserted little dressing room, and made love to me in front of the mirrors. Afterwards, he said, "So come back tonight at 6:30 . . . Well, you know Hunter. Maybe another try at 10:30. But we're determined to get something!"

~

At 1:00 a.m. I drove through the fog to a very deserted street in front of Tosca. Close to where I parked, the van pulled up and Rocky and Jim hopped out. Inside Jim gave me a polite kiss, "Go back in the restroom and get the costume on."

I stepped into the legs of the suit, zipped up the dark fake fur, and slipped on my gold heels. I pinned up my long dark hair so it wouldn't show under the mask. Peering into the mirror I wondered, was it possible to look sexy in a gorilla costume? I thought I heard Missy's voice, then Hunter's. I knew Art and Jim were shooting *Missy's Guidelines to Safe Sex* with her in a few days, but it was shocking that she was here. In an instant, she was in the tiny bathroom with me.

Missy wore a long loose skirt and pink sweater, her blonde hair collar-length, and a pompous expression. She looked like a thirtyish Republican matron. What could a freedom-loving outlaw like Art see in her? I wondered. She was a caricature of everything I thought he hated.

"What are YOU doing here?" she asked.

"I'm in this thing," I said.

"Oh, you mean tonight?"

"Yes."

"Well, I guess I better let you get ready."

"I guess you should, bitch," I said, beginning to smolder with outrage. She left.

"I have two looks," I told Jim. "Butch," I held up my tiger tooth necklace, "and femme," displaying a long scarf of fuchsia chiffon.

"Use both of them," Jim said. "You can play with both of them."

Trying to ignore him completely, I walked past Art.

"I didn't realize she would be here," I said to Hunter.

"Neither did I. She drives me crazy, too," Hunter replied. "Have a good stiff drink, what do you want? No, trust me. Have a drink." I was livid. Alcohol would hardly be a panacea.

"You don't understand," I said. "Too much has happened. I'm not putting up with this!"

"I didn't think they let hookers from Utah in here!" I said to Missy in a clear, angry voice. I delivered this dressed as an ape from the neck down, the mask in my hand.

"Now, don't get crazy," Art cautioned.

"Rocky," she called out, "the car keys, please!"

I walked over to Art, who was acting aloof, and said, "I love you very much."

Missy snickered and turned towards Art for a moment, conspiratorially. "I love you very much," she mimicked. "Sick little girl," she taunted me.

"You're the little girl," I replied.

Art walked away, into the bathroom.

"I really enjoyed fucking him yesterday," I added.

She strode back to the bathroom in search of Artie. I could hear the stall door slam, hard. A couple of times.

Art reemerged and said to me, "I guess the three of us can't be in the same place." To Jim he said, "Do you *enjoy* this?"

She and Art walked out the front door of Tosca into the night.

"I'm sorry," I told Jim. My eyes were wet.

"No, that's brutal . . .. See if we can get Art to stay." Art was part of the skeleton crew, in charge of recording the sound.

I hesitated, for a couple of minutes. Art did not come back into the bar.

"Are you O.K.?" Jim asked me.

I was in the shot as a gorilla, sitting at a table with Hunter, who delivered a never-to-be-heard monologue, and gave me an enthusiastic comradely slap on the back. Later, Jim and Artie would call this film *The Crazy Never Die.*

When the filming was over, I approached Jim, who seemed more than characteristically remote. He had taken some acid Hunter gave him hours before, and had stripped down to an undershirt, revealing surprising muscles from lifting weights.

"I'm sorry," Jim said. "Missy wasn't invited. She already screwed up one shot and I didn't know he would be so coked up."

"If you need me, just give me a call," I told him.

I couldn't sleep.

At 8:30 a.m., Art called me, "No one appreciated what you did last night and I don't know where you were coming from . . ."

I hung up, knowing Missy had badgered Art into delivering this reprimand and was no doubt listening to him scold me. Still, I was hurt and worried. How frustrating it was she was back for another film. Whenever she was around, he did more cocaine.

Stirring up some jealousy and anger heated Art up. Uncertainty kept life exciting—for him, and for the women he spent time with. I thought I knew how great his appetite was for variety, even though I didn't like to dwell on it—but I was only beginning to sense how much he craved complication.

Two hours later Vince called me, "Love is strange . . .. What happened? Jim's out at the golf course trying to calm Hunter down. Art is slamming around here saying you should be fired. Did he call you? What did he say?"

"I had no idea Missy would be at Tosca last night. With everything that has happened it was just too much having to wear that stupid mask with her there."

"Jim wanted you for this production. And if Art insists on dragging her around . . .. They're just going to have to get their shit together. Jesus Christ, it's not like it hasn't happened before. So the whole thing doesn't spill out like some drunken family brawl!"

Vince advised me to change the message I had on my machine since I came back to Mitchell Brothers a year earlier. He thought "Hello, this is the Bastille, the Marquis is all tied up at the moment . . .." might offend Jim or Art if they called right now. "Put something on like 'Hello, this is Heaven,'" Vince suggested, ever the diplomat.

Months more would pass before *The Crazy Never Die* was completed. Much of it was shot away from the theater. Hunter's novel on the O'Farrell, *The Night Manager*, never was published. After being in that scene at Tosca, I would never again see Hunter when he came to the theater. No matter how many women Art played with, he was always possessive of me.

Despite his image as a free spirit, Art developed trust and love slowly, and was terrified of betrayal. Although at times he behaved quite callously, he expected extreme loyalty from the women he cared seriously about. Art's short-lived romances, and the drinking, drugs and partying he did with new women entertained him, kept up his reputation, and were escapist. Because I never betrayed him despite his outrageous tests, over the years he would grow to trust and love me deeply. Vulnerability was a quality he was slow to expose.

~

In a couple of weeks, Art and Jim and the staff viewed the completed version of *Grafenberg Girls Go Fishing* on the movie screen of the Cine-Stage. That afternoon I was doing shows close by, in the Kopenhagen.

160

Art had directed the mixing of the soundtrack. It was cranked up high, so it would echo out into the lobby. Unmistakably, Art's voice and mine, mixed with sounds of our lovemaking, blissfully thundered through the O'Farrell. Through the one-way glass of the Kopenhagen, I watched Art strut into the lobby, proud of this authentic sex soundtrack he created and was flaunting.

"I couldn't stay in there," Paulie said to me. "I started to get turned on. It was too real."

All that afternoon and for the next several days, they played it, loud. "That's you!" another house manager commented.

I loved it. The emotion on the soundtrack was too genuine on both our parts, to be forgotten for long. In a few days, I had a tape of the movie—it was a memento that was priceless.

In May, Art shaved off his beard and mustache, to fly around the country with Missy promoting *Missy's Guidelines to Safe Sex.* The Mitchells hoped in vain to sell the video to high schools and colleges. But by the middle of the summer the tapes—boxed in her favorite color pink—sat with the brothers' dreams for the video potential of safe sex, in tall, unwanted stacks at the O'Farrell.

Part 2

Chapter 9:
Welcome to the Rancho

SEPTEMBER 1987

The fall days were clear and warm, and my heart was full of hope and excitement. Art settled in with me. Weeknights he stayed at my apartment; weekends he spent with his children at the Moraga house with Jim. Anticipating being with Art for so long made my pleasure all the sweeter. There was a calmness and trust between us that was new.

One afternoon he asked me to come to a party he had to put together, "You should see the bachelor, he's such a typical wimp. And I can't stand lawyers." I wore a black silk dress and heels to the party. My hair was highlighted in the darkest shade of blonde, and fell to below my shoulders. Art kissed me hello, and continued to give me loving looks all evening.

I was amazed to see the writer I knew years ago, Greg, at the party. It had been a couple of years since I had run into him. I was happy to have Greg to talk to, as I knew none of the other guests.

Art asked the Kopenhagen dancers, who were gay and did fist fucking in their shows, to lead off with a performance on the pool table. He told one of the women she would get paid $100, and the other, a redhead with gigantic breasts, $200, because she was getting fisted. They felt embarrassed having to perform in front of this sedate group. A loud, friendly coke dealer took the girls into the executive bathroom and gave them some coke to alter their mind-set. He had already given Art quite a bit too, and he was flying, having a great deal of fun being outrageous in front of these straight types.

"The girls said it's O.K., because they are real good friends," Greg said to me. "I thought this was all over for you, that you had done a million shows, that you needed to get into something else."

"It's hard to give up the money you can make dancing. I'm involved with Art. And it's getting better!" I smiled jubilantly.

Art was eager for the show to begin. He could not disappoint all these people. "If they don't do it pretty soon, you'll have to get fist-fucked," he said to me as I stood with Greg.

I knew that wasn't going to happen. These women were experienced at fisting. Art and I had attempted it a few times unsuccessfully; he was too protective to hurt me. Greg thought he was serious. "Sorry, I can't permit you to do that," Greg said. "Simone's a friend of mine, you know."

"She'll do what I want her to," Art said, a little angry.

The redhead lay back on the pool table as Art narrated, "Gentlemen, I understand that there are some lawyers here tonight. Over the past eighteen years, I've given lawyers more than five million dollars, mostly to defend me and my brother in cases that involve the First Amendment. I've been busted nineteen different times, involved in nineteen different court cases. All because the law of this country is so backward, so behind the times and out of step with the way people live today. If me and my brother have achieved anything in our lives, we have stood up for freedom."

"So tonight, gentlemen, you're in for a real treat. You're about to witness an act that is totally illegal in seventeen states. And do you know why? Because it shows how women don't really need men, they don't really need your dicks, they can get off so much better like this, this is just as good, no, better than a real big dick." Art took out a hundred and tossed it onto the girls on the pool table who were fist fucking, and looking serious.

166

"Tip them, gentlemen, give these sluts what they deserve." Then Art walked over and kissed one of the girl's huge tits. His monologue was received in complete silence by the shocked, disapproving group.

When Art said "sluts", I giggled, out of place against the silence. I knew he didn't disapprove of sluts, and thought of himself as a slut. But the group was edgy and unimpressed by their host who was trying so hard.

The next part of the show would be in the Ultra Room. The groom, a semi-hostile short guy who was stone sober, didn't know he was to be tied up and tantalized by two naked dancers. Paulie took me down the back stairs to show me how they had set up the bondage ropes. Into the dark Ultra Room we went, to find the short Chinese projectionist tied up, to test the ropes. I laughed.

When it was showtime, the groom refused to be bound, and kept his distance from the beautiful girls. Next, the party was to go down to the Kopenhagen. The bachelor, afraid someone would force him into some gross sexual act, stayed upstairs in the hallway anxiously waiting for his sister-in-law to arrive.

As soon as everyone else left, Greg shut the office door. Immediately, I opened it. "I can't be in here alone with you, Greg, he's coming back."

"Well, that just makes it that much hotter and dirtier for us. Are you that afraid of him?"

"No. I'm in love with him."

"Oh, Simone, not *him*."

Just as I had expected, Art was back in three minutes. Eying Greg suspiciously, Art ushered him out, authoritatively said "THE SHOW'S DOWN THERE!" and closed the door heavily.

Art turned to me, "You can't stand it, can you. You love your daddy's dick so much . . . Go home. I'll be over in an hour. I'm fed up with these guys. They're getting on my nerves." He threw open the poolroom door and announced to the few men standing around, "YOU CAN COME IN NOW. THE BLOWJOB'S OVER!"

Warren Hinckle's campaign for Mayor of San Francisco was sinking. Despite his having posed on a bulldozer with a huge broom to sweep out City Hall, his new poster "Tired of the Same Old Shit— Vote Hinckle," which displayed a Wayne Thiebaud-style plate of shit, and his limited distribution of condoms, his candidacy wasn't taken seriously. Hinckle was best known as the former editor of *Ramparts Magazine* during its heyday in the radical 60's. He was a rakish, hard-drinking, San Francisco character who wore an eye-patch, and took his beloved basset hound Bentley everywhere. He had been prevented from writing his *San Francisco Examiner* columns since the beginning of his mayoral campaign, because of conflict of interest. In October, the brothers scheduled a political fund raiser for Hinckle. Art was the host that night and Jim was absent. We mingled with the guests. They were businessmen, mostly, who were sitting around talking quietly and sipping drinks.

Just to me Art said, "You're looking at me with that lovelight in your eyes. Do you know what that means? It means I can do anything I want to you, I can tear you up, I can rip your heart out and never see you again, or I can treat you real nice."

I blanched when he spoke of terrorizing me, and hoped he didn't mean it. Why terrorize someone who loves you? It sounded like more destructive game playing. Yet, he behaved lovingly to me that night. Walking with me through the lobby with one of the businessmen Art happily exclaimed, "I'm going to pack her blind."

The entertainment featured Amazons bearing plastic axes, with usual O'Farrell fare, fist fucking and dildoing. It was a bit stronger than these guys wanted to see. Afterwards, Art asked me to come into the hall bathroom with him and two of the girls from the show, to offer them some coke. "Gentlemen, since I've had a vasectomy they tell me I have to have sex four times a day or I'll get cancer," he joked. "It takes five women and an animal to get me off. And it's that time."

When the party ended, Art and I were left alone. He alternately stroked me and pulled away to look in my eyes, mesmerizing me completely. As we walked up the street, he carried a Kopenhagen flashlight to defend us from possible attackers. "You could drive that, except you'd probably wreck it," he said in jest, pointing to his Mercedes.

At my apartment, he disappeared into the bathroom. When he came back in my bedroom, he had put on some of the costume from the mannequin I had dressed as a French maid and handcuffed to the pipes near my tub. The long platinum wig, the French maid's hat, and the cat mask made me burst into laughter. He took them off.

"You never question my motives, my timing, my actions. I'm tired of cold people. You're the girl for me, Simone. I want you to trust me. You're sexier than five years ago. I love you. I'll never hurt you. I didn't hurt you; you've grown stronger. I've made you stronger. They all like you," he added.

In the morning he suggested, "Why don't you come over Saturday, I'll write the directions down, why don't you get there about 11:00 a.m. and you can meet my kids."

My relationship with him was intensifying. I was finally going to meet his children.

～

Near the end of a road overhung with green trees that winds through Moraga, I ran into Art driving out in his blue Ford van. He gave me a clear special look, "The house is just a little further, Simone. Say hello to everyone and make yourself at home. I'll be back soon."

Past a field where a few horses ambled, I took a curved drive up a slight incline to a sprawling ranch house. Inside the formal white door was a dining room with sliding glass doors to an open grassy backyard that sloped gradually uphill. I stepped outside and said hello to Lisa, who had brought a miniature collie dog to play with Jim's children.

Lisa had started working for Jim as his secretary that summer, as well as dancing. Since Jim and Lisa were quiet about their relationship at the beginning and she was still married, I didn't realize they were involved or understand why she was there.

Jim was in the backyard picking fat insects out of the pool with a little net, showing them to his children. "Welcome to the rancho, Simone," he said, with pride. "This is Meta, Rafe, Justin, and Jennifer Mitchell. Kids, this is Simone."

All Jim's kids were from his second marriage. Meta was dark-haired, serious, and the oldest of his children at ten. Rafe was six, and loved to race around the yard in rough play with the other boys. Being younger and smaller at four, Justin had a tendency to whine. Jennifer, who had been born the night of the premiere of *Grafenberg Spot*, was sensitive, sweet, and going on three.

In a few minutes Art was back, his three youngest children ran to him. He gave me a warm kiss. Soon Lisa left, and a little later Jim drove away with his children.

"I named two of my sons after the characters in Steinbeck's *East of Eden*, Aaron and Cal," Art told me. "Steinbeck is a fine writer. *East of Eden's* great, but *The Grapes of Wrath* is the story of my family."

Aaron (also called Ace), Cal (whose full first name is Caleb), and Art's daughter Jasmine (whose nickname was Jazz) were there, and their pleasant Brazilian housekeeper who was very pregnant. Art was saying, "You can come over and hang out with your daddy, I want to integrate you into my family." I was radiantly happy.

Alone in his bedroom, we fell into each other's arms across his sleek, mirrored four-poster bed. It had been part of the set of *Grafenberg Spot* and *Grafenberg Girls Go Fishing*.

"You're a very pretty woman but don't wear makeup," he said. "I know for the biz you feel like you have to—do what you have to for the biz, but don't wear it other than that."

I was dressed in jeans and a sweater, but I had made up my eyes lightly and wore lipstick and a little blush. I took his advice to heart, and washed off the makeup to please him.

Art seemed tired. The housekeeper fixed a dinner of shrimp, rice and salad, but he didn't want to eat. I sat down at the long table with the children.

Aaron, Jasmine and Cal had blond hair and bore a strong resemblance to Art. They also had his boundless energy and outgoing manner. Cal, who was five, inherited Art's temper and his slender build and features. He will look exactly like him, I thought; it seemed uncanny. Aaron, at nine, had Art's quickness, his keen athletic ability, his desire to make an impact in every personal encounter, and his strong will to win. Jasmine was very pretty, and friendly at seven. I liked them a lot. We talked for awhile after dinner. Then Art sent the housekeeper with them to the video store, to get *Blue Velvet* for us, and lighter fare they wanted.

When they were gone, Art and I went to his bedroom in the back and made love again—in his bed, in his home, at last. Against the silence of the big house, the phone rang and rang and rang. Twelve or thirteen rings each attempt. "Missy Manners will get over it," he sounded philosophical.

"How would you like it if Missy were in a room all tied up?" Art asked as he held me. "You could come in and whip her and a whole lot of other people would be waiting there to whip her, too?"

"Art, I went through two miserable years because of that bitch. And I never want to see her again!"

"I tried to pimp Missy for the movie but it didn't work. We used her for too long! You were wronged," he said. "You only imagined that I loved her and I didn't love you—I never love anybody after such a short period of time. I never stopped loving you, not even for one second." I snuggled closer. Outside the trees rustled in the moonlight.

∼

We ate breakfast with the kids and then went outside in the sunshine. Jasmine and Cal gleefully took turns swinging in a tire hung from a tree; I pushed. Art played ball with Aaron and Cal. That afternoon I drove back to the city to do a show at the theater, enchanted by the changes.

At the end of the week, he brought me Anne Rice's *Beauty* trilogy to read because he was thinking of basing a movie on them and planning to meet their author. What a treat—I always loved fiction, after all.

∼

The day before Thanksgiving, Art was clowning around with Paulie's son and jumped up on the pool table, rolled over the eight ball and cracked a rib. It was agonizing, and he had to take painkillers.

"Friday we're having a big poker tournament," Art said. "Why don't you stop by?"

When I looked into the poolroom at 9:30 p.m., the remaining all-male hard core including Jim were playing low-ball poker intently. Art flashed me a smile and said hello. Everyone was absorbed in the game. Several of them wore blue hats embroidered with "Beat Art." He had won for eight years in a row.

"Is his back bothering him?" I asked Paulie.

"He can't feel his back. He's on the painkillers. He can't feel a thing. He's winning. They're playing for thousands."

Chapter 10:
Cabo San Lucas

DECEMBER 2, 1987

"God, my back's bothering me so much," Art said in the morning. "I wonder if a heating pad would help."

That day I picked up a heating pad. When Art showed up at my apartment that evening, he was extremely upset, and a little incoherent. He got on the phone and said, "Is Vince there? Well, who's around? Paulie? Tell Jim I want ten thousand dollars in a bag or I'll Molotov cocktail the lobby. I want the money—I'm getting out!"

I wondered what the hell was happening. Plus he was almost crying, which I had never seen before. I didn't know what to do. Sitting on my bed he picked up an alarm clock and hurled it against the footboard. Broke the clock completely up. "Nobody wants to listen to me anymore. I'm getting out. I've told Jim that I want out—just sell the business, divide it. Sell the house."

I took out the heating pad so he could lie on it. "Oh, you've got a heating pad," he said. "You had one."

"No, I got it today."

He began to cry. "Oh, you got that for me. You don't know how much that means to me." Then he said, "We're going to leave in the morning, go ahead and pack three bags, you're going with me, we're going to Mexico."

Even though I wanted to be with Art, going away when he was so upset was a bit scary.

When Jim got on the phone Art said, "I want ten thousand dollars in a paper bag, I'm sending Simone down to get it." After he hung up

Art told me Jim said, "How about five thousand now, five thousand later?"

I threw a leather jacket over the sweater and jeans I was wearing, and drove down to the O'Farrell. It was 7:00 p.m. and dark. I ran into Jim near the deserted parking lot. "I don't know what's going on," I tried to sound moderate.

"Well, same old stuff. I'm sick of Art. He's a cocaine addict. He's twisted; you've seen it. He's a coke addict. I'm sick of it," Jim looked angry and severe.

"I'm sorry."

"If you go somewhere call, and we'll send more money," Jim added.

In the lobby Paulie put his arm around me, "Oh, boy. Is he out there?"

"No."

He handed me a brown paper bag of money. "There's plenty of love for the both of you," Paulie said.

I took the bag back to the apartment. Art was still very upset. He counted the cash and I brought him dinner, but he took only a couple of bites. His back was killing him, and he lay on top of the heating pad and had me turn out the lights. He said, "Call your father and tell him you're getting married and you're going to Mexico—lie!"

That didn't make me feel too good, either. Hoping Art would relax and drift to sleep, I packed quietly. I was afraid the pad would burn him but I couldn't move him off it. I halfway wondered if he would change his mind overnight and decide not to go.

⁓

In the morning, he went to Moraga to pack, picked me up in the van, and we stopped by Nick's clinic. Nick wanted to take an X-ray, had told him, "It would be good to know if your lung is punctured, Art."

He sent me up the street to get him some rolling papers and a couple of pipes to smoke coke out of, while he went in to see Nick. When I came back he was emerging with a bottle of painkillers, and we took off over the bridge. In the East Bay Art stopped in front of a house, hoping to buy some cocaine. Fortunately, no one was home. Feeling desperate, anxious to get out of town, he got back on the highway and hit it.

"I was fighting with Jim yesterday. He's been on my case for weeks. I told him, 'Your wife had her foot way up your ass to her knee the whole time you were with her!' Jim swung at me. We got into a fistfight. And he actually hurt me; he knocked me over the TV. He shouldn't have done that—he knew I already had a cracked rib. My brother shouldn't have hit me when I was injured. Then I picked up a great big heavy tape dispenser, and held it as Jim walked towards the bathroom. Paulie saw it and thought, 'What do I do?' He backed away, afraid I was going to hurt Jim. I just held it over Jim's head like 'I could kill you, fucker, if I wanted—but I love you, so I won't.' Then I put it down.

"I have a lot of ideas I want to use for the video store. Jeff won't listen to me. Nobody around the O'Farrell takes me seriously and I'm fed up with it. They'll miss my spirit!

"I called up Karen this morning and yelled some stuff and said I'm not going to be picking the kids up this weekend. I'll pick them up the eighteenth or I may never be coming back!

"When I walked into the poolroom this morning Jim said, 'Hi, Art, here's some pills from the Doc.' just like nothing happened. I snatched them, then I went over to the safe, opened it up and took out two or three guns, and stuffed them in my pants. I chewed out Lisa. She's just another slut. Lynx can get anything she wants on the schedule. At least Vince was fair.

"Then I stormed out, just like the song 'Walking down the road with a pistol in your waist, Johnny, you're just too bad . . ..'"

He turned the radio on. Some old rock song was playing a line about eating your pride. "You've had to do that, darlin'," he said, and I smiled, knowing how true that was. I was so happy to be with him. Where we were going didn't matter.

Just south of Salinas, we stopped for a quick hamburger. I would have liked dinner, but Art had to keep moving, kept calling, "Soute! Soute!"

In Pismo Beach, we got a quiet room near the sea. "I came down to Pismo twice this year—one time I came down by myself and did two or three grs of coke, and just stayed in the room. I went out and flirted with some older woman in a bar, even though I couldn't have handled fucking her. Another time I brought the kids and we dug for clams." We found a country western bar and danced a little; Art relaxed and talked warmly to the band. Adorable big red paper bells hung from the ceiling for Christmas, some of them a little bent.

Back at the Sea Crest, for one long moment I watched him walk into the bedroom. He was so sexy, so good looking, successful, tough, and infinitely complex. The sheets never felt softer. I was with a man I deeply desired. The sound of the waves and the high wind over the December sea lulled us asleep. Countless miles away from complications, and from the O'Farrell.

～

"You deserve this vacation," Art told me at breakfast. "I want us to have a good time for all the bad times and uncertain times we've had."

A fortuneteller's sign beckoned near the highway. I had gone there once, years ago. What if we got some weird fortune? I thought. When we were safely past I told him the gypsy's old prediction—I would have more than four children. "Yeah, lady, you're going to have more than five children," he said, as if his children would also be mine. I kissed him.

Artie and I drove south, into a storm. I wondered if we were really going to drive all the way through Mexico, down to the jungles of South America, in the van. In the back, buried under sleeping bags and fishing poles, for protection, were the guns.

It took forever to get to L.A. in the rain. Art decided we would drive to San Diego and get a plane to Cabo San Lucas from there. "I'm tired of living in the cold north," he mused. "I could live anywhere. Karen could move south with the children. It would be sunny. We could live close by and go to the beach all the time. Why not?"

"You know, I'm ready to retire. I want Jim to divide the business," he said. They must have had many serious disagreements over the years for him to say that, I thought. How uprooting it would have been for Art to take off and move somewhere far from the business he'd been in and loved for close to twenty years, and start all over again. I didn't think he wanted to go through that type of change.

As I drove he saw a cute teenager wearing a backpack and called out the window, "Hey, we're going to Mexico, want to come along?" She smiled.

Art pissed in a Heineken bottle as we moved through L.A., tossed it out the window. Soon we slowed to a crawl behind an endless stream of cars. He fidgeted in his seat and hurriedly rolled up a joint. L.A. seemed foreign and surreal. "We're both outcasts, Simone," Art said. "You're an Okie, just like I am."

"Yes," I smiled. "And we're both part Cherokee Indian."

"My mother knows don't get Art started on the Indians," he said. Not knowing better, I had. He believed that Ten Claw, a terrible warrior who killed many people, hung many white scalps from his belt, was his spirit guide—his spirit—who came into Art at times. "Go back, Ten Claw. Go back, Ten Claw!" he said. "If you come through me, who knows what can happen!"

For half an hour, Ten Claw, fierce, remote and thirsty for vengeance, rode next to me in the van. Horrified by the massacres inflicted on the Indians, eyes wet for the Trail of Tears, he wailed in an unearthly tone, "Too many died! Too many have died!" The history was mine, too, but Ten Claw saw it before his eyes, felt every wound, pictured each drop of blood, was filled with heartfelt sorrow. Near crying, I kept silent. "No, Ten Claw, Great Warrior, don't come through me!" He kept repeating. Ten Claw burned with a passionate hatred for the hypocritical ways of the whites, and the desire to take revenge on their oppressive power structure, the government of the United States. "Pornography is my gift to them!" he cried. Ten Claw and Artie were one.

As we approached the many off-ramps of San Diego, Ten Claw withdrew. At the airport, they said the next flight to Cabo San Lucas left in the morning. Artie Mitchell bought the tickets.

⁓

I waited in the terminal the next morning, while he parked. Art came walking up to me, with a bouquet. "Oh, you didn't have to do that," I said. It hit my heart. We looked like newlyweds, which he partly wanted so they would tend less to search our stuff. At the airport in Mexico we rented a car and drove through the desert, on a two-lane highway, stopping for a Pacifico for him and Agua Minerale for me in a sleepy little town. In Cabo San Lucas, he chose the Marina Sol, a high-rise hotel with a still green courtyard and a pool in the center. "I brought you to a nice place, didn't I?" he asked.

I loved the ceiling fan in the bedroom. The afternoons were so hot, we had to take siestas every day. Every siesta I would pamper Art with a warm wet towel. Then we would make love and fall asleep in each other's arms. It was paradise.

The first evening he took me down to an open-air restaurant by the water. Art had the strolling musicians play a song at our table, dedicating it to me, his wife, "por mi esposa."

"When Aaron was five he was playing with some Mexican kids on the beach with firecrackers, and he accidentally set a palapa on fire. I felt so bad. I gave the owner some money and she thanked me profusely, even though Aaron had temporarily destroyed their business.

"That trip I just took Aaron. The night we got here, we were so tired we fell asleep. When we woke up it was too late to get anything to eat. I showed Aaron how to make an air sandwich, that was our first meal in Mexico.

"After the trip, Karen was real upset. She said I'd taken my little boy all the way to Mexico and didn't even feed him properly. Aaron loves being with his dad. He loves me. He told all his friends the story."

"How do you make an air sandwich?" I asked.

"Well, first you take some bread, and open up your jar of mayonnaise," Art pantomimed. "Then you put in whatever you want, turkey, lettuce, whatever . . ." air sandwich stacked high, he took a funny, realistic bite. I wondered about this story. It sounded like dustbowl humor, born from hard times.

"Eat the salsa, Simone. It kills the parasites . . .. Aaron loves whole fish. Mostly that's what he orders, in Cabo."

After dinner we stopped at a beautiful little bar, and sat looking down at the lights on the water.

"They have this great ride here," he said. "You put on water-skis, they strap you into a parachute and pull you way up in the air over the water. It's a gas, you'll have to do it!"

"Oh, I couldn't do that. I really don't like heights."

"You're questioning me. You can't question *me* ..."

"Art, we're going to have differences. It's healthy," I said. "I have to feel free to say what's on my mind!"

He considered this for a couple of moments, then agreed, "Yeah, I guess you're right."

Back in our room he told me, "I'm thinking about calling Karen and having her come down with the kids. I miss my little kids so much, they need me."

It was too soon. I wanted to spend some more time alone with him, feel we had an unshakable relationship, before Karen came to visit. He needed to unwind, too. Karen and Art fought so bitterly it didn't seem the best idea. "Karen is going to resent me," I pleaded. "She was married to you."

"I'll tell Karen, 'Look, I'm down here with my lover.' She's basically a hippie girl, which is one reason I always liked her. Karen's pretty good about meeting guys by herself. She's just loud!"

"Maybe Karen should move down here and the three of us could get a house together with the kids," Art said.

"I think we should do that on one condition," I told him. "Missy Manners should move in, too."

At 5:00 a.m., a rooster began to crow near the hotel, every few seconds, waking us and everyone in the area. Art strode out to the patio to scream, "IF YOU DON'T SHUT UP YOUR MOTHERFUCKING ROOSTER I'M GONNA COME OVER AND CUT HIS NUTS OFF!"

Suddenly there was silence. In the pink dawn, we went back to sleep. For the rest of our stay, we never again heard the rooster.

On his first Pacifico of the day, Art reflected on his whim from the previous night, "Yeah, you're right. I guess it wouldn't work for my ex-wife to move in with us."

That morning, I felt ill. We had been fucking at least three times a day and I had a bladder infection. At the hotel they referred me to Doctor Acosta, and we drove into Cabo and found him. After downing his prescription, I felt fine.

Art bought me some bright gauze dresses, gauze clothing for himself. A pretty girl ran the shop. "When I was trying on pants she brushed up against my dick and blushed," he said after we left. "I'd like to take her to dinner." Typical Artie fantasy.

He bargained for a Mexican wedding dress for me, then we found a quiet restaurant. We were the only customers and slipped our shoes off, in the sand. A pair of brightly-colored parrots eyed us from their cage. Holding my hand close he admired their serenity, "Parrots mate for life, Simone."

That night we met an old friend of Art's, Steve, and his girl for dinner. Steve had moved south to do commercial fishing. He had been a Sausalito cop. His girl had been married to a Mexican before, and had two young sons. Steve was wary of getting married again. Art would say, "You should marry her. She's the best thing that's ever happened to you!"

"I may knock you up," Artie said, just to me. I looked into his capable warm eyes, believing him and wanting his child. "I'll have my vasectomy reversed, it's easy."

"My cojones hang heavy," he told Steve and his girlfriend. "I have six children, and soon, seven."

∼

At 7:30 a.m., we got to the marina. Art wanted blue marlin. "It's my honeymoon," he told the Mexican captain and mate. As soon as we got out the waves were deep blue tipped with white, and rocked the boat steadily. I felt a little seasick.

Blond-bearded, slender and elegantly muscled, Art got in the chair first, and got a hit. Thirty feet off the stern the powerful blue fish leapt into the air and fought for its life, against him. "Marlena," the mate said, in awe of it.

After Art pulled his fish in expertly, with enjoyment that was seasoned, I got in the chair. Certain I had to establish I wasn't weak, with muscle I didn't possess, by will alone, I pulled in my marlin. I was giddy with triumph. "It's a big fish, Simone. It weighs a hundred and thirty-five pounds, easy!" He told the captain to let mine swim free, to keep his. The mate hit it in the head with a club. Artie raised his hand to make the sign of the cross in the air over the bright surface of the sea, in benediction for our taking a life.

On the dock, we had pictures taken with the fish. Art thought I should show Rita the one where I stood alone with the marlin, next to the sign saying "Mitchell," like we'd gotten married.

Artie Mitchell and me with blue marlin, in Cabo San Lucas, Mexico, in December, 1987.

I changed to a red dress for lunch. Somehow, Art came up with a red carnation. I sat looking at him enraptured, twisting a strand of my hair.

"Don't do that," he said. "I never want to see you do that again."

My face fell. "It's just something I do naturally . . .. But if you don't like it, I won't do it."

He began to cry, seeing how easily he could frighten me after the reversals of so many years, "Don't worry. Never stop doing it. I want you to always do it. I love it. I love you, Simone."

I stretched my hand across the table to touch his face.

"Drink my tears," he said. "I love you."

Art wanted the full red carnation in my teeth, in bed.

In the evening while I waited for the photographer to bring the pictures of our fish, Art went into the bar. I found him in wild loud conversation with a drunk, buxom woman who was wearing an umbrella hat. She said she was the mayor of Cabo.

He was flirting outrageously. He showed her his O'Farrell Bic lighter with all the movies listed on it. She leaned closer, curious, "Are you really who you say you are?" Then she would look at me, not understanding.

"I'm in love with him. Nothing he does offends me," I told her.

Art said to me, "You're so serene that everyone just wonders at it."

The bartender eyed us suspiciously. I was thinking, oh, God, does Art want some kind of three-way with this old overweight woman in a muumuu? He had totally charmed her. In a little while she was so close to passing out she had to leave.

We drove to the Chinese disco, a big odd round place with loud pulsating music. He wanted me to grab his ass and he would bat my hand away, "If other guys see this, they'll think—that's the guy that's going to get a real good blowjob and whatever he wants." He loved putting on a show.

Two paunchy guys in their forties approached. He thought they were D.E.A. agents trying to set him up. One of them offered to sell him some real cheap cocaine, ridiculous, Art said, almost a joke. He saw through it and was insulting to them. Then they tried to flirt with me and I was all eyes for Art. There weren't too many American women and the Mexican girls don't have much to do with the white guys. "I'm glad I brought my own girl," Art said.

He started playing a game with some young guys. Picking up a penny, throwing it over his shoulder, trying to find it, for luck. But if you stepped on it you'd be dead within six weeks. Artie's spirited style, performing even this simple trick, gathered a crowd. He led them outside to continue the game, and the two disgruntled older guys followed, jealous of Artie for being the charismatic ringmaster, with a woman who adored him. One of them was so angry he stomped on the penny, inviting doom and ruining the pleasure of the game.

"FOOL!" Art said to him. "In six weeks you'll be dead!"

"I smell trouble," he told me. "Let's get out of here."

$\sim$

Friday we went into Cabo to call back to the States. Art got the O'Farrell and told Vince, "There are so many fish down here I'm walking across their backs. We're staying at the Marina Sol, if you need to reach me, but you don't want to reach *me*! Call Karen and tell her I'll be back on the eighteenth."

I didn't want to go back that soon, but we would still have another week. "There is something to be said for just totally kicking back and relaxing and having some time to yourself," I said.

We drove to the airport to see about return tickets. Art talked affectionately about Karen's father, a world-renowned sailor. Artie financed a catamaran he built years ago, and sailed to his place in Guatemala when Aaron was a baby. "Guatemala's dangerous, it's crawling with armed troops. In Guatemala City, the old man took us to his kind of a place—a real cheap hotel with straw on the beds. I told him 'You can find me at the Hilton!' You'll have to meet him," he said, admiring the older man's machismo.

Because of the drive that day, we didn't get a siesta. Back in our room he said, "Let's get dressed and go get a hamburger."

"You want that two nights in a row?"

"That's it. We've been together more than we ever have before. Go over and have dinner by yourself. They've seen you there with me. They'll watch over you. I'll go get my hamburger. Then we'll get together. Meet me at the bar in an hour and a half."

After dinner, I walked down the dirt road towards the bar. In the darkness Art leaned against the wall of an abandoned building, puking. He had been drinking a lot of tequila. That morning he had eaten the worm. We found a bar with a band and danced the night away. At the table, tears in his eyes, he told me how much he loved his father, "I miss him so much. My dad taught me all there is to know about cards, and how to be an outlaw, but an honest outlaw."

Art told me about the trip to Japan when he and Jim took Marilyn Chambers to promote the original *Behind the Green Door*. "One of the Yakuza wanted to fuck Marilyn for five thousand dollars. We were young. We didn't know. We told him it was impossible.

"In Tokyo they took us to a whorehouse. Me, Jim, and Chuck Traynor got to go. First they brought out three very pretty girls but I know you don't take the first thing that's offered to you. Jim did. He took this average looking Japanese girl. Since I had been so hard to please, they brought me a real fox.

"She massaged me, rubbed her tit on me in concentric circles. I was getting a raging hard-on. She bathed me. And she climbed on top, fucked me just slightly, and seemed real surprised when I didn't get off.

I turned her over and Okie long-dicked her. She had to be coming, but it also must have really hurt.

"The Yakuza presented Marilyn with a exquisite strand of pearls. Then Marilyn admired a wedding kimono and the Japanese have this custom—out of politeness, they gave it to her. I felt embarrassed .. .. I'd like to open a club in Tokyo. Marilyn still has it. She could be mistress of ceremonies. Most clubs have two years when they're hot.

"My father did ten years at the most notorious prison in Texas, for a gambling scam. The FBI finally caught him," Art said. "When I was ten or eleven years old my father told me, 'Son, If you ever kill someone, never tell anyone about it and you'll get away with it.'" He looked at me, serious. "That's a family secret, Simone. Don't tell anybody. When my dad told me, I could just tell by the way he said it, that he had killed. I never asked him . . .. That was the point of the story."

"I won't say anything," I promised.

"Tonight we're staying home. Saturday night the Mexicans get roaring drunk and drive like maniacs. They only have enough money to do that once a week."

After dinner, *Godfather II* was on television. Art said the guys at the theater knew all the lines from that movie. "We're bigger than U.S. Steel." was a favorite. So was "This is the business we have chosen."

We wandered into a restaurant that had a sleek black crow in a cage twenty feet away from our table. Artie carried a single tortilla chip at a time over to the crow. Pretty soon, the charmed crow was cawing to get him to come back, give him another chip. Just like Artie's women. Art began cawing, too, loud, saying, "I'm Arturo Cuervo, "CAW!" That afternoon I learned to caw, too.

"We should move down here, Simone, and get a house, big enough for the children."

That evening we went to the Giggling Marlin bar, with Steve. "Americans can't handle money here," Steve explained. "You have to marry a Mexican to have your own business."

"You can marry a Mexican deaf-mute, Simone," Art joked. "Then we'll start our own empire!"

⁓

Artie bought a box of Havana cigars, Romeo y Julieta's, to smuggle in for Christmas presents. "I'll wrap fifty dollar bills around the cigars of the big guys, hundreds around the small guys." Never politically correct, he added, "Big men are judged by the way they treat little men." At the Twin Dolphins hotel, he bought two huge blue and white bath towels for us. In the gift shop he asked, "Do you see anything you want?"

"No." I figured he had been with some pretty grasping women. I didn't want to be like that with him.

Art picked out two baseball caps. "I'll give one of these to Jim," he said.

He had started thinking about going back. Art still liked his brother, really. Maybe the rift between them wasn't that wide. A lot of this talk about moving to Cabo might not pan out, I thought.

On the wide terrace we sat holding hands. Below the cliff far out on the blue expanse of water two whales sprang into the air again and again, before crashing into the sea, foreplay to the primal ritual of their mating. "I'm going to marry you, Simone. Because I really trust you," he said. "I need you. I need a woman, not a little girl." Life looked magical. We had been so happy in Mexico, I hated to think of returning to San Francisco. What would happen when we got back?

That night Steve drove us in his truck with no windshield out to his house. Artie held one of their sons lovingly in his arms, "I miss my kids so much."

Later we went back to our favorite bar and looked out at the flickering lights over the water. "I'd be a fool to ever let you go, Simone," he said.

"I love you so much, Art. I want to always be with you."

Conscious it was our last night in Cabo, he began clowning around. He had his dope can with him and made a trip into the restroom to stick it down his pants. Then he started limping across the bar, having me hold it, acting like his johnson was so big that someone had to help him carry it. We had an audience. Since I was sober, I felt a little embarrassed. To get into the spirit of some of Art's antics it would have helped if I had been high.

When he tried to pay with a hundred, the owner of the bar said he couldn't break it. Art was outraged, "I'm never coming back to this place again!" After that, he was so drunk he tried to get into another place that was all-dark. We went back to the hotel and to bed. He had to have been feeling funny about coming back. He wasn't ready, either.

"I'm not taking any dope or dope paraphernalia back across the border," Art said as we packed. "I'm already smuggling in the Havana cigars. I know they'll check me." The whole time we were in Mexico if we passed a Federali he would say "Don't look over in his direction, because these guys, they'll run you in for nothing!"

On the way to the airport he hiked off into the desert and hid his dope can in a cactus—near the 25-click mark out of Cabo. The can held the remnants of the weed he'd brought with him, rolling papers, and the two pipes. When he came back his hands were bleeding a little, "The next time we're here I'll see if that can is still where I left it. It would be someone's lucky day if they found it, though!"

At the airport, we sat at the bar. Art drank and I kept kissing his neck. The bartenders kept saying, "You bought that."

"No," Art was proud. "You can't buy this." I was so affectionate with him. And then from out of the blue he said, "You know, just because I took you on this trip it means nothing. I could get rid of you tomorrow—I could leave you tomorrow."

I felt so hurt. I went off to the bathroom, crushed. When I came back Art asked, "How about a kiss?"

"No! You just told me you're leaving me. Don't say that. It just completely takes the pleasure I have out of being with you when you do that!"

I felt terrified. Everything had been fine. *Until then.*

There were only seven other people on the plane to Tijuana. Art sat in the window seat looking very tense. "Aero-Mexico is not very safe," he said. "They have crashes all the time. My mother is a witch. She's psychic. She says to imagine yourself inside a pink bubble when you're taking off and landing, and nothing will happen."

Sex should turn his mood around, I thought. When the seatbelt sign went off, we went in the bathroom to get it on; he didn't come.

"I think you'd get really fat and lazy as my wife," he said. "I'm never marrying anyone again. Ever!"

It was a ghastly flight. I was coming down off the trip, worried about what would happen, then he blurted out all this hurtful stuff, too. Uneasy about going back and facing Jim, even though he had to, Art had also been sweating the border, certain he looked like someone no governmental agent would let into the United States. After we got through with no complications, he relaxed a bit.

Driving through L.A. in the van, Art's mood picked up and I felt buoyant. "Well, we had our first fight," he said. "I'm sorry. Sometimes I can really be mean!" Beyond the freeway, lights sparkled. He told me about a trip to Europe with his brother right after high school, "Jim and I hooked up with two *Playboy* bunnies on the ship. My girl was afraid to have sex with me when she found out I was only seventeen.

But I convinced her it wouldn't be a crime, because we were on the high seas! . . . Until I was twenty-seven, I was trying to get a hard-off!"

Art's stories usually made me laugh, and always gave me a window into his macho perspective.

"When we were traveling in Europe, Jim was fucking this girl—he fucked her tampon all the way up past where she could get it out, so we had to go to a hospital to have it taken out! My brother is so weird! In Germany, we picked up these two hookers. I'm easy; I got off. And my brother kept fucking and fucking this hooker who was older for hours, and not getting a nut. She wanted her money. Jim kept saying, 'No, I'm not paying you. I haven't gotten my nut!'"

As our Mexico trip ended, I realized our relationship had changed. For the first time ever we had been together constantly for more than two weeks. Art had won my heart by his expressions of love, but some of his attitudes and behavior had surprised and disappointed me. Although we had great sexual chemistry, much shared experience, and deepening affection, we didn't have much in common when it came to our backgrounds or interests. Still I was optimistic, knowing no relationship is perfect. Despite our differences, I was head over heels in love with him.

Art was hell-for-leather bent to get back. It seemed strange to me, as so recently he had been in such a frenzy to leave. Over the Grapevine, it was snowing and the road was icy. Even though it was freezing, for awhile we rested in the back. I found a sleeping bag and crawled in but it was kid size, only came up to my waist. Soon he was eager to get back on the road. We drove all night, all the way to San Francisco. I would have given anything to stop at a motel, but Art was determined to get us back as quickly as possible, back to whatever was waiting.

Chapter 11:
East of Eden

SUNDAY, FEBRUARY 3, 1988—MORAGA

Artie and I, the children, and Jim climbed up the lush green hillside above their place. At the peak Jim's gaze was dynastic, here we are, the Mitchell brothers, on top of our hill. We made it. And we're still on top; we've brought our offspring up here, too. Jim stepped back to try out his new camera, and took a few shots of us silhouetted against the heavy clouds. Artie bent down to wrap a blanket around his niece Jenny's two-year old shoulders; she was cold.

I felt fulfilled. Finally, I was sharing Art's bed and his life. Of course, he was also sharing the house with Jim, whose bedroom was just a few feet across the hall. Weekends and holidays were fast paced—Art's children played, competed, and roamed with Jim's children in spirited chaos. When the younger Mitchells weren't there, the long ranch house seemed almost too large. That house had an ever-shifting, semi-public atmosphere almost as fluid as the O'Farrell.

Art's life—which was enmeshed with my own—was much more complex and spontaneous than I had imagined. Countless people were attracted by his charismatic, friendly personality, his appetite for drugs, booze, and sexual adventure, and his success and money. Art had a lot of fun with this, and gave his phone number out endlessly. Many of the people he met wanted something. Some drifted through the house. There were other intrusions that were much more insidious.

"When the phone rings, don't answer it, Simone," he said. "Karen is saying if you're here, she won't let me see the kids."

I agreed, but I felt bad about it. Although they had split up four years earlier, and their divorce had been final for a long time, Art said Karen was livid that he had taken me to Mexico. "You've got nothing to worry about," he consoled me. "You calm me down, that's the important thing."

While the children were happily playing in the backyard, Art and I went into the garage for a private moment, crawled into an ancient car of Jim's, on blocks. During the blowjob, Jim wandered into the garage. He laughed, "The forty Ford."

"Yeah, I always knew this Ford was good for something," Art said. We climbed out of the car. I was embarrassed, but laughing.

"Feel his chest," Art joked. "Doesn't it seem similar, genetically?"

A little later in the backyard Art said, "Go up to Jim, go find him. He was perving these Catholic girls last night when we went to the basketball game. They were trying real hard to be cute, but he was really perved out over them. Go up to Jim and say, Art sent me on a mission. He sent me to give you a blowjob."

I was psyched up wanting to please Art. I thought this was some kind of old joke involving one-upmanship between them that wouldn't be taken seriously. Usually I could play along with his fantasies enough to satisfy him, and they wouldn't materialize. "I don't really want you to do it," Art explained to me once. "I just want you to say yes."

I approached the kitchen, in search of Jim, even though he was intimidating and always sedate, and I didn't feel comfortable enough with him to joke. After all, he was the president of the Mitchell Brothers' corporation, my boss, and a man who took his own authority very seriously. Humor is a great equalizer. Jim certainly didn't consider me his equal—I was a woman, and an employee. All the more reason to break through this, I thought. When I found Jim, I was speechless and retreated, to Artie.

"I just want to share something really fine with him," Art sounded serious. "You really enjoy sex."

Standing near the blue counter-top, I felt like a fool. "Uh, Art sent me on a mission," I said. "He has to be kidding. He said I should give you . . ." I couldn't say it.

"A BJ."

"Yeah."

Jim stared. Somebody six years old threw open the door, dressed like Rambo, "Daddy! Look!" He held up a lizard.

"I gotta leave," Jim said coolly. "I'll take a rain check."

I fled back to Art, mortified, "Was he offended?"

"Oh, no," Art said, savoring I would play along with such an outrageous joke, just because he asked me. "Don't worry. I'll set you up with him." He added mischievously, "You should suck both dicks. It's the *Mitchell brothers!*"

I was so relieved to see Jim leaving. What the devil did he think of me? Art sat on the diving board; I tried to hide behind him.

Sex with Jim never came up again.

〰

Art picked up his youngest three children after school in Corte Madera on Friday, for the whole weekend. His teenage kids visited, but were busy with their own lives.

Art's older children were polite, and were tall and blond like his first wife, Meredith. His son Storm, who was fifteen, seemed quiet— Art called him "The Diplomat." His daughter Mariah was fourteen and articulate. Liberty, his oldest daughter, was in her senior year of high school on the East Coast.

Like his father, Cal was full of mischief. He threw little tantrums from time to time. Aaron was bright and willful and daring; he enjoyed the way I listened to him, like he was an adult. Jasmine missed her mom and dad being together, but seemed to like me. She asked me to tell her fairy tales, and to leave the nightlight that looked like a blue balloon on, at bedtime.

~

In bed, Art told me one night last week he was at the theater and a new dancer, who was nineteen and into coke, told him it was a real slow night. He offered her a hundred, they went down to the Ultra Room and he fucked her. Soon there were some nights he didn't spend with me. Lisa said he was doing a lot of cocaine again.

Art was sprucing up his bedroom, which the last owner had papered in pink and blue flowers. I ordered drapes, and he had asked me to choose fresh wallpaper, but his mother bought some on sale and had driven down from Sacramento and hung it that week. I had looked forward to finding something especially nice, and felt disappointed. The new paper was white with a generic pattern in dark yellow.

"I'd like you to pick out the carpet, Simone. Do you think green would go with this?"

Rocky and Art were painting the woodwork in there green, like the door in Art's favorite movie. Art was disheartened and edgy, "Karen's had a breakdown for the 9,000th time. She's demanding I co-sign for a car or she's holding the kids!"

~

At the theater Jim asked me to design costumes for a new show, Topless Shoeshine. He wanted bras and g-strings with shoeshine rags attached to them so girls could polish the customers' shoes with their tits and pussies—while dancing for tips, of course. I knew the dancers wouldn't go for it, but Jim already had expensive leather shoeshine chairs installed along one wall of the Green Door Room, and bought shoe polish, and brushes. It was one of those ideas that was better left as a fantasy.

~

"Simone, can you watch the kids tomorrow? Jim and I got invited to the Olympic Club Golf Course."

Next to a sleeping Art, I lay staring at the canopy over our heads willing myself to win. My presence would dominate and pervade that bed, I told myself. No one else could last.

In the morning, he gave me fifty bucks to take the kids out for breakfast, and left to play golf. Jasmine, Cal, Aaron and I had the house all to ourselves. I felt closer to him being with the children he loved so much. I just have to do my best in my portion of Art's life to outlast the others, I thought, and love him.

Sunlight hit the fish tank. Art's dad, J.R. Mitchell, looking a bit like Jim, smiled elusively from a little pewter frame on Art's dresser.

On the trip back up the hill from breakfast Cal yelled from the back of the van "It's a bird, it's a plane, it's super dick!"

"Caleb! Be quiet!" Jasmine objected. I smiled to myself. It sounded like Cal would grow up to be as outrageous as Artie Mitchell.

We went swimming, and they raced from one lively game to another. Art called, "Let's go to dinner at Bennihana's tonight. Don't tell the kids, it'll be a surprise."

It was hot. I was watching the kids by the pool when Art got home and poured himself vodka over ice in a glass from Dan White's campaign fund. He walked outside with the cocktail, and kissed me, affectionately playing the returning loving husband to the wife, watching over the kids. The children were so happy to see their dad, and yelled for him to get in the water. He dove in to swim with them for a few minutes. Then Art and I went back in the bedroom, locked the door, peeled off my black swimsuit fast.

At 6:00 p.m. we drove the five children to the restaurant and waited. The teenagers talked to Aaron, Cal and Jasmine with affection.

"One Father's Day dinner I brought the kids here and it took forever to get served. Finally when they seated us there was no fried rice on the menu, and they refused to fix it! That's the only dish Cal and Jasmine would eat. I was real drunk that night. I started screaming, 'No fried rice!'"

Thirty minutes after the drinks, we were seated. The little kids began throwing ice onto the grill a couple of tables away, enjoying the hiss. I was starving. Artie was getting louder, "If they don't serve us pretty *goddamn soon* we're getting the fuck out of here!"

"Why don't you do *just that*," some man at the next table suggested.

Finally, a waitress wearing a kimono arrived with soup, some salad. But in five minutes, with no entree in sight, Art went to the register, defiant, "You Japs. You're giving me such lousy service! I'm never coming back here again!" He slapped down a fifty and stalked out. The other six of us followed.

Art drove to Chuck E. Cheeze. I was near tears. The kids ran up the stairs to the arcade. Art and I considered the menu.

"What do you want to eat?" he asked.

"I don't want anything here . . .. Can we leave, can we just leave?"

"Well, they're doing their thing. Order two medium pizzas. One pepperoni, one cheese. I'm waiting in the car."

Upstairs over pinball I found Mariah, "I thought he was just kidding until we actually got up."

"He does this from time to time," she said.

~

In the middle of April, Rita Ricardo married Charles De Santos in a church on Larkin Street, followed by a reception in North Beach. I was maid of honor. Art didn't show, so I spent some time with a friend of Charles's, who was also a filmmaker.

It was a little frustrating to me that while Rita and Charles were getting married after being involved for only three years, Art had not been able to make a serious commitment to me yet. Although I still needed space for myself, I felt some envy of the marriage of my friends. Art's drug and alcohol problems made me long for more leverage with him. And since now I was spending a lot of time with his children, too, part of me was beginning to crave a relationship that was more stable. And I would have liked to have been treated with more respect by his family, by people at the theater, and by others who touched our lives.

～

Sunday, Art and I took the kids to Marine World. After I fixed Cornish game hens for dinner and Jasmine mixed the batter for brownies, we all watched a movie together. When the children went to bed, I locked the bedroom door, pulled the heavy drapes closed, and climbed into bed with him. Around 11:00 p.m. I heard the bell. "Art," I nudged him awake. "The doorbell's ringing. Could it be Jim or somebody, who could it be?"

"I don't know. I don't care who the fuck it is. I'm not going to answer it!"

Way down the hallway the door opened and footsteps came closer, to our door. Eerily, someone tried the handle. "Artie, open the door. Artie, open the fucking door."

The doorway was outlined in light as we sat up on the bed, in darkness.

Art said, "Go away or I'll call the fucking cops, Missy."

"Open the fucking door, Artie!"

"You're breaking into my house."

I couldn't resist, "Well if it isn't Miss Manners."

Suddenly she was angry and very loud, "OH, YOU'RE REALLY STOOPING LOW TO FUCK A WHORE THAT'S SO LOW

YOU ALWAYS SAID YOU'D NEVER EVER FUCK. YOU'RE
FUCKING SUCH A LOW WHORE AS SIMONE CORDAY!
WATER SINKS TO ITS OWN LEVEL, ARTIE!" She pounded
hard against the door and kicked it with all her might, like a cartoon
character on a rampage.

I stood up and leaned forward so she could hear, "You're a liar,
Missy. A mean, vicious liar! We all know that!" I thought the door
would burst open, but it didn't.

"I'm calling the cops, Missy," he said. "I'm picking up the phone
right now and calling the cops!" He dialed, "I'm way up on Bollinger
Canyon Road and my ex-girlfriend has broken into my house. She's
trying to terrorize my present girlfriend . . . .. Oh, I don't know, the last
time I saw her she was driving a Volkswagen."

Suddenly it was quiet. After a couple of minutes when it seemed
safe, he opened the door. I felt stunned. The door was badly scarred,
with black curved marks and a deep hole, made by a high heel. He
went to the front to look around.

"She's gone."

"Are you sure? She has no right to call me a whore."

"I know," he said. "Sticks and stones will break your bones,
Simone, but words will never hurt you. I guess I should file a formal
complaint against her. I could have knocked her down but it's not
worth it. I've seen it all—then *you've* hurt *them*. She'd like to do me
in if she could. Let the police deal with it. She's just a drunk. She's
crazy!" Art hugged me and laughed, "Never a dull moment!"

After that night, I never went to sleep without making sure the
doors were locked. Art was more trusting, and believed no one would
harm him.

In the morning Jasmine and Cal, who had slept only fifteen feet
away, didn't mention hearing a thing. Had they listened to rampages
like that before, I wondered, did they think screaming was normal? I

took another look at the hole in the bedroom door, that door Artie
had wanted to paint green.

MAY 7, 1988 — MOTHER'S DAY

Art and I went away to Pismo Beach with the kids. Sunday
we took a long walk along the water, and had fun digging clams.
Prudently, we left early, so the children could have dinner with Karen.
The clams would be her present, for Mother's Day.

The next time I saw Art he was in shock. Karen had made a
staggering Mother's day announcement. She was pregnant, by a
"ship in the night," with twins. Karen was going to have them, and
use Artie's support for five children, not just for his three. She was
maneuvering him into supporting eight kids; not just his own six.

What a blow this was! Their marriage was over with. But
whenever Art was worried about his children and Karen, he pulled
away from me. She wouldn't let go.

Art's first wife, Meredith, went to law school after she divorced
him, even though she had three young children, too. She had been
one of the brothers' attorneys in the late 70's until 1981, when Jim fired
her. Karen had met Art when she was eighteen, and had been raising
his children for ten years, since she was twenty. Although she had
plenty of moxie, Karen didn't have Meredith's academic background
or the motivation to develop a career for herself—yet. From her
perspective, it made sense to have a couple more kids—no matter who
the father was—and hold onto Art's financial support for dear life.

"My ex- has cracked. She calls me up," Art said. "She is going to
visit her grandparents, and she asks me would it be O.K. if she tells
them the twins are mine. She is too embarrassed to tell them the way
it is, that it was a 'ship in the night.' So I said, 'It's always better to tell

the truth.' Then one of my friends ran into her over in Sausalito and she told him, 'Yes, Artie and I have been getting along real well lately, and *I'm pregnant.*' but he knew I had a vasectomy."

"That's insane. Why is she saying that?" I asked.

"I don't know. Whether she just has too many things on her mind now with this pregnancy or what it is. Everybody knows that with twins you stay up all night with them for months, when they're born it's just the beginning. And it's twice as hard for years."

"If Karen's saying those twins are yours, she's just trying to get more support, because the more people that believe it the greater chance there is of her getting it."

"Well, maybe so, but it's not so easy nowadays with all the tests."

"You might have to get a letter proving you had a vasectomy."

"All it would take is one test and—No Sperm."

~

Late one afternoon, I was sitting in the audience of the New York show when I glanced to my left. At long last, there sat my crazy old fan Harvey, in the seat next to me. Maybe he had gone off his medication and was having a relapse of his obsession. I left the audience fast. By the next evening a final creepy package of letters was waiting at the box office for me, beginning with, "Yes, it's really me, Harvey."

~

Friday afternoon after school we took the children to Clear Lake. I loved going on trips with Art; whenever we were away together life was relaxing and uncomplicated. He and I sat in the bar near a big group of Kiwanis and talked about getting a house up there. "It would be great for the kids during the summers," he said.

Sharing the Moraga house had been convenient for Art and Jim a couple of years earlier when they had live-in housekeepers and all the kids were younger. Like their father, Art's kids were fun loving

200

and wild. Art took his children on a lot of trips, and was relaxed and permissive with them. Jim was more cautious and worried, and didn't like traveling much. Neither brother wanted their children overly influenced by the parenting style or lifestyle of the other. It was confusing enough for each family of children to be dividing their time between two parents. As much as they could, Art and Jim were alternating weekends away and weekends home.

I didn't like Art's living arrangement with Jim. It seemed odd to me that two brothers in their forties would even consider living together, especially when they were business partners. The falling out they had six months earlier was an indication they needed a break from each other. It made it tougher for Art to grow towards a more balanced relationship with me, when he was living with his brother. "Sharing that house with Jim is pretty intense," I said, "when you work together, too."

"Right. Yeah, it's intense. I know one thing. The next place will be a tight little spot. This dump may have finished me forever on the big house. It's just too much trouble. And I'm tired of driving back and forth from the East Bay all the way to Marin."

So was I. We had to get up at 6:30 a.m. to get his kids to school.

～

Art found a watch with a large black "X" on a white face and was joking with me, "Now, the X-rated time is . . .."

That weekend, Jim and Lisa and his kids were at the Moraga house, too. Jasmine wanted *Preppies* at the video store. I thought it was O.K. Art let them choose most of their movies. When we brought it home, a couple of the kids went in the back to watch it.

"I found them totally engrossed in that movie," Lisa said. "It showed frat boys on their knees on dog leashes, and sorority girls with their tits out!"

201

"God. The box looked tame enough. Jasmine knew the title and asked for it," I said. "I didn't think anything of it."

"I told them 'Nobody watches this movie!' and turned it off. It was directed by Chuck Vincent," she said. We hid the tape high in a kitchen cabinet.

Lisa had danced at the O'Farrell since the late 70's, and had been arrested in one of the raids when the dancers were nude in the audience. As Lysa Thatcher she had starred in porn movies, including *Neon Nights, Coed Fever, Satisfiers of Alpha Blue,* and *American Desire* (26 films which she appears in are listed on Adult Film Database). She was confident, cool, soft-spoken, and always looked immaculate. Customers bought Lisa expensive jewelry and even a mink. She made outstanding money at the O'Farrell. But by that summer, she had grown tired of working there. She was nearly thirty and had been dancing for ten years.

Of course, I was beginning to burn out dancing, too. It was exhausting to balance caring for Art, spending time with his children, and driving the long distances between our places, with doing shows at the theater, and having time to myself.

The dressing room gossip was that six years earlier, Lisa had married an attractive guy in his twenties who played in a band and drove a cab. They had bought a house in Marin County, where Lisa trained briefly as a dog groomer. Outside the sex industry, her high school diploma didn't qualify her for jobs where she could make the money she was used to earning. "My favorite section of the newspaper is the Macy's magazine," she would say. Months earlier, Lisa left her young husband and began a single-minded campaign for Jim, who was forty-five.

What was happening between Lisa and Jim intrigued me, even though we had been dealt a very different hand of cards. Lisa and I were as dissimilar as Jim and Art. Captivating Jim was different than dealing with changeable Art and his wild binges. Yet, both Mitchell brothers expected their women to center their lives around them and their children.

Jim wanted help with his kids on a regular basis. He also wanted a woman to give him steady emotional support. Underneath Jim's orderly, slow-paced, quiet personality ran an undercurrent of anxiety. I never saw him break loose and have fun. He had a chip on his shoulder. Jim longed for the kind of respectability he had found out an Okie pornographer couldn't buy.

Lisa had to establish that she would be an invaluable asset, and prove how conscientious a caregiver she had become. As Jim's liaison, she had the dancers sign papers changing their employment status from employees to independent contractors. Lisa was succeeding in proving her devotion. For the last two months, she and Jim had been acting more serious and aloof. Day by day, their inner world was becoming very private.

Art was unhappy with Jim for moving Lisa in, "*That's* against the rules. The other night Lisa said to me, 'Gee, we didn't know you liked cheese cannelloni, Art. We thought you wanted spaghetti, like the kids!'

"Paulie says Lisa is doing a lot of stuff in the audience," Art said to me. "No. I won't tell Jim, yet, that Lisa's breaking the rules. Not yet," he joked, "not until she satisfies my every whim! Paulie asked me 'What am I going to do? *The boss's girl*. All the other girls will take her lead.' That's another reason *I* have to get out of here!"

∾

Artie's first wife Meredith had her three kids sign papers to change their last name from Mitchell to Bradford (her maiden name), on their birth certificates and everything. Art was furious. On the phone, he told his teenagers, "If you disinherit your father, don't come at me for the money!" Then he slammed the door to the kitchen, hard. Cal

203

kept on talking to me in the living room about Big Bird, like it hadn't even happened.

Most likely, the teenagers' names were changed to distance them from the Mitchell notoriety in the X-rated industry—a notoriety Art was very proud of having achieved. He loved all his children dearly, and was generous with them far beyond making his support payments. This name change was a rejection he didn't deserve.

The next day we picked up Mariah, then went to Nordstrom's to pick up sunglasses for Art. She wanted a sweater, then shoes. He wouldn't buy them. He led her empty-handed, probably for the first time ever, back to the van. Mariah was indignant, "Mom says that's your job!"

"What? To increase her real estate holdings? Is she using her support that's supposed to be for you and your clothing for that, Miss *Bradford*?"

Years later, I would learn that Art's first wife received so much less child support than his second wife Karen did, that his older children were understandably resentful.

By the next weekend, Artie had forgiven the insult. He was talking about buying Mariah a $25,000.00 horse.

~

Because Karen wouldn't let him have the kids on Father's Day weekend, Art canceled his plans with me and said he was going to drive to Santa Barbara by himself. All weekend I was seething.

When he was back, I phoned over there, Jim answered and gave it to his brother.

I told Art how disappointed I had been, I wanted to spend some time alone with him, too, not just with him and the children. "I'm angry, Art. We haven't gone out for weeks. I'm not going to put up with it. If big men are judged by the way they treat little men, what about the way they treat their women? I want to be treated like a girlfriend you love and respect, not like someone you don't care about."

"Well, that makes sense," he said. "Bye."

He was quite angry. For the next few weeks of the summer, he didn't have me around his kids much, and the nights we spent together were more sporadic. I enjoyed the break and went out with friends, although I missed Art very much. But for there to be any positive change I had to protest, then wait for him to want to get tight with me again.

Of course, many women wouldn't accept the peaks and valleys of my relationship with Artie. Most wouldn't tolerate his drug and alcohol binges and flings with other women, and take him back as I did. In the O'Farrell backwater that was mine, his behavior was accepted. As his alcoholism progressed at a gradual pace, I hardly noticed. He was still worth it, to me. Great sex, a bond of affection, and excitement kept me with him. The times we spent apart allowed me to recoup and build energy for the times we were together.

At work, Lisa told me, she and Jim had finished moving to San Francisco, near Ocean Beach. "It's a really cozy spot, in fact sometime you'll have to come over. It's out by the ocean, and I've always wanted to live out there. I don't mind the fog at all."

At 8:00 p.m. Art called me, "Simone, do you still want that certain something in your mouth? Put on something sexy, heels, stockings, something black. I'm going to fuck you all night."

Art kissed me hello, then asked me to fix him something to eat, and even for dessert. All I could offer for that was some candy.

"Did Jasmine like her birthday present?" I asked.

"Oh, yes. And she especially liked the card. Come over here and sit near me. Aren't you glad to see me? I love you. I wouldn't stay with you for ten years if I didn't love you. Don't you realize what a great man you have? You love me, don't you?"

"Yes."

"I love the way you try to fight me. You just can't, because you love me."

We alternated between sex, conversation, the meal, and Art's drinking beer and some shots of Vodka and Old Grand-Dad.

"There's one thing that's important to me, Simone, and it's not love and it's not anything else. It's freedom. Don't try to swim upstream. Go with the flow. Whoever's been giving you advice is wrong."

How maddening. I hadn't made any outrageous demands of him and had done nothing wrong. But over and over again, Art had to prove he was in charge.

"I know you're brilliant. I know you have a thousand cutting remarks to say to me. But don't say them," he continued. "You have what you always wanted. You have a sexual mate for life. You're so lucky. You have a guy that really knows how to fuck you. I've stayed with you longer than either of my two wives, and you're the only girl I ever wanted to fuck for four or five hours, all night. We can't be an ordinary couple, because our desires are not ordinary desires. I'm the only one whose sexual appetite is almost equal to your own."

"I want you to be happy. I need you, Art."

While he was in my tub, I showed him three surrealistic cards I found that week. One of them pictured a woman on a high stool, which he called a pedestal, in vague bondage. She was viewed by two short men, one of which looked like a fat perverted Napoleon. It was called "The Little General."

"There you have it, woman on a pedestal, and these two guys are just typical guys. Not like me."

"I don't fuck, much, anymore, I'm getting too old," he went on. "When I do I want it to be quality fucking. When I fuck the pigs, I wear rubbers. And when I really want to fuck, I come over here. . . . My job is to mess with your mind and torture you and fuck you. I'm a hell of a fun guy."

I laughed.

"I've never seen a woman so in love as you. And it tears you up when you know your daddy's fucking some other girl because you know I'm fucking her a hundred different ways and she's falling in love with me. Every girl I fuck falls in love with me, Simone, because I'm a man. There's only a few men and a lot of boys out there. And the boys don't know how to fuck.

"My job, and it was given me by God, and you can call it whatever you want, but it's a convenient term, a catch word, is to be your master. I'll always be with you. I'll never leave you. And I never will. You've had such a good life."

He started saying he wanted me to be his slave.

"Art, you're an unkind man. Anyone you're with is going to have some emotions, otherwise it would be just like being with my mannequin in the living room."

"But I like your mannequin."

"Have you ever read *Venus in Furs*?"

"No. What is it?"

"It's an old S and M novel written in the 1890's by Leopold von Sacher-Masoch. Marianne Faithfull is a descendant of his."

"Never heard of it. The title's neat, though, *Venus in Furs*."

It's a classic S and M novel, the language is very flowery, and it's boring and hard to get through the entire thing. The main character is a guy named Severin who becomes a total slave to a woman, called Venus in Furs. But she becomes bored with him. At the end she gets a new boyfriend, and she's about to have him whip Severin when finally a light goes off in Severin's head. He realizes that his total adoration of his mistress only led to her despising him. At the end Severin says 'He who allows himself to be whipped deserves to be whipped.'"

"Oh, he loved it."

"No, he didn't. That was the point. If I became your slave, you would just get bored with me. . . . So, do you want me to put my fur coat on and roll around on top of you?"

"No, that's O.K."

"I want to go out with you, more," I said.

"O.K. I'll take you anywhere you want," he replied.

" . . . Will you do anything I say, anything?"

"Yes," I said it to humor him, momentarily.

"I'm going to eat your pussy. Your favorite thing."

"I want your dick, too."

"I know, but this is special to you, am I right? . . . So, instead of just eating the toffee or his girl's pussy, he chose to do both." Art bit a piece of the candy.

"You can write books, you can talk, you can do anything, but you'll always be my woman, Simone, until you die . . . .. You might even be able to have me every night."

~

Saturday I had dinner in Moraga with Art and the children, who seemed happy to see me. Blissfully, now the whole house was ours.

"As soon as Jim moved, I could feel this sense of relief," said Art. "And I bet he does too. There were just too many kids, and adults, plus add a couple of friends!"

Chapter 12:
23 *Mohawk Avenue*

AUGUST 9, 1988

"There's been a rumble at the theater."

Scratched up, bruised and very upset, Art got to my place at quarter to 1:00 a.m. I hugged him, cleaned up his wounds, and brought a Heineken to him in the bedroom.

"You know Danielle—Danielle from Hell—we hired her even though she doesn't meet O'Farrell standards, because this old friend of mine who's a poet recommended her—she attacked me. I went up to her, all I did was give her a hug. And she claws my head. I wasn't expecting it—I just reacted—I took her by the hair and bounced her head eighteen inches off the rug."

"Oh, no, Art." I was shocked.

"All the girls in the dressing room were putting on makeup and didn't see her claw me, they just saw her head bounce off the floor. I decked her. Then she went on stage and danced three songs. All the dancers were freaked. Then I went up to her and said, 'I'm sorry this happened. You're not fired. Can we talk about this?

"So she says 'If I'm fired I'll start a *federal lawsuit*.' Then she claws at my leg through my jeans and tried to knee me in the nuts again, missing. Then she takes off her shoe with a metal heel and threw it at me, but it just caught the corner of my jacket. I picked the shoe up and threw it through a window. Then I told her get out, you're fired!

"After that I went out and yelled out over the audience from upstairs, 'The O'Farrell is finished. You swine sluts can go down and work at Market Street where you belong. You dykes have broken my heart!' It must have sounded like the voice of God. No more beaver, the customers would have heard. 'Oh, no, not that! Anything but that!' It was so heavy that no one even dared back talk. The Whoremaster doesn't speak very often," Art added, "but when the Whoremaster speaks!"

I laughed at his words, but the story was very scary. I had trouble believing he had done anything so violent, and that anything like this could happen at the theater.

His leg looked terrible. Danielle was a good street fighter.

"Some swine gave me speed Sunday night, and I did it. I shouldn't do the drugs the swine give me." That's why he couldn't sleep the previous two nights. "Danielle is a good hostile street poet, her stuff's brutal, sadomasochistic. She gave me her book and I read it and liked it. I like to think the O'Farrell is a place for everyone."

At 9:30 a.m., Art left for the theater to face the music. Going down the steps in haste he forgot to give me a kiss, turned back and kissed me, saying, "I didn't want you to worry all day."

By evening he was mellow, "Jim said 'I heard six bad reports about *you* last night.' to me. I told him, 'I don't even want to talk about it. Yes. O.K. I did it all. I beat the shit out of the girl. You're going to believe that, anyway.' I didn't want to get into it with *him*. I'm not one of those wimps that thinks business should be normal!"

I laughed.

"The revolt of the dykes is coming. I can feel it. I'm going to start a new policy of not talking to any of the dancers."

～

"We went to Vanessi's," Art said to me in bed. "They said we have some coke, do you want to do some coke? And unlike years before, I said yes, I want to do some coke, but not until after dinner. Then I put on a Kopenhagen show for the bachelor, and he didn't even go down there. That little brunette knocked on the door and said business is slow, so I put her in the office with the guy and he didn't even try to fuck her or get head or anything, he just talked to her."

"Well, isn't that usually the case," I said. "It's more the bachelor's friends that want him to do something, the bachelor usually doesn't want to."

"Yeah. . . . Now my bachelor party was really something else. First we went to Vanessi's, had dinner. And someone invited a street wino to come along and he thought—great, a free meal, a lot of booze. So when we're sitting in Vanessi's, Huey Newton came in dressed—and Huey always could dress—just to the nines. The wino took one look at Huey and fled. After dinner we went to some Korean massage parlor and Jim laid down twelve hundred dollars, "We've come to PARTY." So Nick was up on stage singing into the mike. Everyone was dancing. Next, we went over to the Mab. And to Finnochio's. Alex showed up dressed all in Vietnam gear, like he just got back from 'Nam. When we went back to the O'Farrell, they got the Ultra Room ready for me. Huey comes up to me, puts his head right in my face, and says, 'People are waiting for you. You must not disappoint them.' They tied me up in there. Girls were giving me blowjobs and fucking me and I was so drunk. It was when there were no windows and guys were pulling the girls into the booths and fucking them right there, all over. So after my bachelor party, it's sort of hard to compare."

~

Thursday evening Art called, exuberant, and asked me to cook spaghetti. He wanted me in the room with him, wanted food immediately, kept drinking and drinking so he had to go in the bathroom and get sick before dinner.

"You know what, I love you," he told me. "I can date and play the games but the first time something happens—*I'm gone.* I know you love me. I've had the most fulfilling sex of my life with you, Simone.

211

. . . For your birthday I'm going to take you on a vacation with my kids—you deserve something special."

That Friday, Hunter Thompson's former editor, David McCumber, was flying in to watch *The Crazy Never Die* and meet with Art and Jim that evening, before taking the tape back to show Hunter in Colorado.

"Don't answer the phone this weekend, Simone," Art said. "Karen told me if you're going on the vacation the kids can't go."

How aggravating. This made me feel powerless, not like Art's established partner. How did I fit into Aaron, Jasmine and Cal's lives? Because their parents were constantly fighting, the three youngest children felt anxious and unhappy at times. To try to make up for this, Art turned every weekend and vacation into party time for them, and showered them with gifts. He truly enjoyed spending time with his children. Art went on every amusement park ride with them, took them fishing from Clear Lake to Mexico, was an appreciate audience for their performances, and happily funded it all. The rest of the younger kids' time was spent with Karen, who seemed to be always pressuring Art for more money, even though he was paying her $4500 a month in alimony and child support. I wondered if Art and Karen's three children were learning to value much besides money, power, and pleasure.

At 1:30 a.m. Art came back from the meeting, shaken, "The Moraga cops stopped me for drunk driving," he said. "I wasn't drunk, but I took some acid tonight. I'm worried it might show up on the test. I fixed them, though. I puked in the back seat of the cop car and rubbed it into the rug with my shoe. They hate that, it stinks."

Saturday night after the kids settled down, Art put on a tape of the Hunter movie. *The Crazy Never Die* opened with Hunter Thompson swigging out a of a bottle of Chivas in the back of a car rolling past icy fields, as morose Jimi Hendrix-like guitar droned "My Old Kentucky

Home." We watched a bit of the movie, and Art fast-forwarded to show me in the gorilla costume with Hunter at Tosca.

He smiled, "It made the last cut."

When we were in bed, he asked, "So how big is Hunter's dick?"

"I don't know. I never fucked him."

"You didn't?"

"He was my friend. Besides, it's better this way. Think about it. Anyway, you're the only one who ever fucked me right and I love you. I didn't think about fucking Hunter."

Sunday, Art's mother Georgia Mae drove down from Sacramento and I met her for the first time. Lisa and Jim came over with his kids, too. A brunette in her sixties, Georgia Mae was cagey, very proud of her sons' material success, interested in all the children, and curious about Lisa and me. Lisa had met her on a trip to Sacramento in June. She told me Georgia Mae talked a lot about all the children's past lives, and served deep-fried Okie meals and white bread. I told Georgia Mae I had been a teacher, because Art said she had taught third grade. "What are you doing now?" she asked.

"I'm dancing at the theater."

"Oh," she said slowly, with subtle disapproval, "I guess the tips can be pretty good."

"Liberty made me feel pretty bad," Artie said to Georgia Mae. "She says she doesn't want to see me. She's upset about the business her dad is in. I sent her an expensive handbag with $500 in it for her birthday, and she didn't even mention it."

"She'll get past that. Liberty's smart, and she's a good kid. She won't always feel that way," Georgia Mae said.

When the children went outside with Art and Jim, Georgia Mae, Lisa and I sat at the table. Georgia Mae remarked, "And Simone's a dancer, do you know a few good dance steps, Simone?"

"A few, I suppose."

"I'm going to alter that square dancing dress you gave me for Meta," Lisa said.

It sounded like I was the only woman at the table who had worked as a stripper. Jim and Lisa must have kept Lisa's having danced at the theater for ten years and starred in porn movies a secret. I didn't expose Lisa. But because I had been honest about my dancing at the O'Farrell, I would be seen as the more disreputable girlfriend.

According to Jim and Georgia Mae's thinking, it was smart to profit from the sex business, but it wasn't respectable to work in it as a performer.

～

On Monday, Art and I left on a five-day trip with Aaron, Jasmine and Cal in the van. In Disneyland, Art took us on all the rides. We were in an upbeat mood. He and I made a couple of trips out to the van so he could smoke a joint and drink a beer for a break. On a bench near Tomorrowland, Art rested his head on my lap. Gently, I stroked his hair. "When the kids are grown I want to cut loose and do more traveling. It'll be fun," he said. "Liberty starts college next month. They're growing up fast. All my alimony and support payments will be over with when Cal turns eighteen, in the year 2000!"

～

A few nights after we were back, a famous rock group was coming in for a late party at the theater. Jim had asked Art to entertain the group and to try to get some music for *The Crazy Never Die*. Art was getting some of the younger dancers together for an after-hours show, and they were excited. I knew he was going to ask the girls to do sexual stuff with the group, and he would probably be doing some drugs; I didn't want anything to do with it. At noon the next day he called, "How come you didn't stay for the party? I know, you're like my brother, you don't like parties."

"I knew there was something going on, but I felt like going home."

"Well, one of those rock stars finally broke loose and tried to get his dick in four or five of them, they're happy. He got soaked. We had it in the shower show."

That summer, Art and Jim had shower heads installed over the stage of the Green Door Room, where *Green Door II* had been shot, and some hand-held shower massage fixtures hung on the back wall. Once the dancers did their set in the mist and toweled off, they table danced for tips. I didn't like the format, but tried it once for the experience. They still hadn't worked out getting enough hot water. Although this show satisfied some fantasies, I didn't like it because I stayed cold all day.

Soon Art complained that they had entertained that rock group for nothing. They weren't able to get music for the Hunter movie after all.

Tuesday I met Art at a bar where he was waiting for Hinckle; then we had dinner. After we were home Art gave me a big smile, "You've really got it made, Simone. You're the best. Your shows are so good. You're so sexy. Maybe I'll make you a superstar."

"At forty? I want to get out of dancing. One day you're making great money, the next day it can be bad, and the next day you can be out. I know that by now."

He looked at me in disbelief, "Look at your hair, Simone, you're beautiful. You can stay in the business another ten years!"

"Oh, Art—that way you can still be the boss and I can still be doing the Ultra Room when I'm fifty, do you think I want that?"

"You want to retire, don't you?"

"Well, from dancing, I do. I'm getting too old for it."

"How about if you just take care of me, that's a full-time job. I'm thinking about moving in here with you. We'll tear all this shit out—he looked over at my two hundred-year-old English prints—and put the kids' bunk beds in here. They'll love it. We'll live out of trailers.

"I think I'll start paying the rent. And take care of expenses. It'll be a good way to stack up some money real fast. Then I'm thinking about buying a place either in—I like the Marina, or in Corte Madera, because my kids are there."

I certainly didn't want him to toss out my beloved artwork, but this dream was enticing. I wanted to believe that living together full-time would bring us more intimacy, that he would use less alcohol and drugs, and would treat me better.

By morning, Artie had backed away from the idea. I was disappointed and angry. To avoid alienating him I had held in a lot of resentments for months—that day they spilled out. "When you do something that hurts me and I overlook it, that doesn't mean I think what you've done was O.K. It just means I've forgiven you," I said. "I'm larger than you are, Art, because I'm capable of compassion."

"What's most important to me, Simone, is not having a relationship. What's important to me is being able to do whatever the fuck I want to when I want to. And if you can't handle it, you're finished. I'm gone."

"No. Since we've been together so much, I've been acting more human with you, that has to happen. I've just been more assertive, that's all. I'm not a blow-up doll. I have emotions and my feelings get hurt. You are just very good at manipulation. You're a master at it, better than anyone I'll ever meet."

"It's my job," he said with a smile.

"All you're saying is you want your way all the time and fuck what anybody else wants. I can see through that by now. It's just allowing you to continue to be totally selfish." When he left, I slammed the door as hard as I could.

An hour later he called me. "I'm sorry. I just got my feelings hurt. I thought you wanted to live together when you said it last night," I said.

"Oh, it was totally my fault," Art said.

I believed he was capable of changing in a positive way, even if it took a long time. What I didn't know was that time would run out for him.

◈

It was time to harvest Art and Jim's marijuana crop. Art and I spent the night in the Moraga house. In the morning, one of their buddies rang the bell, looking shocked to see me there as the whole cutting and caravan operation was to begin any minute and was top secret.

"Why don't you look for a place in Corte Madera today," Art suggested. That afternoon I drove around the area and found only one place with a "For Rent" sign, a tacky white tract house trimmed in royal blue a block away from the kids' elementary school. The address was 23 Mohawk Avenue.

It seemed an unlikely place for a pornographer to want to move, not secluded enough for my taste. But Art wanted to be only in the flat area between the freeway and Christmas Tree Hill, where Karen's house was.

In the morning, we drove over the Golden Gate Bridge to Corte Madera. Art said he managed a video store in San Francisco and introduced me as his wife, and we filled out a rental application. Two small bedrooms faced the back yard. A den opened off the living room, but could be separated with a folding wooden door. The place seemed small to me, but it was light and airy, and had a solar-heated pool. "It's a hippie pad," Art whispered. "I love it." The landlady was

217

a friendly nurse. She and her husband were fond of the house, and the view of Mt. Tamalpais from the kitchen window.

~

The owner of the house said it would be ready in two weeks. Friday Art gave me $2200 in cash to have a check made out to "Simone Mitchell" to rent it. "I need a partner like you," he grinned. "No, I need a partner that is you."

~

I need someone to help out in the office," Vince said. "Lisa told me she'll be too busy with Jim's children to work. Would you want to try it?"

Lisa had been dancing, doing office work for Jim, and helping Vince with the schedule until she and Jim got a place together in July.

I told Vince yes, and said I would come in Monday afternoon.

In May, Vince had taken a small office in an old brick building a block away from the O'Farrell, on Geary. All the Mitchell Brothers' dancers began dropping by the office to get their schedules and pay the new stage fees (originally $12.50 a shift), and dancers came in to apply for work. Outside, street hustlers and dealers hung out. At night as the street people yelled to each other outside, Art and Jim's cousin Rocky slept on the floor, until the theater closed at 1:00 a.m. and he headed over there to clean the place. A friend of Vince's came by and painted "Dancers Guild International" on the door.

Vince and I agreed I could come in at 1:00 p.m. every afternoon because Art had been sleeping late. I would have time to fix breakfast first, and drive Art down to the O'Farrell, since he took cabs to my place at night instead of driving, if he was fairly drunk.

Why did Vince ask me to work in his office? I'd been dancing at the theater for seven years, had a reputation for being reliable, and had a longtime relationship with Artie. Years earlier, Karen Mitchell

218

had helped with scheduling the dancers until Aaron was born; for the last year Lisa had done it. Since I had just turned forty and wouldn't be dancing forever, it made sense to me to try some other aspect of the business. Although I didn't dwell on it, I knew it would be tough transitioning from dancing to a straight job. That summer I had gone to the costume shop of the San Francisco Opera to explore getting back into designing, but was discouraged by their long hours and low pay.

Monday I started at Vince's, and for a couple of days, I didn't hear from Art at all.

Towards the end of the week Vince held up a pair of glasses, "Hunter dropped these last night in the parking lot and then jumped on them, completely smashing them, saying they're wrecked now. Jim gave them to me and said 'Save these for the archives.'"

Underground cartoonist Dan O'Neill dropped by Vince's office proudly carrying two copies of his book *The Reagan Years*, which he just sold. He told Vince and me, "I'm a total womanizer. And up in Nevada City the women take these things seriously. Some of them pack guns. I've had them miss each other by minutes. And once I had to ask one to leave, it was just too dangerous!"

"Is Art mad at me? I haven't seen him for days," I asked O'Neill.

"Oh, I wouldn't worry about it," he said. "He's probably just out wandering around. He thinks of you as the only person who's ever been kind to him."

"I know Karen's twins are due pretty soon."

"Oh, yeah. *That*. It's as though fate finally figured out a way to really kick him. One night Art and I went over to the Music Hall and were upstairs during a piano concerto, and Art said 'Dan, you have to draw the pianist's portrait so she'll fall totally in love with me.' So I went to work and finished the thing. And she was playing a long concerto and building up to the finale and the audience was sitting in rapt silence, waiting for the final note. Art folded the drawing into a paper airplane. I said 'No, don't!' But Art sailed the thing down perfectly, and just as she was building up to the final note the thing hit the microphone and instead of the beautiful note the whole audience had been waiting for all over the hall everyone heard a loud, harsh, awful thud. That's what it took at that moment for Art to feel better, he needed to wreck everybody else's pleasure."

Chapter 13:
Party in New York

OCTOBER 24, 1988

Al Goldstein was throwing a twentieth-anniversary party for *Screw* magazine in New York. Art told me his brother wanted him to take a bodyguard, "Jim can't go anywhere. He's too afraid Lisa will fuck some guys . . . . I think I'll take you," he said.

"Really, you mean I get to go?"

It was 6:00 in the morning, the plane took off at 8:00. I blew him, and later in the dark, Art said, "My cock was made for your mouth, Simone. . . . . You sucked me so good, I kept my hard-on even after I came. . . . Do you want this big cock?"

"Absolutely."

When the alarm went off, I blended him a banana and papaya protein drink. Art put on a tie-dye shirt in earth tones I'd given him, a blue-grey overshirt, jeans and a camouflage general's cap. I wore a dressy violet sweater, jeans and a coat. We packed quickly: a velvet miniskirt and heels for me, plus Art's patent leather dancing shoes, and a gift from Hunter. Then we were off.

At the TWA counter, I saw that Art had first class tickets made out to Mr. and Mrs. A. Mitchell. I was amazed. He must have planned this. Why not tell me before 6:00 that morning?

"Do you like surprises," he asked, "or do you like to know?"

"Oh, I like surprises. But I like to know, too."

After a stop at the bar, we were on the plane. "The dirtiest tennies and the most money," he said. "All the rest of these people are

Republicans. They're the only ones in the country that can afford first class.

"I watched Hunter in action the other night. He had a new move, he takes a Bic lighter and throws it just right against the edge of a TV or something, so when it hits it flares up high. Pretty cool move."

"Did he like the music and the tape?" I asked.

"Oh, yeah. His eyes sort of glazed over when he heard it. The painting Steadman did is really cool, it's this drawing of Hunter as a skeleton in motion like he's running, he's coming out of a coffin and the colors he used are these brilliant shades of red orange."

Ralph Steadman was the British artist with a dark, whimsical style who illustrated Hunter's books. Having him do a painting for the movie was a coup.

We made out during the whole flight, more or less surreptitiously, and went upstairs to the lounge to scout out the bathroom, but there were too many people around for us to slip in there together. Art spread my fox coat over my lap just before we were supposed to land, and fingered me to orgasm. Neither of us cared if anyone noticed.

In New York, it was late afternoon and still warm. In the limo, I poured Art bourbon over ice and got some apple juice for myself. He called *Screw* to find out where the Goldstein party was being held. The secretary said the drinks were $4.50, but we could get drunk first and then come. Art laughed. "Just like Goldstein, too fucking cheap to buy the liquor," he told the limo driver. "I came all the way from California to show my respect for him on his twentieth anniversary."

As the limo sped into Manhattan, Art wanted to do some role-playing and have some oral sex on the backseat—to "turn the driver on, to educate him." "Yes, if you want me to, my Master," got him immediately rock-hard.

At Elaine's the restaurant was nearly empty, and we got a table in the back and ordered—salad, scampi, and some pasta the waiter endorsed as the "king of the pastas." We held hands. Art said, "You know, I could have come by myself, but what would I do? I would be alone in Elaine's at seven o'clock in Manhattan. It wouldn't be any fun." When I looked into his brown eyes he said, "I feel the same way."

Art told me about previous trips to New York with Jim when the original *Green Door* came out, "When you've made it, New York kisses your ass like nowhere else, and for one week we had *really* made it. This guy got down on his hands and knees in a restaurant to beg us, beg us to let Marilyn Chambers do another press conference. We were embarrassed. But finally we agreed to it, and that's when the whole thing took off."

He told about the Mafia boss they met years before who loved them and took care of their *Green Door* tapes being pirated. Art said the scary part was walking into his place down this hallway lined with young toughs, jealous of the closeness their Don felt for these Okie outsiders. They loved this man, who reminded Art of his own father. They sent a limousine with a young black hooker to give him a blowjob when he got to San Francisco. He was too embarrassed to do anything, but he loved it. "Nobody had ever done anything like that for him before," Art said. She, of course, told them all about it. They had to tell him to slow down visiting them, though, because the FBI began following them and thought they were in the mob. Soon after they got to know him well, he died of a heart attack. Ignorant that only Mafia people were welcome at such events, Art and Jim naively went back to his funeral to show respect.

They learned an important lesson from one of the Mafia boss's promoters, a midget whose office was down in a basement. "'Boys,' he said to us, 'just tell me what you want to do.' We spilled our guts out, telling him everything we wanted to do. And after we were through, he said, 'But that's impossible. What you want is impossible. Why don't you tell me what you want to do?'"

In that way the brothers learned the power of initially being agreeable, then limiting and rejecting people's ideas after they totally spilled out their plans.

When *Green Door* first opened, one winter they came back with ten or twelve of their people to check how things were going in the theaters, which were spread out all over New York. They sent John Fontana and another guy out to a tough black neighborhood. When they got there the theater was unheated but packed, the breath of the customers' mist in the cold air above them.

We lingered over the meal, not eating much of it. The Spanish waiters knew we were making out, and it was driving them crazy. Back in the limo, Art put on a shaggy black wig that Hunter had given him a couple of days before, to wear to the party. He joked about going up to the top of the Empire State Building, asked the driver where it was and we went. Some foreign tourists snapped his picture, thinking he was an outrageous American punk. When I got on the escalator, Art reached under my black velvet miniskirt and ripped out the crotch of my pantyhose. When we reached the top, the height terrified me. I crept along close to the building, while Art urged me to put my head through a hole in the fence to better see the view. "I love you very much, but I can't do that," I said.

He laughed, realized I was freaking, and we went back inside and down. "You really have—what do they call it—vertigo, don't you?"

"Yes."

"You were creeping around out there like a little mouse. It made my dick hard."

The driver took us to Goldstein's party at the Hot Rod. Music was playing, but the dance floor was empty, although the place was crowded. Art threw my heavy purse over his shoulder. We began to dance, uninhibited and looking at each other with love, as lights from cameras flashed. People were posing and watching each other.

Veronica Vera in red latex, and a shapely transvestite walked by. We said hello to Al Goldstein, who was wearing a handmade vest decorated with patches. His mother and his teenage daughter were there for the festivities, and his slender young girlfriend accompanied him everywhere.

Art recognized two men in their fifties from the Sex Institute in San Francisco, who came to present Goldstein an award. "Next year we're giving an award to you and Jim. They're going to be after you guys next, Art," one of them said. "We're entering a very conservative time. It doesn't look good for pornography right now." The case that started in 1982, when the brothers were given six-month sentences, had to be ruled on a second time by the California State Supreme Court.

"Sometimes I want to go to jail. You don't know how much I *hate* them," Art said to me. "My dad did ten years at Uncle Bud's in Texas. It was a hellhole. One of the prisoners pulled another's teeth out one by one so he could fuck his mouth. My father's friend couldn't stand the pace of working in the fields, so he asked my dad to chop his foot off so he could be with the cripples and have an easier life. To help him, my father chopped the guy's foot off. Each day when they left the fields after working all day this prisoner would say to one of the guards 'Boss, can I fuck that mule? Can I fuck that mule, Boss?' 'Yeah,' the guard would say. 'You can fuck that mule.'"

Art found a connection to buying some cocaine, and we left the party in a cab while he bought it from a former porn star he knew. A dazed-looking guy in his twenties, lover of the guy selling coke, let us into a spare modern apartment. Art was told he could go back but I had to stay in the living room. With balloons from the party bound to my wrist with silvery ribbon, I talked to the guy, who was friendly and missed California. Near us was a very still fat parakeet in a cage, but when I looked closer, it was painted wood.

"It's strange you never heard of my friend," he said. "He was really famous."

"I only started dancing a few years ago. I don't know much about movies."

As soon as Art returned, we grabbed a cab. "You won't believe this," he told me. "I go back there and he's sitting there, totally naked with this great big johnson, smoking coke. He offers me some. I fake a hit. He says to me 'I wanted to go to the party, Art. But I just couldn't. I want you to tell everyone that I look good. I do look good, don't I Art?'

"'Of course, you do. What makes you think you don't look good?' He looked on his deathbed, a skeleton with sunken eyes and a great big dick. I just wanted to get out of there. It was creepy. The first time I got to New York there were posters in every taxicab with his picture—'Mr. Ten and a Half'. Maybe he does have a ten and a half-inch dick. It looked that big."

As we sped through the dark streets, this death's head image faded. This would be the only time I was with Art when he bought drugs. I felt slightly uncomfortable, but he had made the rest of the trip so special, I hardly felt like objecting.

Neither of us remembered the address of the party correctly, and the driver dropped us off several blocks away. It was cold and we hurried along, holding hands.

"If I have to take my shoes off to use them as weapons, watch out." Art said, "People in New York are crazy."

Back at the party, we found a room filled with old convertible cars you could sit in and watch old documentary-looking porn from the late sixties. Art lit up a "j" and passed it along to the guys in the next car, but he was pretty loud and they kept their distance. We watched a couple of minutes of a brunette fucking Santa Claus. Art said, "That looks like my old girlfriend!"

We went back in the other room and danced. Balloons hovered above us, and Art began playing with them, getting me to pull them back and forth by their silvery streamers between his legs. Then he started sitting on the balloons, and I sat on them with him, to pop them. In a little while, Goldstein was presented his award, and Art gave a speech congratulating him for enduring in such a tough business.

The only porn star Art knew well who was attending the party was Jamie Gillis. He had brought a stunning, tall blonde who worked as a private investigator as his date. She told me they met doing legitimate acting. They had been to San Francisco recently and had gone to the O'Farrell, so she asked me some questions about the business.

Lisa had a romance with Jamie and starred in films with him in the late 70's. Jamie said to Art, "I couldn't believe Jim wouldn't even let Lisa talk to me."

"I know," Art said. "I can't even look at her."

When the party ended around 2:00 a.m., Art offered to drop Jamie and his girlfriend off in the Village. Our limo was back and Art berated the driver for taking off during the middle of the party, "Where were you, my man, when we came out to get the drugs you were gone! How could you do that to us!"

Art and I nestled together while Jamie's girl leaned her head languorously on his shoulder, suddenly looking remote. When they got out, we said friendly good nights.

Art hadn't reserved a room, and had the driver call the Plaza, but they were booked. A couple of other places were booked too, so he had the driver head out toward the airport and call some more hotels on the way.

As we huddled together in the darkness, Art said, "Jamie's girl came up to me at the beginning of the party and said, 'There's something I want, but Jamie says no.' I was really surprised. She wanted to fuck me—she wanted to fuck us. And Jamie was so jealous, he wouldn't let her. It would have been fun."

"She was really nice and friendly," I said, not believing Artie's story.

"I know. You guys were having fun, talking and laughing. Jamie is a very talented guy. Real imaginative. He'd like to direct. He'd be good at it, too. . . . It would have been great. I would have traded your ass in a minute. He would have fucked you good—he has a great big dick. But I know what it was—Jamie is a working stiff. He doesn't want to lose his girl to some guy with lots of money with a little faster lifestyle. He's afraid of losing her. But he's blowing it because the first time she wants something—it's No. He already has lost her—did you see how unhappy she looked?"

"She seemed upset," I added. She had looked tired. "Something was wrong."

"Yeah, of course there was. She'll come out and we'll fuck her. You'll see. She can stay in your apartment. She was so pretty."

I knew most of Art's fantasies never materialized, but I had to nurture them to make him happy. I had my doubts as to whether Jamie's girl said anything at all to Art. The only remark she made to me about him was "Is he always high?"

The lobby at the hotel was brightly lit and nearly empty. In our room, we fell into bed, quite tired and feeling very close. After we made love I fell asleep snuggled up to Art's back, my arm curled around him.

By the next afternoon, we were back in San Francisco. Art turned to me, "So does this count as a date for this week?"

"It certainly does," I said. "I'm very happy you took me with you, and I had such a good time. I'll be nice to you forever."

"You know, Simone, you and I really showed them how to have fun," he said. "Everyone else was so uptight. And you know why, don't you? Because we're really in love. We showed them how two people act when they totally love each other."

Around 4:00 p.m. Art said, "It's about time for me to get down to the theater. Right about now is when my brother will start to get worried. "You and I showed them how to party," he said. "We were smoking!"

Chapter 14:
This House is for the Little People

In a saloon in the Marina, Art and I sat with Dan O'Neill and
a lawyer friend of his. O'Neill had begun a lawsuit because one of
his cartoon characters, a rabbit named Roger, closely resembled the
drawings in the Disney movie *Roger Rabbit*. Years ago O'Neill drew
a pornographic comic book series based on Disney characters, called
"Air Pirates." Disney won a suit and had "Air Pirates" outlawed. Art
and the lawyer counseled Dan not to expect a huge settlement, to be
cooperative and agree to keep his mouth shut—otherwise the Disney
people would balk and he would get nothing. O'Neill wanted to ask
for huge sums of money and expose the story in the papers.

When O'Neill wandered off towards the bathroom, past a table
where future San Francisco Mayor Willie Brown was dining quietly
with a pretty young woman, the lawyer said, "I've been helping
support Dan for years. He's driving my car."

"I know. Every time Dan asks me for money, I never say no. I
know he needs it," Art said. "He can survive until this suit comes
through though, he's been living on the edge since the 60's." I
thought of O'Neill on a gold-panning trip we had taken with the kids,
singing "Every little breeze seems to whisper Louise," after ripping
an embarrassing tear in the seat of his pants. He had paddled upriver
with a large salad spoon, in an alligator raft that was slowly sinking.

Back at our table, O'Neill sang a funny song he'd written. I leafed
through a couple of issues of "Air Pirates" O'Neill pulled out of a

brown paper package. A caterpillar said to another bug, "Want to suck about a million tits, how about licking half a million clits?"

"I learned from the brothers that there are no limits!" O'Neill grinned like a Cheshire cat.

~

After work I bought Art a blender for a housewarming gift, packed my stuff and drove forty-five minutes to his new place in Marin County, exhausted.

Art was in the living room watching ESPN, drinking Stoly. He was pleased with the present. "Well, look around, tell me what you think of the house."

It was less than half the size of his last place. The hall bathroom had been converted from a bedroom, had print fabric wallpaper, and a matted down bright blue carpet which was separating from the sides of the blue Jacuzzi. The boy's bunk beds sat in the small den adjoining the long living room. There were lots of windows, and sliding glass doors, a couple of skylights. The place was warm, and much more convenient than the house in Moraga. I felt excited and full of hope.

"It's a good house, Art."

"You know, three girls called up tonight and said they were totally on fire and wanted to come over but I wasn't interested. Because right now you and I are on fire. You don't even know how hot you are."

Art's new bedroom wasn't big enough for the four poster bed and dresser from Moraga, his box springs and mattress lay on the floor. For the first time, we made love in that house. Sunlight flooded the bedroom in the morning.

"I went to talk to the witch, Karen, yesterday," Art said. "She's been calling and calling. Karen showed me a letter from her attorney. She says that the guy who fathered the twins is married and has three children. She probably fucked fifty guys and picked this guy because he has the most money. She says 'He really made me feel special. I

went to my lawyer, Art, and he said to go ahead and sue the guy,'
and she *actually* said this, 'If I work this right I'll never have to work
again. I can just take care of my five children. You know *he* makes
even more money than *you do!*' Then she said 'My attorney tells me I
can either sue him or you can adopt the twins and accept all financial
responsibility.' I told her 'Don't come at *me* for the money.' And the
letter was at least a couple of weeks old, she already mailed it."

"But she didn't even tell this guy she was pregnant, and now she's
nine-months along and she's suing him—that doesn't seem right.
How can she win?"

"Well, that's just it."

Art was hyper and asked me to help him clean the floors. Then I
started papering the shelves. "You should arrange things so they'll be
convenient for you, Simone."

"Come here for a minute." I followed him to the entrance hall.
Art held a gold-framed print and I helped him level it. "I'm hanging
the pictures low on the walls so the children can enjoy them," he said.
"This house is for the little people."

∾

That night Art stayed with me in the city. I felt much freer making
love in my apartment than at his house. The tiny bedroom at the back
of the Mohawk Avenue place with its sliding doors close to the pool
never felt secluded.

Once in awhile I would find jewelry, makeup, women's clothing, a
vibrator casually thrown onto the closet floor in Moraga. Rita said I
had to ignore it. I could enjoy being Art's main girlfriend, but I might
never be his only girlfriend.

∾

Art's teenage daughter Mariah and her friend went on a walk to
get ice cream, bought a dozen eggs and egged all the cars on the street.

Then they took a sad looking chocolate cake from the fridge and left it on some neighbor's doorstep. They came back laughing and told Art.

"You and Cal are just like me," he said to Mariah. "You're doing just the same things we did as kids. You're bad. You have more Mitchell in you than any of the rest!"

Having been drinking and doing a bit of coke all day, Art was very talkative and started a card game with the kids, telling them stories about his gambler father. We sat enthralled at the long table, Aaron excited, at ten, about how soon he would be good enough to play in the poker tournament.

"You have the gift, my boy. You're going to be a genius at cards," Art fondly predicted, and Aaron was bright-eyed. "When Aaron was born I put aces up in his room; that's why Aaron's called 'Ace.' One Mitchell in each generation has it—my Dad, then me, now Aaron."

We walked outside while he smoked a joint. "You know, Karen has this fantasy that we're going to get back together. She came and stood out in front of my house in Moraga and cried and cried and I finally had to tell her to go home. Oh, I have thought about it. But there's just no way. It would be good for the kids' sake. But I just hate her too much. And I've told her—*Never. No.* I'm not getting back together with *You.* I haven't said that to you, you know. But we don't have that much garbage between us. Oh, we have some. But not mega-garbage, like Karen and I do."

"But these twins. They're welcome. All children are welcome to Uncle Arturo. I'll probably like them more than all the others. You and I are going to have to raise them, you know!"

∽

Monday night I hoped Art would come over after the shows, but he didn't. I couldn't sleep. After all the energy I poured into pleasing him, that bastard was probably with some other woman. I hated the feeling I was being taken advantage of. And day by day it was becoming more awkward for me to work for someone I had a relationship with—he had too much of the power.

In the morning, I was very tired. Around three-thirty, I picked up the phone at Vince's. "Hello, Dancers' Guild," Art said quickly. "Is Vince available?"

When I looked over occasionally, Vince was smiling and I tried to catch what they were talking about.

"Oh, the blonde," Vince said, causing my eyes to look directly his way. In a few moments he said, "Don't send her the money. She can spend the money. And then you get nothing. But if you send the tickets, then she'll use them. Well, I suppose she could sell the tickets, but it's better."

When I heard the words "blonde" and "tickets," I started to burn. It sounded like Art was bringing the blonde we met in New York out here for some kind of three-way. I hated the idea. At 4:30 p.m. Vince said I could go, and I grabbed up his heavy black ledger book to finish a little work at home and walked out the door, feeling quite depressed.

"Hi," I heard and looked up. Art stood on the corner and gave me a shy smile.

Something broke inside of me. "FUCK YOU!" I yelled, so mad I began backing away from Art into the street, "JUST FUCK YOU!"

First surprise, then a mean angry look come over his face. We needed to talk. The light changed and I walked along with him towards the O'Farrell.

"Have a hard day at work?" he asked.

"Well, I guess so." I paused. "First you call up, and you don't even say hello to me. Then you start talking about that blonde from New York. She's coming out here, isn't she?"

"What? You must be on acid. First, I had just made about a hundred telephone calls, it's tiring. That I didn't say hello to you

234

means nothing. And as far as that other—you're imagining things. Do you know what that was about? Remember Isadora?"

"Yeah. I do." She was an O'Farrell dancer who had left hoping to do performance art in Europe that summer.

"Well, she's stuck in Barcelona, Spain. She went over there and there's nothing happening. So I get this call from some relative—in Minnesota—that I've never met, asking me for a loan for a ticket for her to get back here. So we're spending a thousand dollars of company money to bring her back."

"Oh." I had accused him wrongly of something when actually he had been performing a humanitarian act. What bad timing. We were in front of the door of the O'Farrell now and I was afraid. I had never yelled at him before. "I'm sorry, Art. I was upset."

"Don't worry. We're having a big party for all the politicians tonight. It's Election Day. Are you doing anything right now?"

I was still angry. "I have to drop off my car. I'm sorry. When you don't show up I figure you're probably with someone else and I just can't stand it."

I spent a quiet melancholy evening, hoping Art would show up after the party. At 2:00 a.m., my phone rang. "I thought I should call before I come over tonight. Boy, you were pretty mad, today. What was that about some blonde from New York?"

"I'm sorry. I was upset. I didn't mean to yell at you. I was overtired. I worked yesterday afternoon and then. . . ."

Art cut me off, "I think you just need some good packing. The party's winding down. The last of Jack Davis' gay friends are leaving, so I'm about through. I'll be over pretty soon."

He never showed up.

"I haven't heard anything from Art for a couple of days. And I'm too mad at him to call," I told Vince. "Last weekend I washed about five thousand dishes."

"Dishes? Oh, no! He hasn't been around the theater, either." I explained about my yelling. Vince thought Art would have gotten off on it.

When I went back to my apartment that afternoon, there was a note on my desk:

"Simone—Good Bye—A.J."

He had taken most of his clothes. Even his weed was gone. Totally shaken, I called the theater.

"Was it a goodbye note or a suicide note?" the day manager asked.

"Goodbye, I think."

"He was really on a roll last night," said Paulie, meaning Art was doing a lot of drugs.

Whether he was high or sober, Art never hit me, never threatened or ridiculed me. His chief cruelty was his total unwillingness to be considerate of my needs, or to compromise. His flirtations with other women, and his withdrawals from time to time, became less devastating once I realized they were temporary.

Chapter 15:
Dancers' Guild

NOVEMBER 14, 1988

Monday my car was blocked by a white Dodge that belonged to the soundman.

"Oh, I recognize you from the movie," he said. "You were in *Green Door*. And I just watched you in this one." He showed me the box they were using to package *The Crazy Never Die*: the Ralph Steadman painting of Hunter Thompson as a skeleton on the front, on the back a photo of Hunter firing a gun. Spatters meant to represent blood decorated the background—how tasteless.

"When they see the box, people will buy this," the soundman said. "It will really sell it!"

∼

On Sunday, I reached Art, who sounded distant, and cocky. "I'll call you next week and settle this," he said.

I told Vince what Art said on the phone and he asked, "Settle what?"

"I don't know," I answered.

"I know you're in love with him," Vince said. "You picked somebody who's really not your typical shmoo. Artie likes to capture the intensity. . . ." Trying to cheer me up, Vince whistled a few bars of "Jingle Bells."

How ironic. I laughed.

∼

237

Lynx was a slender woman with blue-black hair, who had danced on the road. Her gravely voice gave the impression that she was tough. When I asked about Art in the dressing room she told me, "Everybody says he's going out with Krystal Rose. But I don't think so. I just think she probably partied with him back in the office like I used to do, only I don't drink anymore, so I don't do that. I could ask her—but who would admit that kind of thing? I wouldn't."

"She's pretty young, isn't she?" I asked.

"She's twenty-two."

As I was leaving the dressing room, Krystal Gypsy Rose had just come in wearing tie-dye leggings and a tee shirt, beaded earrings. She was an average looking girl, 5' 3", with brown hair. I wondered if she was waiting for Art and how opened up emotionally she was to him. When she started working at the theater a couple of months before, I had complimented her on her dancing. She said she had worked in New Orleans and followed the Grateful Dead, dancing for tips in bars in towns where they were playing.

Late in the afternoon, Krystal Rose came into Vince's wearing an ankle-length black rabbit coat. Rocky and Vince gave her one of those looks I have seen so many times. On the most basic level, it means—look at this new hot piece of flesh. Or it can mean—I've heard all about what it's like to fuck you, honey.

Now Krystal had the arrogance I saw in Missy, when she was basking in Art's seductive attention. She would be glowing with excitement—on stage and off—charged with the confidence and vitality Art inspired when he turned on to a woman.

~

As I slipped on a black trench coat for my espionage show, Justine was putting on her police officer's costume for stage and cueing up the "Miami Vice" theme song. "Hey, take a look at this," she said. Posted on the O'Farrell bulletin board was a sign-up sheet for a rock n' roll party with Jefferson Starship:

"Girls who are planning to go who need transportation must be at the theater in costume and ready to perform/entertain at 10:00 p.m. Pay will be pass-the-hat. No boyfriends. Any questions—speak to Artie personally."

Ten girls signed up, Krystal Rose—second on the list. "He does provide girls for things like this," said Justine. "The only thing the girls that went last time got were free tickets. They were all fucking like bunnies backstage. Just because they want to fuck the rock stars."

∽

"Karen had her twins last night and they each weigh seven pounds," Vince said. "Art told me Karen's trying to work both ends of the deal, she's trying to get money from him and money from the father. Art dislocated his shoulder golfing and is taking Demerol."

I was alone in Vince's office when Rob, who had worked for Art and Jim for many years on their films and had been the senior DJ at the time I was hired, called, "I wanted to let Vince know my wife just had a baby boy. She was on the same floor of the hospital as Karen. I didn't go over to see Karen, though, because then you're involved."

I explained about the twins. "I knew it was something weird," Rob said. "They can never do it normal. Either there's no father or no money or something."

Rob had left the O'Farrell two years earlier to work in film and video, around the time he married a woman outside the sex business. "I'm glad you've been able to get out," I told him. "I haven't said anything to Vince, but I'm going to have to, too. You're really talented, and I think anybody that is has to get out."

"Getting ahead at Mitchell Brothers' doesn't happen because you're talented, it happens if you're there to roll one up. It's always been insular and it always will be. They make people come to them.

239

You and I have really paid our dues there, Simone. You can imagine the price Vince and Mez and Jeff have to pay; they would never make the kind of money they're making anywhere else."

Like the strippers with twenties tucked into their stockings, the management was locked into the O'Farrell cash flow, too.

The next day I stayed late at Vince's, trying to get six girls with bikinis for Bill Graham's Christmas party the next night. "Try to get some foxettes!" Vince had urged. Only one big blonde agreed to go, but she didn't own a bikini.

That evening I drove Rita to the Condor at Broadway and Columbus in North Beach, with its towering blonde likeness of Carol Doda flashing light bulb nipples, and "Rita Ricardo—XXX Film Star" signs advertising their new star. I hung out with her as she changed sequined gowns and feather boas in her dressing room, preparing to make her grand entrance on the Condor's notorious piano.

For years, Carol Doda descended to the Condor's stage on a piano with a hydraulic lift. Then, in November 1983, a petite blonde O'Farrell dancer got very drunk and high with the Condor's assistant manager, in the early hours of the morning when the club was closed. While they were having sex on the piano, it rose, pinning her and her heavy-set partner against the ceiling. He had a heart attack and died, lying on top of her. Hours later, someone heard her screams, and she was freed. The police were never able to uncover how the up-switch was thrown. The Condor's white baby grand trimmed in gold became known as the "killer piano."

Rita and I stayed upstairs talking between shows in the musty old building until closing time. The Condor always was dead. Burlesque houses each have their own atmosphere. Late at night, when they are almost empty, leftover triumphs and tragedies hang in the air like still vivid dreams.

⌁

Vince told me last night Art got into an argument with Lady T., said she was trying to spiderweb Terry, the new Filipino girl.

"Spiderweb? You mean come on to her?"

"Well, yeah, date her, whatever. Art said she got all pushed out of shape and clawed his back. He said she has no sense of humor, which is true. So the first time he called he wanted her fired and he's going to get on the phone and make sure she doesn't work anywhere in San Francisco. Lady T. called me and asked 'So, am I fired?' and I said yes. 'Why?' Well, because they own the theater."

"Then Art called back a little while ago and now he wants to be the nice guy and give her a thirty or sixty day suspension and he says Krystal Rose wants to kill her. He said 'I'm just tired of being beat up by all these dykes.' Lady T.'s supposed to come in this afternoon but you can take her off her shifts."

When Lady T., an intelligent, regally thin brunette, came in, I listened to her version. It sounded like Art had gotten into a terrible drunken funk and frightened her.

Vince was apologetic. "What do you want to do?" he asked.

"I want to work," she said. Vince explained about her being suspended. He said softly that especially when Art had been drinking a lot he did things that Jim, his brother, worried a lot about. "We appreciate your being cool about this," he added.

Lady T. walked out of the office so fast I couldn't see her expression, but her story was believable.

"Did you hear that?" Vince asked.

"Part of it. It sounded like a totally different version of the story," I said. "Maybe it reminded Art of the thing with Danielle."

"Oh, no. With Danielle, he knew he'd been a bad boy. There were several objects being picked up and used as weapons, and people flying off the walls, and the audience was involved. After that he didn't come around for a week."

"I know. He came over after it happened."

"I need to win the lotto," Vince said. "If I do I'll probably live to eighty-five or ninety, but at this rate I'll probably only live to sixty-five, fifteen years more! So Art's been calling in today from wherever he's holed up at—North Bay, South Bay, East Bay, wherever. After twenty years I know enough not to ask 'Where are you?' I asked the new DJ if he had a happy New Year and he said, 'Well, everything's been as usual, a one-man party.' Art's been doing a lot of heavy drinking lately," Vince added, "I don't know what he's into, it isn't the new girlfriend."

At the root of his latest skirmishes at work, beneath the drugs, Art was angry. In addition to his tensions with Jim, and Karen's pressures for more money—Karen's having another man's twins was insulting to Art's macho ego. Fate dealt him a winning hand so early in life, he had hoped to fulfill all of his dreams, even if they were contradictory.

The dancers told me Art spent New Years' Eve hanging out at the theater alone and very loaded on acid. He made one trip on stage with a garbage can over his head. After the can fell off, he threw it around on stage while customers left the first row, afraid of being hit by it. Later he got on stage again and sang. In the dancers' bathroom he hung by his heels from a pipe and fell off, landing on his back. Then he scrawled some nasty graffiti over the dressing room walls. Quietly, it was painted over the next day. The worst moment was when he had his hands around a dancer's throat, choking her. Justine pulled him off, saying, Artie, remember lawsuits—you're setting yourself up for one! "He was just too high," she said. "I'm used to that."

In the shadow of Art's fights with Danielle and Lady T., the frenzied way he rang in the New Year was terrifying. It seemed like something really bad could happen. I felt angry towards his new drug partner. I had never seen him in such a crazed state. And since he had backed away from our relationship and was only seeing me occasionally, I felt powerless.

When this cycle of bingeing ended, I knew he would come back to me—but how long would I have to wait? It had been a rough couple of months already. Maybe I would have an affair, I thought. Maybe that would help me get through this horrible time.

~

In the lobby lay a stack of new posters drawn by underground cartoonist Spain. A giant naked figure of Cicciolina waded calf-deep in the bay, her ass inches above the Golden Gate Bridge, joining California and the Continent. A banner announced her as "Minister, Chamber of Deputies, Italian Parliament," above the dates for her American debut performance at Mitchell Brothers', and the slogan "She's Got Diplomatic Immunity." A porn star and a politician, she had to be tough. Cicciolina would later marry and have a child with pop artist Jeffrey Koons, and pose for a series of paintings by him.

Some theater in New York had offered her big bucks—sixty-five-thousand dollars for two weeks—a year and a half ago and couldn't get her in, Vince heard. The immigration lawyer they hired hadn't been able to do anything.

Vince was trying to humor and calm one of the dancers on the phone, "A lot of people at the theater have a lot of affection for him, and feel totally at a loss as to what to do. . . . There has been a whole upsurge of people—managers, dancers, and friends—complaining about Artie's behavior, and talking to Jim about getting some help for him."

Even though that week there was a flurry of talk about Art's need to dry out, no one ever took any positive action. The emphasis was always to protect the O'Farrell, maintain its image as a party house, and deny anything could be wrong.

Like others at the theater, I thought Art was just a heavy drinker and was choosing to binge. Entertaining the endless stream of visitors to the O'Farrell was Art's job. He took his outrageous, hard-partying public image very seriously, and considered it his vital contribution to the place.

"It's twenty years being PR for the business," said Vince. "I don't think he's ever stopped doing drugs, what with the stuff people bring in, and then when he gets into the cocaine!"

~

Wednesday I did Kopenhagen shows with a woman who had just moved here from New York. She was street-smart, and friendly. Her boyfriend was a construction worker who just had a bad accident, falling, landing on a beam. Until he recovered, she was supporting him. A few days earlier, Art had called her because a couple of well-known entertainers had been in, and one of them needed a blowjob. "Vince, Art and Jim were all back there in the poolroom with the guy," she said. "I told Jim, 'I've known Lisa for ten years, I did movies with her in New York.' He got really mad, he said 'So have I!' I made all of them leave, except for the guy. I got money from him, and tickets to their show, but I don't want to go see it. When it was over, Jim was so rude to me. He said, 'Get out of my office!'"

~

The next week Vince said, "Jim had a talk with Artie and said he took it really well." That sounded like a distortion. I knew Art too well to believe it.

Even when Art was away, I thought about him. He had the most profound understanding of sex. Even when I thought about baby-sitting, cooking, rushing to please him, the madness, how inconsiderate he was, none of it mattered. It was beyond my power to choose not to love him, by then. It was that strong.

~

Vince said they needed a key to the city to present to Cicciolina and asked me to work on it. They thought she might arrive Sunday. I checked out the official key to the city, painted a phoenix rising from flames. On the three-foot gold key I printed, "O'Farrell Theater—1989; Cicciolina—Put the 'X' in Sex."

"It's beautiful," Vince said Friday. "But Cicciolina's not coming, at least not yet. She went into the embassy in Rome with a tape recorder concealed under her teddy bear's panties and was caught. Outside she pulled up her top, and said, 'Is the United States Government afraid of Cicciolina's breasts?' The Italian police arrested her. Now she needs another lawyer!"

Chapter 16:
On Fire

JANUARY, 1989

Rita and Charles were shooting a film on the weekend, so Saturday I took some costumes to the location, a lovely Victorian mansion filled with antiques. Jamie Gillis was starring in the movie. I hadn't seen him since the party in New York. After appearing in three thousand films, Jamie was above the general chit-chat on the set and seemed to view the whole porn scene with a wry sense of humor. With his dark handsome features, he could have passed for a latter-day Lord Byron or Elliott Gould in his prime. Jamie was so tempting I couldn't help thinking about taking some very sweet revenge. Remembering the party, he asked, "Do you hang out with Art a lot or was that something unusual?"

"I have for years, but we have an off and on thing, and right now it's mostly off."

Sunday around 1:00 p.m. my phone rang.

"Did you hear about the fire?" Vince asked.

"What fire?"

"There was a bad fire in our building yesterday afternoon. I went down there this morning with Rocky to look around and none of the records or anything much was destroyed, but the room where your desk is, is in pretty bad shape. I talked to Jim and he said we can move into the O'Farrell temporarily if we have to."

Christ. The fire started around the time I was blowing Jamie.

In the morning, I couldn't bring myself to go in until the last possible moment. The place reeked of smoke. They gave Vince the office space next door—so we still had the long narrow "war room" and an outer reception room. The room that had been mine was a shambles—bits of waterlogged paper and glass lay on the soggy rug. Supposedly, someone threw a burning cigarette in a bag down the garbage shoot, right in back of the Dancers' Guild office. The fire spread up, burning out ten apartments on the fifth floor.

I pinned up our decorations: three posters for the Exotic Erotic Ball; an article on Marilyn Chambers. Our still-living Christmas tree stood in the war room next to the window, wearing a baseball cap on its top to scare off the street hustlers and drug dealers that passed by. Vince started a coffee pot system under the bathroom tap to fill the toilet tank. All his records, and the dancers' schedules, were miraculously untouched by the fire.

That night my Ultra Room partner told me Art was upstairs, so I put on my black leather costume and went down near the room to wait, and avoid him. I didn't want Art to try to have sex with me in the O'Farrell instead of spending the entire night at my place. Forty-five minutes later, when I was feeling like I had outfoxed him, Kenny found me, "Art wants you in the office."

"Hi, beautiful," Art said, and flashed me a smile.

"Did you like the key?" I asked, knowing he had seen it that afternoon. Vince told me they loved it.

"Yes. It's great. You're very talented. Do you want me to come over tonight?"

"Of course I do."

"I've thought about it, and I like you better than I like my new young girlfriend. I'm going to tell her I'm leaving her and going back to you. Do you love me? Are you sure?"

"Of course, I love you."

"We'll see."

When I climbed into bed with him at my place he said, "You think you don't need me but when your baby's here everything's different, isn't it?"

Art had been unable to eat for days, since he went to the dentist and had his teeth ground down. "I didn't know what I was getting into, I thought you could go in and two hours later walk away with new teeth. The pain's been unbelievable. He gave me some heavy painkillers—they must be morphine but they don't say that. They say 'May be addictive'—I've broken off five temporaries since then. I told the Chinese dentist, 'If I get my teeth Monday, you get a blowjob by Marilyn Chambers. By Wednesday, you get a blowjob by Nina Hartley. But if it's Friday you won't be able to call off the contract I'll have out on you!' When he asked me to pick out the color of my teeth I waved away the 'more natural' colors and told him to give me the whitest white, like Rock Hudson before AIDS. If I'm paying for these, I want them whiter than the whitest color you see on cars!"

We watched an old 1930's gangster movie on TV with Alan Ladd and a young Jack Webb. We laughed as several men were shot and all kept their hats on. Art had shot after shot of Cuervo, and after that was gone Old Grand-Dad, along with some beers. For the first time in three months he was laughing and having a good time with me. "You never, ever gave up on me, did you?"

"No." I put my arms around him.

"I like it when you kiss me," he said." Nobody likes me. Nobody has ever been nice to me. My father. My mother, a little bit. She's trying to make up for it now, but it's too late."

"Everyone sure likes you a lot better now that I dropped you like a rock. And when they saw the key, they kept saying, 'Oh, she is so talented.' They are all pulling for you, Simone. Vince loves you. You're doing a fantastic job. I, for one, am glad to have you over there."

"Sure you are," I thought. "How convenient to still have me under your thumb."

"From now on I'm calling myself 'Performance Art,' not Party Artie! Performance Art really suits me. It's a lot hotter.

"We've sold some of the Hunter videos through Publishers' Clearinghouse, they're wild about it! It's ninety percent my brother's movie; I helped out, but it's mostly his. *No one* likes it."

The Crazy Never Die was a big disappointment. Some scenes were shot at the O'Farrell and around San Francisco, others were shot on the road or in college auditoriums where Hunter spoke to large crowds. Jim and Art filmed this themselves with a skeleton crew; almost everyone involved was drunk or high. By the production's end, there was almost no recorded sound. New sound that would sync at least somewhat with the action was dubbed in later, but it had been impossible to recapture Hunter's speeches and the questions and reactions of everyone else in the film.

"Hunter phoned up and said he had shown the tape to a couple of his friends, and they told Hunter the tape would ruin his career. They're from Hollywood. They're all on cocaine. What do they know?" Art said. "I haven't done any of that shit for three months!"

What has he been doing? I wondered.

He stuck his fingers deep into me. "This is your cervix. That's where babies come from. And this is your g-spot." He hit it exactly, my eyes opened wide. "And then there's these two glands." He turned his fingers and touched them, it was exquisite. "Scary, isn't it, how I can know more than you do about your own pussy?"

He was quite sick from the combination of booze and painkillers, but insisted I set the alarm for 6:45 a.m. for a golf match. On the way to the theater, he was quiet and not feeling well. "Art, you really should be eating. If you want, I'll fix you dinner tonight."

"I don't know what'll be happening by tonight. I might be in the hospital by then. Thanks for everything," he said, and gave me a kiss.

~

Lynx came to Vince's complaining that Sharon Mitchell, our porn star for the week, didn't want to do shows with her. She just wanted Lynx to hand her her towel after she stepped out of the shower show, and put her shoes on her feet. Demeaning for anyone, but funny it would happen to somebody with Lynx's ego.

"The first good head job and you'll own her," Vince smiled at Lynx. The brothers always thought lesbian shows were an outrageous turn-on, and preferred them.

Jim came in and talked to Vince at length about trying to get a new show together for the Cine Stage. They would turn it into a dance floor featuring dirty dancers to dance with the customers for tips, and an all-girl naked band to play. They would try to secure an electric guitarist who danced at the theater, to get it together. "Maybe the musicians could taxi-dance in-between the sets for tips, so they won't have to be paid!" said Jim. When I said it would be important to get people who could actually play, they spun off into planning to have good-looking girls with big tits and pussies out who could lip synch. "Who cares if they actually can play? We'll do a video, make a record. We'll mix it in the studio," said Jim. "It'll be our fist-fucking forty-five!"

"We're rolling now," Jim turned to me and said. "It all started with the key. Put the 'X' back in sex!"

"Oh, you liked it," I said. "Good."

~

Monday evening Jamie called me. He was in town, staying at a hotel, going to the races.

"I'm really attracted to you," I told him.

"That's good," he said. "That makes it easy."

Why was I drawn to Jamie? Of course I needed some diversion and a bit of revenge, but he had a serene mystique that was quite a contrast to Art. And Jamie didn't abuse alcohol or use drugs. People who have been successful in porn can possess an intelligent, irreverent sense of humor, a heightened sensuality, and an enviable capacity for survival. Having worked in the sex industry for seven years, I knew I wouldn't have much in common with anyone who wasn't a part of it. Ninety-nine percent of men outside the sex business cannot accept that their girlfriend has worked as a stripper or porn actress. Nothing is more valuable than understanding and acceptance. I could hardly date someone "safe" and conservative after being involved with Artie.

When I got to Vince's office, he was on the phone. Rocky sat across from him. "Last night that little gay guy picked up some guy in a bar and brought him back here. The guy killed him, then he set the bed on fire, to cover up the evidence," Rocky said. "Somebody saw smoke coming out from his door and called the fire department. I was coming up the street and saw the fire trucks, then about twelve cop cars were out in front of the building. I didn't even try to come in here to sleep—who could sleep with all that going on!"

Vince put the receiver down, looking serious. "The building manager is really upset. First the fire, and he was her right hand man, he was helping out a lot," he said. "He was like a son to her. It's a good lesson. Don't pick up anyone in a gay bar."

"Do they have any idea who did it?" I asked.

"Well, they probably got a description of the guy when he was in the bar. They'll probably get him. Of course, he could be a serial killer. There have been a few in this area, just not for awhile. He did all of her schlepping. He was a vital part of the operation. She's really sick about it. Get some long stem roses, something nice, for her,"

Vince said, handing me the money. "They left his body out in the hall for hours. *Murder One*."

∼

Jamie called and invited me to a party. "What should I wear?" I asked him.

"Anything that's comfortable. If you want to wear your leather skirt, you can. Janet said if I want to wear some sort of costume I could, but I'm such a legend, whatever I wear, everyone will be wearing to the next party, anyway!"

"You know, maybe you should mention this to Art," Jamie suggested. "It might help, you know. He might think, well, if another world-class stud is seeing you. . . ."

"I don't think I should," I said. "I don't know what might happen."

I didn't want to risk telling Art. After all his suspicions about Hunter, I knew Art couldn't handle jealousy. Finding out I was seeing a major porn star would be especially threatening to him.

In a few months, Jamie would come up with an original concept and shoot some videos called *On the Prowl*. Jamie, a porn actress, and a cameraman would cruise the streets in a limo and pick up a guy off the street to film having sex with the actress in the limo's back seat. Although it was hard to film in such a tight space, and the legalities of using such impromptu talent were questionable, it was great cinema verite. *On the Prowl* was later adapted in a wonderful "On the Lookout" scene with Burt Reynolds as the porn director and Heather Graham as the porn star "Roller Girl" in the mainstream movie *Boogie Nights*.

∼

"What I'm about to tell you has to be top secret," Vince said. "In twenty minutes or so a sergeant from the robbery detail will be here to talk to me. The cops got a tip that I'll be robbed today on my way to the bank. They're coming in to fit me with a bulletproof vest."

"Oh, Jeez," I said, and touched his shoulder.

"That's for luck," said Rocky.

"Don't tell anyone about this. Not Ron, not anyone. It has to remain top secret. They're going to cover us today and if nothing happens today, next Monday, too. When the girls come in try to shoo them away. If they come in, that's all right, but don't let them hang out with any bullshit. No one can know about this."

Soon two cops, one heavy-set and one lean, arrived and had Vince put on the vest. "This will stop anything," one of them said. "Yeah, anything but a .36," said the other.

"It'll even stop knives."

"It'll protect your upper body, but what about your arms and your face?" Vince asked. He and Rocky were going together. They would take Rocky's truck, not Vince's Mercedes. Vince had been robbed a year earlier.

The vest looked bulky and odd under his sweater and he was about to put on a raincoat, too. He had sprayed on some K-L Homme. "So, you want to have sex while I still have this on?" Vince said as they were getting ready to leave.

"Yes," I tried to joke, concerned about him. "Good luck."

"Luck, we'll need more than luck!" Rocky answered.

While my boss took a tough walk south on Polk Street tailed by undercover cops, I held the fort at Dancers' Guild, feeling a bit vulnerable. In the last three months my world had become much more dangerous—with my lover headlong into drugs and booze, rampaging through his theater; the fire; the S/M murder; and now this!

Around 1:00 p.m., Vince and Rocky came back nervously jubilant and went in the back room. "Simone, answer the phones. We need to debrief." The former male employee they knew was involved had been standing on the corner but was scared off. In a few minutes they emerged, Vince pinched me, said they would be gone for half an hour. When his wife called, I explained.

"Oh," she said, relieved. "He came back!"

~

Art brought some coke to my apartment, was doing some lines. Rarely had he done cocaine in front of me. He seemed to be much more in a fog than he had a couple of weeks earlier.

"Nick, Rocky and I were doing some heavy drinking tonight," he said. "Nick picked Rocky up, yelled Geronimo and threw him back over his shoulders. Rocky landed on his head, he might have a concussion—it sort of shortened his neck. I was passed out on the floor with towels over my face trying to sober up. Afterwards we tried to kick Nick out, but he was so high he didn't want to leave."

"I'm so glad we're back together again," he said. "Hinckle is getting married in New York. To some uptight, filthy rich, bluenose society broad named Susan Cheever. She hates *us*."

In the middle of the night, we were both awake. "I'll always love you," he said, "even after all the other ones are gone."

~

In May, the New Century Theater opened up on Larkin Street, just a block away from the O'Farrell. Since it offered the same types of shows, and was freshly decorated and glitzy, the Mitchells were quite worried about competition. Jim decided to save money by canceling the stars. At the end of June, he scheduled a "Spirit of the O'Farrell" meeting for the dancers.

"The Strip-Rock band is off. Every woman musician we interviewed on the phone refused to consider playing nude," Vince said, "and there's a rumor our guitarist is doing heroin. Jim is *very* disappointed." Because Jim had said he wanted to talk to me personally, Vince suggested I go to the meeting, to find out what he wanted.

At the previous "Spirit of the O'Farrell" meeting, Jim had announced to a full audience of dancers, "Ninety-eight percent of you are sluts and whores." It was a peculiar judgment call for someone responsible for setting up the financial dynamics of the O'Farrell, where the dancers earned tips only and were now paying stage fees to work. Some soliciting of tips was necessary, since more than twenty women were dancing each shift, and we were competing with the brand new Century and their dancers nearby.

Twelve dancers sat around the poolroom as Jim addressed us. "The word on the street is twenty dollars in the Kopenhagen and you can feel pussy," Jim began in irritation. "We need a lot more hard core shows! I want—we need you to use strap-on dildos, you need to be more inventive. Some of you are pushing forty."

I looked around. Jim could only have been referring to a couple of us.

"Now it's the 80's, it's not enough for you to be just yourselves!"

It was a typical O'Farrell employee meeting. One ambitious new dancer said some enthusiastic stuff that sounded phony. All the other women sat safely quiet.

"Simone used to have the hottest show around here," Jim startled me. "She had this gorilla costume that she'd put on with a big strap-on hanging off of it—and if she jumped on you, you were really fucked! I want to bring that back. I want to make you House Gorilla!"

Such sensitivity. "No, no, that's all over with," I said. "No, I'm not doing that. I'll explain to you later personally, why."

Jim must have singled me out as somebody who would be supportive, and all the other dancers would think, we have got to get into the spirit, too!

When the meeting was over, I went up to Jim. He loosely put his arms around me and I put my arms around him. "You know," I said, "that show was very personal to me, and Art's been really out there lately. The last thing I need to do right now is to be running around in that gorilla costume. Because too much has happened in connection with it."

"There are a lot of bad memories? You know it is your fault," Jim said, but I was concentrating on the gorilla issue.

"I haven't done the New York show in a year, because I don't make any money in it."

"Well, we can fix it so you do make some money in it," Jim said.

By this point, I was completely burned-out on sitting in the audience, and preferred doing the Ultra Room or Kopenhagen shows. I had just done the gorilla show for special occasions. Wearing that hot gorilla mask for a fifteen-minute show always ruined my hairstyle for the rest of the evening, and to make good tips you had to look your best. The management never understood the dynamics of earning money from the dancers' perspective.

"If you have any trouble with Art," Jim urged, "come to me and I'll help you."

To placate him momentarily I said, "I'll bring the suit in—and you can have it."

"I want to see you in it," Jim persisted. "I want to make you in charge of it!"

None of the other dancers would have wanted to do that show.

I felt shocked, and embarrassed, and after I was home, I got angry. It was a put-down to have Jim make this rude employer/employee demand when I had been involved with his brother for years, even if Art and I weren't tight at the moment. Since he had been so unsympathetic, I hardly felt like going to him for help with Art. It felt good standing up to Jim. How could he think anyone would want to be "House Gorilla?"

In a few days, one of the dancers called me, crying, at Vince's, "Last night I was in the shower show. Just before we were supposed to go on, Jim insisted that all four of us wear strap-on dildos. Then he made each of us pay $35.00 for the strap-ons they were selling in the showcase. We were all too afraid of being fired to say no. When the curtain went up and the customers saw us, they all turned around and walked out. It was so humiliating! After that we told Jim we wouldn't do the show like that anymore."

I mentioned this to Art the next time I saw him.

"I don't know what Lisa is doing to him," Art said. "Whether she's been wearing some kind of dildo on her head, or what. He's got this thing about dildos right now, he's always talking about them."

By the middle of the summer, Krystal looked dowdy and depressed. She was strung-out on crystal methadrine, she told Vince, but she had been able to quit. Vince was booking her in the shower show. Through the wet mist, she seemed hostile and bored, fifteen pounds heavier since the previous fall.

In the morning, I went into Vince's office to work on the September dancers' schedule. "Did you hear about Artie's accident?" Vince asked. "He was playing golf over in the East Bay and got hit with a golf club, and all of a sudden his elbow blew up the size of a tennis ball! He went to an emergency room over there, they drained it and found a blood clot."

"Oh, God. I never heard of anything like that," I said. "It doesn't sound good."

"It's not. . . . It's still bothering him a lot, too."

Vince left to meet with Art and Jim; around 2:00 p.m. he came back to the office. "They went over a list of the girls that they want to not have work at the theater and Art was adamant about you," he said. "I just want to warn you."

I was shocked.

"You're taking September off, anyway," Vince added. "See what happens." When I left, he gave me a thumb's-up.

I had a feeling something was up, since the week before Art and Jim told Vince they wanted to go over the schedule of dancers personally. I was uptight, but resigned, who knew what they would be thinking by Monday, they were so changeable. Since the previous fall, it had become more difficult for me to work at Art's theater and maintain a relationship with him. I had been looking forward to taking a break, and it was time to do something else. I was almost relieved, but I didn't quite believe it.

Many dancers burn out—as in any other career. As you get older, the audience contact and the competitive nature of the business get harder.

~

"Well, it's official," Vince told me Monday.

He and I had to finish off the September schedule fast, eliminating the twenty-two names, about twenty-percent of the total number of dancers.

I took a close look at the list. Dancers they were getting rid of included women who looked over thirty, had danced at Mitchell Brothers' longer than five years, were doing too many drugs too flagrantly, or were outspoken. Danielle and Lady T., who both had personal run-ins with Art, were on it, too.

"Call everyone on the list," Vince told me. "Tell them they're fired." Saying I was being fired, too, made it easier. What a grim assignment I had; some people were totally shaken, and insulted. A dancer who had been at the O'Farrell for six years came in crying and left Vince a note, "I can't think of what I've done except keep one of the best looking bods in the theater."

A thin, moody dancer from Eastern Europe was totally distraught, thinking it was because one of the DJs had come on to her and she never responded, "People say I'm pretty," she murmured sadly. "I don't know."

"If I were your age, I'd just go over to the Century and dance there," I told her.

One girl came in wearing a tube top, gold glitter smeared over her shoulders, carrying a ghetto blaster and a stuffed animal, looking stoned out of her mind. Vince was uncandid but polite, "The person that has the most problem with you is Paulie. You need to talk to Paulie."

"In your case it's got to be personal," I told Lady T. When she talked to Jim he said, "You don't have the typical voluptuous body of a stripper."

That evening, Rita and Charles took me out to dinner in North Beach. "You should have fired everyone," Charles joked. "Then what you should do is call a theatrical agency and put in a request for eleven-year-old girls to show up at the O'Farrell to audition for a movie on the life of Marilyn Chambers—like the musical based on the life of Gypsy Rose Lee. They would all come with their mothers. That would really confuse them!"

Everyone on the list could work until the last day of August. I didn't try to talk to Art, or to Jim. Not saying anything was stronger than whining to them. It was an odd, frozen time—the final few shifts I danced at the O'Farrell, knowing they were my last.

Chapter 17:
At Home in Corte Madera

AUGUST 27, 1989

At noon on Sunday, I came home and found a message on my machine in the voice that melted me every time I heard it:

"Simone, you know I love you. I'm taking you to Guatemala, give me a call."

Art, sounding soulful and passionate and real. Hearing what I had longed to hear, not just the words, but the tangible feeling behind them, went straight to my heart.

In Corte Madera, Art gave me a wide warm smile and put his arms around me. "I love you," he said. "Welcome back."

"Well, I guess you're not going to be dancing any more," he said. "Never let it be said that you haven't had an illustrious career. Now I need you with me."

I laughed and hugged him.

His elbow looked swollen and red, he explained about the accident.

How blissfully uncanny it was to be back there. When he made love to me, it was different in tone from the past months, serious and sweet and full of joy.

～

The next afternoon I drove in to the theater to do my final Ultra Room. Dressed in short red velvet as the Queen of Hearts, I cued up "White Rabbit," and other Ultraland tunes. After my first show I called Vince, "Art and I are getting back together. I know how

260

changeable he is. But this morning he was talking about wanting to go to Nevada City. I'd really like to go with him."

"My, how the tide changes."

"Yeah, it's just hard to tell which way it's running."

After my last show, I drove home. To my delight, Art's van was there. O'Neill's aged VW was parked next to it.

In my living room Aaron and Cal were gleefully trying out the guillotine with a silvery foam rubber blade I'd had built for my French Revolution show; Hulk Hogan was winning on TV. When I was leaving to pick up dinner, Art and O'Neill stood on my porch high above the street smoking a joint. Art yelled out, "Get fucked good lately? . . . I couldn't tell, by that smile on your face!"

We shared the meal while the boys cheered their favorites, Art chuckled with glee. He put his arms around me. "You're so brilliant and intelligent that I can't let you think you can be sure of me," he said. "It keeps us happier that way."

In the morning, we went deep-sea fishing. Cal caught a thirty-pound salmon, and was so proud. "I'm going to call him Fish Mitchell!' Art said. "Aaron was in the poker tournament in August and did great! They're all fucking gamblers!"

～

At 10:00 a.m., Art's mother phoned. He had forgotten to let her know we weren't leaving for Nevada City yet, so she was cooking sausage and eggs and was looking out the window at 9:00, and where were we?

All of a sudden, Art decided he couldn't disappoint his mother. He was hungover, irritated. We stopped at the outdoor fast-food hut of the monolithic Nut Tree restaurant, he wanted French fries for the boys and they didn't have any. "No French fries!" he started screaming at the top of his lungs, shocking the audience of mild-mannered customers. I got sodas, ice tea, and we were gone.

A blanket of clothes, toys, and baseball cards covered the back of the van where the boys rode, with the fishing poles and bags of snacks. Every so often, Art would get mad at them for fighting and making so much noise. "You want to go?" he would glower in a Dust Bowl drawl, "I'm going to pull over to the side of the road and whip your ass!" not meaning it. Hilarious, but tiring.

Finally we got to Sacramento and found his mother's tidy blue and white house. Soon his mother, Georgia Mae, arrived, looking irked. Does she think I'm a good example for Art's kids? I wondered. Jasmine was with her, probably surprised to see me, looking a little more adult and independent at nine, and more mischievous.

"The thing *I* get irritated with is she's *not* thirteen. There were certain things I just couldn't buy, so we got some jeans, and these have to be considered stylish," said Georgia Mae, holding up a little pair of black shoes with buckles.

Art hadn't brought Georgia Mae's birthday gift. "I'm sorry, I forgot to bring your present. I have something very special for you," he said.

"You're going to have to get it together," she said. "Hello, Simone, how are you?" she added, not too friendly.

In a few minutes, we got back in the van with the kids and roared off to the gold rush town Nevada City. Art had run out of marijuana, and was touchy. At the hotel, they gave us two adjacent two-story chalets. When I let the kids in their chalet, immediately they started sliding down the banister with the greatest of ease, gleefully jumping off onto the bed, with their dad's fearlessness and physical joy. When Art appeared they simmered down, then Dan O'Neill arrived.

At the end of a deserted gravel road where mosquitoes buzzed in the heat, we placed a few tin cans on the hillside, formed a firing line, and O'Neill unpacked a rifle and a handgun. The kids and I had never shot before, but Art was a good marksman, and a patient, encouraging teacher, stressing how important safety is. He was slender and elegant, with the most masculine sexual presence I will ever lay eyes on. Jasmine held the rifle a little too close to her mouth, unfortunately it recoiled and hit her. She wasn't hurt, but when we tried to comfort her, she crawled inside the van and cried and cried.

On the way back, we picked up sodas, tequila and limes. In the adult chalet, we settled at the kitchen table. Art began showing off to O'Neill that he was in charge of our renewed relationship, meaner since he started on the Cuervo and we hadn't eaten yet. Since this time Art was serious, I felt braver, and there were a lot of things I had needed to say for months. Somehow, O'Neill's presence made for a safe reconciliation exchange.

"You're only as good as your last five minutes!" Art said to me.

"You're a real mean son of a bitch, aren't you? One minute you want me, and one minute you don't, then you fire me. No wonder I'm tense, it's been a difficult time these last months, Art."

"Once in a while I have to grab a young one 'cause that really makes her hot."

"That's totally untrue. And what he does, is completely ignore me at the theater and flirt with all the other dancers and then show up at my house!"

"And I'd fuck her hard, too."

O'Neill told a joke, I laughed. "And she even gets the jokes," O'Neill muttered.

"Yeah, it must have been boring with nobody getting the jokes, wasn't it?" I said.

He acted slightly offended, "You fucked up, didn't you. I punished you for quite awhile. . . . Now I think of it as my identity crises. But from now on there'll be no more young girlfriends, no more rock concerts." He smiled affectionately, "I figure with Simone I can just drift."

The next evening Cal wore one of his dad's t-shirts printed with a box of Ivory Snow, autographed "Fuck me hard, XXXOOO, Marilyn Chambers," to dinner, oblivious of the meaning. "Who are these people?" joked O'Neill. Characteristically, Art paid the check; O'Neill performed a trick, transforming a linen napkin miraculously into a rat, put pepper on it, made the waiter jump, and all of us laugh.

O'Neill's house had a grand flavor of intellectual decay. Fat upholstered couches sat in the back yard with leaves all over them, ripe for a surrealistic painting. Cartoons of true talent and hilarious dementia hung in his living room in the dust. So Jasmine could take a shower, he handed me a screwdriver to turn on the hot water. O'Neill had fathered many children, but hadn't made any real money since his cartoons were popular years ago. "All the ex-wives couldn't believe it when the money only lasted ten months," he said with lilting artistic detachment. "It was great while it lasted, and then it was gone forever!"

We drove back to Marin Sunday night, even though Art had sprained his ankle stepping off one of Nevada City's high sidewalks. When we woke up, Karen was on the phone, she hadn't seen the kids all week and wanted them to come home right away. At the moment, she had a boyfriend and had begun speaking to me instead of screaming. Art had put the twins on his medical insurance.

Like his dad, Aaron had been growing his blond hair long for months, and was very proud of it. Then Karen had chopped off Aaron's hair. Art said, "It's sad to see a kid cry when he has to go home and see his mother."

"Tomorrow morning I have to go to a funeral—a buddy from Antioch. I don't want to go, I have to go. I have to be a Mitchell brother. I'm tired of it," he said. "I'm tired of being a Mitchell brother."

"I don't like fucking other girls anymore, Simone. I just want to make love to you. Sex isn't anything without love, you know," he said, giving me a clear, convinced look. "The girls at the theater—they want to do some drugs, I just fuck 'em a little, shoot a wad in their face. And it's over. I *don't like it* anymore. Besides, I have a relationship with you."

~

Around 9:00 a.m., he left to rendezvous with Jim and attend the funeral, ace bandage on his foot, his soft blond longish hair a little rumpled, in a sweatshirt and Levi's.

Pretty soon, he was back. Jim had complained about the way Art was dressed, "That uptight, what about the way he dresses!"

I pictured Jim the last time I'd seen him—overfed and color-coordinated, in a polo shirt and jeans in canary yellow.

Still upset by the recent murder of their old friend Huey Newton, Art got maudlin, started crying, "I don't *want* to go to a *funeral*. My brother's Mr. Perfect."

"That kind of thing is really thin, anyway," I said.

"Jim looked at me this morning and he said 'You look like you're going to be the next one to die.' And I looked at him and he was smoking the poison herb (cigarettes)."

"I'm taking you for my woman, Simone. I want you with me, I want you to be my wife. I want you to be a good example for my kids," he brought tears to my eyes. "But if you get jealous once, if you fuck up once, you're out!"

"Art, you've pulled away from me so many times I'm terrified of you. And I don't know what you expect."

"You're not human. You're something else," he said. "I want you to be perfect. Talk to Lisa, she knows what's needed. My brother thinks that you're the best person for me. I'll give you money. No more dancing."

I felt overwhelmed.

We drove to the Lark Creek Inn for dinner. Art was in an exuberant, confident mood. "I really want to thank you for loving me so well for so long and for sticking with me despite the son of a bitch I've been. I don't know how you did it," he said. "I want you to live with me, and help me with the children. It'll be just the same as being my wife, except without the benefits!"

I smiled, accepted, and gave him a kiss.

"It doesn't get any better than this, Simone. That's something I'm sure of!"

⌇

Even though Art said the kids had put in a vote for the guillotine and my really boss mannequins, it made sense to keep my apartment. It was my personal haven, and a convenient place in the city for nights we wanted to stay there. Since we love each other, if I'm tolerant, loving and strong, our living together should work out, I thought.

In the morning, he took me out for breakfast. "You're going to have a good life now, Simone," he said confidently. "Of course I'll take care of all the expenses. And I'm going to give you money and some cash to hold for me in a safe deposit box. You can still work for Vince."

We took the children to a movie, *Sea of Love*, they trooped down close to the screen. Art and I sat together and held hands.

"When my brother and I took girls to the movies in high school we'd open up the bottom of the boxes the popcorn came in and stick our dicks up inside. My date would be watching the movie, eating popcorn, and suddenly she'd reach in and find my slick dick!"

I laughed, "What happened then?"

"Well, it depended on the girl."

⌇

266

Art filled his house with Nintendos and toys and plenty of love for the children. "Children are very activity-oriented," he said, and planned a smorgasbord of things to keep them and their friends entertained. Aaron, Jasmine and Caleb spent the weekends with Artie and dropped by after school during the week. They ran to him with a chorus of "Dad's"—to settle each dispute, grant every request, and to share every possible moment with him.

Sunday Karen Mitchell's tattooed biker brother came to visit with a friend. While the children played outside the men talked, "Hey, Art, I always wanted to know—when you had the Mercedes—do they really work with women?"

"Yeah. It works. Well, you know the difference between a Mercedes and a Rolls, don't you? In a Mercedes you have to take the girls' panties off, but in a Rolls they take them off for you!"

"They're all in awe of me," Art said with a grin to me. "They're all thinking you're the one that's getting the royal dick at night!"

The doorbell rang; I was surprised to see Martha the cleaning lady, wearing short shorts, with wild alarmed eyes insisting, "I have to talk to Artie." Why was she here on her day off?

Later when I walked into the backyard, Martha was manicuring Art's nails at the round umbrella table and gazing into his eyes enraptured; he was enjoying playing lord of the manor. I cringed momentarily. "I had to talk to Artie," she said on her way out, "I just found out I might be in a lot of trouble with welfare!"

Since the previous fall, Art had acquired a tall combination safe, for cash and valuables, because he kept his doors unlocked, in case one of his children needed to get in to the house. He had installed a hot tub in the backyard close to the pool, and mounted a collage of photographs on his far bedroom closet.

Art sent me shopping for presents for Cal's seventh birthday. Karen was buying him a child-size pool table. Art picked out a bike.

We had fifteen young guests, and took them bowling; Art showed them how, and cheered them on. Afterwards they ate cake and ice cream, watched *Roger Rabbit*, and played for hours.

"That party was terrible," Cal said months later to my surprise. "It was worse than an ordinary day!" Like Art, he had an unquenchable appetite for satisfaction—enjoying most pleasures for a moment, and casting them aside immediately for the next amusement. Aaron, Cal and Jasmine had a strong sense of entitlement, and were often temperamental, and discontent. Nothing was ever quite enough.

The boys put pizza down the toilet, climbed in windows, bickered and chased each other through the house in relentless rivalry. They minded Art, and tested me. When Jasmine spent the night out with her girlfriends, the boys took over her room and trashed it, Aaron donned a girl's bathing suit with rumba ruffles for laughs and jumped up and down on her mattress defiantly.

Art had favorite menus he knew the kids would eat. They were finicky, especially Cal and Jasmine. My cooking was improving. "In a year you'll be good," Art said.

We kept a fairly regular schedule that began when Art woke up at 6:00 a.m. and turned on the news. Weekdays he left for the theater at 9:00 a.m., and I drove to Vince's office for a few hours to work. I made the liquor store runs, for Cristall Stoly and Heineken, never buying more than one six-pack, one bottle of vodka at a time. Art was taking naps, passing out early watching big screen TV in the bedroom, and rarely wanted to go out in the evening.

"You're drunk!" Cal piped up one evening. Art felt insulted.

"You're the best person for Art right now," Vince told me. "I think you are, and the people I know think so, too. You don't drink, not at all, so there can't be 'You're drinking too, what gives you the right to say anything.'"

"I'm not sure how to deal with his drinking," I said. "Do you think it would help if I talked to him about it?"

"I think you shouldn't say anything about his drinking—that'll just egg him on. Just you're being there not drinking will help."

That fall I knew little about alcoholism as a progressive illness. I still thought of Art as a heavy drinker, not as an alcoholic. Vince knew his character as well as anyone. Art was so willful, such an outlaw, that quitting drinking would have had to have been his decision. He had been drinking so long and so much, he would have needed to detox in a hospital.

～

Jasmine wanted to be Medusa for Halloween; I promised her I would make a costume. After work, I found a mythology book for inspiration. Art said he would be over later and we would spend the night in the city, but he didn't show. I was worried, since it was the first night we had been apart since getting back together, this time.

In the morning, I called Rita. Before Charles, she had been married to a Michigan nightclub owner who was killed in a random shooting in Detroit. "Art is going to fuck up occasionally," she said. "For most club owners, having sex is casual, it's no more serious than having a drink with somebody is to other people. It's game playing. You have to expect him to do that from time to time. The best thing to do is not to be upset—he has shown a lot of indication he wants you with him. I would call him, accept the situation and let him know you love him. If you talk about it, let him know what counts to you is that he has a relationship with you, and that he's treating you well."

I called him at the theater, acting like nothing had happened. That evening Art looked exhausted, "I fucked another girl last night," he said.

"Does she think she's your girlfriend?"

"Oh no. Far from it."

"Then I don't care."

Upset but trying to hide it, I got dressed in the look he loved—a silk chemise and heels—and came back into the bedroom without much effect. He was too tired. I felt hurt, but I gave him a kiss and nestled against his back. "I love you, Simone," he said.

One of those precious mornings when we were completely alone, Art and I climbed into the hot tub for awhile, stumbled inside to the bed and he made love to me so perfectly I wanted to cry. I wanted to stay in bed all day with him and drift away, on wave after orgasmic wave.

～

Another sunny morning in the hot tub he came up with a plan, "Call the airlines and see if you can get tickets leaving in a couple of weeks, for Zihuatanejo/Ixtapa. We'll make a run down there, take the kids, Storm and maybe Liberty can go.

"Oh, that'll be fun. They'll love it!"

"I wouldn't try to do something like this without you, Simone. It's too ambitious!"

Late at night when everyone was asleep, I walked out in front of the house where the full moon was shining, completely happy. It's going to be my time now, I thought. From now on, it's going to be my time.

Chapter 18:
Earthquake Boogie

OCTOBER 17, 1989

"My brother found out about this great insurance policy, that would be good for the kids in case anything ever happened," Art said in the morning. "I had to laugh—Jim and I went in together to take the physical for it and this doctor gives me a serious look and says, 'Your brother doesn't use any drugs, does he?' So I say, 'No. He *better not*! If I ever catch him smoking any of that funny stuff he'll be in *real* trouble!'"

Since we were leaving for Mexico in two days, I went to visit Karen for the first time in her house on Christmas Tree Hill, to get her to sign a letter permitting me to travel with the children when they were out of the country, in case there was an emergency. Karen agreed to sign if I came up to see her and brought the $50.00 Art promised her—for buying ice and driving down to take care of him when he was sick and throwing up from drinking a couple of weeks earlier, the night he hadn't spent at my place in the city as planned.

Only in the last couple of months had Karen been able to speak to me in a sane tone instead of screaming, so I was nervous. Just after we made our reservations, Art told me she wanted him to take her and the twins on the trip. He told her no, Simone is going. Karen hadn't liked that. As soon as we got back, she was leaving with Jasmine and the twins for Hawaii to even things out.

A white uniformed housekeeper pursued the twins, Karlan and Austin, into the next room.

271

"You know Artie's an alcoholic, Simone. I'm very worried about it. And it's very important that he doesn't allow the children to drink alcohol in Mexico," said Karen. "Once he let Karlan drink some beer at his house, and I found out about it!"

"He did? I've never seen him let any of the kids have alcohol. He's very concerned about them, about their eating properly. . . ."

"The children and I have started going to counseling sessions at Ross Clinic about his drinking. Maybe that's something you might want to participate in!"

I paused, considering my answer. Karen was the first person I ever heard call Artie an alcoholic. Ever since I had known Art, he drank and did drugs. His behavior hadn't changed dramatically. I didn't want to believe anything serious was wrong with his health, although some of his symptoms that fall were frightening.

Art would have viewed my going behind his back to cooperate with Karen on something like this as a great betrayal. Karen was probably planning to use the Ross counseling sessions as evidence for a new lawsuit, as leverage to demand more money from him. I didn't think she had his best interests at heart—concerning liquor or anything else. Karen was the last person I felt I could trust.

I said, "I don't drink at all or use drugs, but what's tended to happen in the past is sometimes Art runs into somebody who does and he'll go off with them and do it, and I haven't been around at those times. But I am aware he has a drinking problem. I know how important it is for him to eat. And I certainly won't let anything happen where the kids will be drinking in Mexico!"

"It does make me feel better that you don't drink, since you're watching my children."

"Good."

I gave Karen the $50. "Thanks, it's hard to get these little tidbits out of him!" she said, and signed the letter. I explained I had to be going. Karen reached out a small tight hand, grasped mine, and gave me a smile.

Although I didn't know it, just as I pulled onto the freeway and headed towards San Francisco, in the inner sanctum office of the O'Farrell Art was signing an agreement for a million-dollar life insurance policy. In the event of his death, the money was payable—not to his children, whom he loved so much—but to Cinema 7, Inc., Mitchell Brothers' principal corporation, and to its president, Jim Mitchell.

In the city, it was hot and still. I worked for a couple of hours at Vince's, then left to pack for the trip. Around 5:00 p.m. I stopped in a health food store, when I felt the ground moving. It was the biggest Bay Area earthquake in nearly a century. The lights went off, hanging lamps swayed overhead, packages toppled off the shelves, and customers fled for the door. Potrero Hill is granite; I couldn't have been safer. I drove a few blocks to my apartment, noticed one picture slightly ajar and found some candles. I didn't know about the freeway disaster in Oakland, part of the Bay Bridge collapsing, and the death and destruction along hundreds of California miles.

When I tried calling the Marin house and the O'Farrell that evening I couldn't get through, but I did reach a few friends and heard how terrible the damage was everywhere else. At 11:00 p.m. I reached Vince at home, "Is Art O.K.?"

"Oh, yeah, I saw him around 5:30. I think he and Rocky are going to stay in the theater tonight because they're afraid of looting," he sounded typically nonchalant.

On television, they were saying the airport was closed, and there could be a sizable aftershock. I spent an uneasy night.

At 10:00 a.m., Art called from the pay phone at the O'Farrell. "All the kids are fine," he said. "If the airport's open by tomorrow, let's go on the trip!" I warily drove over the Golden Gate Bridge. I was so relieved to see him. We were both shaken.

When it happened, Art was in the poolroom. He got up and started to dance, saying, "Whenever there's an earthquake, you better get up and start to boogie. Do the earthquake boogie, 'cause you never know when it's going to be your last dance!"

～

It was dark when we left Marin, and most of the traffic lights were still out from the earthquake along Lombard. Aaron and Cal did some token homework on the plane and joked with Storm. Then we stepped into a primeval, sultry world.

The road to Zihuatanejo was steamy and lined with thick vegetation and palm trees, much deeper in Mexico than Cabo. Silhouetted against the moving green, Art looked toughly beautiful. I felt so deeply happy.

The Sotovento stood on top of the cliffs at Zihuatanejo like a fortress. Art heard it was built by some Nazi in the early 60's. We'd booked three rooms in a row—big humid rooms cooled by blue metal ceiling fans we kept at high speed, ours wobbling dangerously over our bed with a mesmerizing hum.

Liberty was tall with short blonde hair, in her second year at USC, and wanted to become an actress. Because she had been away at school on the East Coast and visited her father occasionally, I had only met her once before.

"I can't believe Dad's found somebody his age who's mellow, too!" she said.

"I've known your father a long time," I told her, "for seven years."

"Seven years! I can imagine what *you've* been through in *that* amount of time!"

Art told Liberty she could bring a friend, he would pay for the trip—so she invited her roommate in LA, who was also nineteen.

"Why is Liberty so uppity?" Art said to me in our room, "She's just a party slut, she's only taking two classes at USC and partying all the time!"

"Two classes?"

"That's all she signed up for. It's costing me a fortune."

"What about UCLA? It has a good reputation, and it's cheaper."

"I know. She heard USC has a good drama department."

At night we walked way down the beach and had dinner. Art was in high spirits, happy to have brought his family together in such a special faraway place. After the meal, the kids raced ahead to the hotel. Art and I took our time wading in the warm water and through the sand alone in the darkness, laughing and stopping every ten feet to play. Beyond the balcony outside our room, the wide calm sea looked eerie and limitless.

Every morning the boys took their boogie boards to the water, Art and I sat at the nearly deserted bar, sipped drinks and talked. Later the girls would come down.

Art went in the water with the boys. He was so strikingly good looking, even at a distance but somehow looked vulnerable, the metal insignia on his cap gleaming, bobbing up and down in the waves.

~

Sunday the beach got crowded, with tourists and local people. Art struck up a conversation with some Norwegian guys who worked for an airline, and I went up to our room and took a shower. When I came back, Art was reclining in a lounge chair with an iguana on his head—it was huge, as big as a dog with a thick, long scaly tail.

"Norwegians don't eat lunch on Sunday, they just drink," one of his new pals said. Art had gotten into a drinking bout with them and was plastered, "Simone, come here and hold the iguana!"

"No thanks." It was snakelike, muscular, and scary, but balanced on Art's head it looked hilarious.

"Simone, come over here, hold the iguana! . . . This is my secretary/girlfriend," he told the Norwegians. "I need a secretary/girlfriend. I like the way she treats me and she's efficient!" Storm looked at me sideways.

A couple of Mexican boys darted around in the sand. Someone had bought some peanuts from a vendor, and one of the boys began throwing peanuts towards Art from a distance and he was catching them in his mouth. Soon both of them were pelting Art with peanuts, "Senor, senor!" and howling with laughter.

They were laughing a little too hard at him, it wasn't fun anymore. Art was getting nastier and yelling for more drinks to be brought. I had to get away from his dark mood and went back to the room. Ten minutes later he burst in yelling, "SHE'S A DISCO SLUT!"

Liberty and her friend came upstairs and slammed their door. Art was furious and jumped out in the hall, "I'M CUTTING YOU OFF!" he screamed. "I'M NOT CARRYING SOME DISCO SLUT!" Then he came back inside, banging the door passionately behind him.

"Do you know what Meredith said to me, do you know what she said? She said 'GET OUT OF MY LIFE.'" He started to cry. "That's what I ought to tell Liberty, just get out of my life! I don't need this. You're NINETEEN years old—get a job. WE had to do it. MAKE something of yourself. 'Cause I'M NOT CARRYING IT ANYMORE, I'M NOT PAYING FOR SOME DISCO SLUT!"

I hadn't known how deeply Art was hurt by Meredith's divorcing him. He had never given any woman the power to hurt him quite as much. No wonder he drifted in and out with me, keeping me guessing. I didn't know what nasty exchange had taken place at the beach, but hardly felt like questioning him about it when he was so angry.

Art calmed down, and we took a siesta. When we got up he seemed quite sober, and we walked down the beach and had supper by ourselves.

Later Cal and I went to buy some cold drinks to take back to our rooms. Sitting at the bar were Liberty and Storm. "Papa needs to comer (eat)." Storm said.

"I'm sorry, your dad just had too much to drink," I said to Liberty. "I know he feels bad about it. . ."

She glowered, "He'll probably just fuck himself to death!"

Some of Art's drunken behavior was embarrassing and hurtful, especially to his older children and to me. At the time I felt at a loss as to what to do or say about it, and believed he would launch into an angry tirade if I objected. Now, I regret not speaking out more.

For the rest of the trip, Art limited the amount he was drinking and controlled his temper. Although beneath the surface there was tension, he enjoyed the time with his kids and me.

Back on Mohawk Avenue, Karen came down for dinner wearing a snug outfit by Body Glove that looked oddly teenage, bringing Jasmine and the twins. At the table, everyone was peaceable, but the small talk sounded overly polite and fake. I wondered what was actually running through Karen's mind. I wanted her to like me, and finally accept my being with Art and sharing his life. We deserved to be happy!

Jasmine played "If I Could Turn Back Time" by Cher and danced, with her slender good looks and sprightliness and long, soft blonde hair. Art and Karen beamed proudly, and took turns dancing with her.

Because Karen was getting one of her cars fixed, the Cadillac, I gave her a ride home with Jasmine and the twins, who were ten months old then.

"Oh, by the way, we're going to Hawaii for two weeks, not one; we're leaving in the morning. Don't tell Art until we're gone. I don't want him to get mad at me and start yelling!" Karen said, putting me in a hell of a spot, right in the middle. Since we went away for one week, Karen was going away for two.

When I got home I told him, and he just accepted it.

∼

Monday Art went into work with a mischievous grin, wearing an outfit he'd picked up in Mexico—a battered straw hat, a tie-dye shirt, and shorts printed with huge leaves of marijuana.

Because the Bay Bridge was closed for earthquake repair, getting into San Francisco and back was a problem. Art and I had to leave the city for Marin at 1:30 p.m. and creep along bumper-to-bumper onto the Golden Gate Bridge, to be home when the boys got out of school.

After dinner, Art sat at the table and read with Cal, who loved attention from his father. Then Aaron read, eager to shine in his dad's eyes, gliding so fast over the words he was mixing up the meanings. I helped with his social studies.

Half an hour later, the boys went back to video games.

For awhile, Art read with them every weeknight after dinner. One night he was impatient when they began complaining. "You guys are just spoiled brats. You'll never be Mitchell brothers!" Art said. "You don't have it!" Then he walked back to our bedroom and slammed the door. A couple of minutes later when I went back there, he had fallen asleep.

∼

On a clear Indian Summer Friday afternoon, we took Cal, Aaron and one of their friends to Clear Lake, and rented a cabin. With cool detachment, Aaron watched a fish he had caught squirming for air on the dock. "I won't have to worry about him," Art said. "He's got the killer instinct. He's a Mitchell."

Frost and loneliness hung in the fall trees. After breakfast, we made a trip to the store for food and more booze, Art rushing me along the aisles. Back at the cabin I checked in the freezer, and felt alarmed. He had finished a big bottle of Stoly already, plus a six-pack and a half of Heineken, and we only checked in twenty-four hours earlier.

I could feel Art's restlessness, even though he said nothing about it, and I was frightened. We had had Cal and Aaron with us for four weeks solid.

"My mother called and she invited us for Thanksgiving," Art said.

"Oh, great!" I answered.

≈

In a few days, Karen was back and the boys went to stay at her place. She dropped Cal and Jasmine off at Art's house on the way to school. They were all excited about the live turkey Karen was keeping in a cage, and planning to kill for Thanksgiving. "Mom's getting the turkey drunk, Dad," Cal said. "You should see him. When he's *drunk*, he walks funny!"

I winced.

"You're going to come to Thanksgiving dinner, aren't you, Daddy?" asked Jasmine.

"I might not even be invited."

"Oh, yes, you are. Why, my mother would certainly invite her *husband*."

When we were alone I said, "Art, if I'm with you, I should be with you on holidays."

"Oh, come on," he said.

How infuriating. I glared.

≈

Monday night I called him at the theater, "Hinckle is here with some friends," Art said, "and I think I'll go have some dinner with them and go out later."

"Oh, can I come?"

"No, Simone. You never can."

I felt sick. He had to have done quite a bit of cocaine to sound so menacing.

"I'm going to get up really early and play some golf."

"Should I drive over later or do you want to spend the night in the city?"

"Do what you want. Do you get a feeling of what I'm doing?"

I was really scared then. I didn't know if he just meant he wanted the night off. It sounded worse. I spent a restless night in my apartment.

Now I know that people with drug and alcohol problems want to be with someone who will get high with them when they have the urge to binge, but at the time I didn't fully understand this.

As our relationship progressed and his alcoholism advanced, Art cast me against my will in an overly serious role. Over time this was depressing, and *did* make me more serious. It seems ironic, as my forte had been doing shows that were funny.

Late the next afternoon, I phoned him. "I've been thinking," Art said. "It's not working out. I need to live by myself. Come over and. . . ."

I was in tears. "No, I don't want it to be this way. Art, I really love you. . . . "

"I love you, too."

NOVEMBER 23, 1989, THANKSGIVING

I let another day go by, hoping he would change his mind, and called him on Thursday. "Yeah, come on over, I have to leave about 3:30 p.m. to go up for dinner," he said, "but come on over."

I drove there in a solemn mood. Art looked serious, sober and controlled. The home I had come to think of as bright with possibility and as mine, was gloomy and inhospitable. Storm seemed ignorant of what was happening, and stayed in the bedroom watching TV. Art talked with me in the living room. When I tried to press up close, he wouldn't respond; when I tried to kiss him, he was cold. He was directing and, as always, playing the lead, in a dark scene I hated being cast in.

"I love you very much, Art. I want to be with you."

"It's better this way. . . . That money I had you put in the safety deposit box, I want you to have it. It'll be the biggest birthday/ Christmas present you've ever had."

"Oh. Thanks." I wanted Art, not a stack of bills. I felt crushed but furious. He was acting so remote.

"Don't tell anyone about the money," he added, worried Karen might hear of it and give him a tough time seeing the kids.

"I won't."

"Well, Storm and I have to make a move," Art said, and they left for Karen Mitchell's for dinner with the children—freshly slaughtered, drunk turkey.

In the silent house, I packed up my possessions, stuffed them in my car, and took my confused black cat. I drove away from Corte Madera disheartened, angry, and harder. "Since you've done this, Art, you can't slip in and out of living with me again so easily," I decided going over the bridge, "next time you have to be committed."

Back in San Francisco, I felt just as wrapped up with Art as if I was still at 23 Mohawk Avenue. I had loved him through so many changes for too many years for one afternoon to destroy. Even "without the benefits"—which was what he had proposed—I felt like Art Mitchell's wife.

～

By morning, in the quiet of my own apartment, what had taken place took on a different light. His asking me to leave just before Thanksgiving seemed like some weird ploy to pacify Karen Mitchell for the holidays, and it would free him to get high with other women for the duration of party season. Art had many different desires he tried to satisfy. Knowing him, his domestic side might surface again in a couple of months and he would want me back with him in Marin.

Being alone in my own world gave me time to think. That fall we had shared much happiness. Still, living with him and the children full-time was like being caught in a whirlwind of Art's creation, without having any power. Most of my time had been spent keeping his household running, and pleasing his children and their friends. He had a constant need to interact with a lot of people I found uninteresting. Art and I had seldom gone out by ourselves and done anything adult, and I'd had almost none of the time by myself that I was accustomed to enjoying.

I felt deeply disappointed. How frustrating it was that Art wanted to dominate every decision, and that he had compartmentalized me in the world of his children, isolated from the adult mental stimulation I needed. How sad that he was so rigid and closed to the possibilities of trying to make the life I was sharing with him more fulfilling and more to my taste. I had also failed, in trying too hard to please Art and not insisting that my own needs were met. His alcoholism and drug use was such a seamless part of our lives, then I didn't fully realize the major role it was playing.

"If I were you, I'd take some of the money and pay off your credit cards," he had told me. But since I didn't have a full-time job, and was determined I wasn't going back to dancing, I couldn't. Facing the straight work world was a scary reality. I had to find a job before I went through his gift!

~

I steeled myself and went into work at Vince's office Monday. Within a few days, the embarrassing news I was no longer living with Art would be all over the O'Farrell. Even if he didn't take up with Krystal again, pretty soon he would be getting loaded with some other young dancer. It was like I was battling a legion of demons—as soon as one of Art's girlfriend/drug buddies was gone, another took her place. Maybe they were materializing out of the legendary amounts of white powder Artie spilled on the O'Farrell rugs over the years. It was hateful being in that little office watching the saga unfold.

Krystal came in to see Vince that afternoon in a frisky mood, laughing with him and giving me an occasional smirk. She made a run to the corner store for a six pack of Heineken and drank bottle after bottle herself, staying so long I had to make a call to Art while she was still simpering in the background. I wanted to catch him early, when he was still sober enough to be attentive. "Call me at home tonight. It's important," I said. A few minutes later, Krystal opened the door on her way out and projected a loud belch toward the hall.

Since Thanksgiving, I realized I should tell Art about Karen's counseling sessions for his alcoholism; even if he hated hearing about it, he needed to know. Whatever Karen's motives were, I knew she didn't have Art's well being in mind. I hadn't wanted to tell him on the Zihuatanejo trip, because it would have upset him and might have spoiled the relaxed fun time he wanted with his children; I dreaded telling him at all.

After we got back from Mexico, I asked his cleaning lady Martha about it, because she knew Karen. I was surprised she had attended one counseling session. "Aaron ran out of the room the time I was there," she said.

"I don't want anything to do with it," I had told her. "I have to be on Art's side."

At 8:00 p.m. he called, still sounding aloof, and I explained what Karen had said to me. "You fucked up, didn't you," Art said with cold irritation. "That's why you're telling me now. She was probably tape-recording you!"

"God, I hadn't even thought of that. I don't think she was."

Karen would use the counseling sessions as evidence against Art in the child custody hearings held in February 1991, days before his death.

The next evening he came over and made love to me passionately. The nights he spent with me that first week reassured me that our relationship was important to him. I could deal with whatever path he momentarily needed to explore.

I did realize I could no longer tolerate working in the office with the pool of dancers he would be coming onto. Vince and I agreed I could do his work at home. That would work out better because soon I had to find an additional job anyway. A couple of times a week Vince and I would discuss what needed to be done over the phone.

I spent an afternoon with Justine at my apartment. We talked for hours; she was familiar with a whole underside of the O'Farrell I had no idea of:

"Artie's been 86'd from most of the clubs in the city. He can't even get in now," she remarked with some glee.

"I didn't know that. Why?"

"For coming in totally fucked up and acting like he owns the place. For being an asshole."

"Just in the last year?" I said. No wonder he didn't like going out much.

"Mostly."

"Things have changed a lot for him," I said. "I think Karen's pressuring him has had a lot to do with his getting so messed up. He's not handling the booze well anymore. He's probably feeling older. He must hate it."

"Oh, he does! When he first got together with Karen, she had her own apartment in the city. She really *had him* for awhile, she did everything she could think of to please him. He was totally into it. But after she started having babies, he just got tired of taking her out and started partying without her, separate. She hated that, it ate at her more and more. Oh, they did their family trip with the kids but it never seemed very real or satisfying to them.

"Oh, want to hear something really juicy I heard about," she continued. "Lynx was over at Jim and Lisa's house this one night and she and Lisa put on a wild show for Jim. Lisa really likes being told what to do."

Although I hadn't been present to witness these events, they had a ring of truth to them that fit the inner world of the O'Farrell well. It made sense that other women who wanted Artie or Jim had done extreme things to captivate them. Maybe my dressing up as a gorilla during a three-way to please Artie hadn't been that outrageous, after all.

Justine consoled me about him, "You guys have been together too long. He's going to come back. Whatever he says, he's going to come back."

I put on my fox coat and leather pants, Justine wore Art's Guatemalan jacket, "It's so unquestionably his," she said with the pretty sparkle of an ingenue, and off we went to dinner. Afterwards we stopped at a couple of clubs and dropped by the O'Farrell. Then Justine went to the Century to dance.

~

Art went on a short December binge, then he asked me to spend Christmas with him and the children in Marin, which I did. In January, I began job hunting and spent time with him more sporadically. Rita asked me to come to Canada with her, so I just got on the plane. I was thinking, let him wonder where *I am* for a change. The next afternoon when I checked my machine from Windsor, Ontario, Art had left four messages, each sounding progressively drunker; the last was: "Simone, where are you, where the fuck are you?"

As Rita and I watched the wintry landscape from the train, and trudged through the snow in Toronto, my longing for Art never left me—but I was also thinking, I'm not going to get pushed around. He has to be more considerate.

Back in San Francisco I gave him a T-shirt printed with: "Detroit, the City Where the Weak Are Killed and Eaten," and a skull and crossbones.

"This is my favorite shirt," he said, beaming. "You like seeing me in your stuff, don't you?" He put on the muskrat trooper's hat I had given him for Christmas. "You've done more to keep me alive in the last ten years than anyone else, Simone."

Now party season was over, he seemed mellower. My having been away for a couple of weeks made him more loving. I told myself, if he gets a charge out of collecting sexual nuances, let him—it has been his basic nature all his life. Since flirting and having occasional sex with other women seemed to keep him more turned on when he was making love to me—I was benefiting. I love him and I'm going to make this work, I thought.

From the relaxed friendly way the children were acting, I sensed they and Art were ready for me to be there again.

"You're a wonderful woman, Simone, but I'm a hard man," he said. "You chose me, you know. You're so sexy. . . . You know why you chose me, don't you? Because I'm a survivor—women do that—you picked the toughest, most intelligent guy you could find. Someone that would be a match for you."

He left for the theater, and called me at 1:00 p.m., "I don't know if we should try this, but I've got this raging hard on. . . . Do you want to come back here tonight?"

"Of course I do," I told him. I explained that I had signed up to take computer lessons and was supposed to go that night, so we agreed that I would come over right after that. From the interviews I'd been on, I knew finding a straight job in the 90's could depend on my learning to use computers. I felt Art should be able to accommodate something that *I* needed to do!

My teacher was late and I lost track of the time; I wasn't through until 10:00 p.m. When I heard Art's drunken message on my machine I was in tears, "You fucked up, didn't you. Don't come over." I dialed his number and gave my very reasonable excuse. "No, I don't want you to come over," he fumed. "Martha my maid's here and I haven't fucked her yet, but I'm thinking about it!"

"Art. You're being so unfair. ART!"

Part 3

Chapter 19:
Near Drowning

MARCH 20, 1990

Tuesday I gave Vince a call about the schedule. "Did you hear about the accident Art and Jim had, about Artie almost drowning?" he asked.

"DROWNING? NO! What do you mean?" My heart was racing.

"It happened at Ocean Beach," he began.

God! Art almost *drowned* and I didn't even hear about it? The idea of the power of the ocean swallowing up someone I loved so much stunned me. I wanted to fly to his side.

No one had tried to reach me—not even Jim or Lisa. I felt powerless to do anything to help and very excluded.

I sent flowers to the Marin house. The newspaper ran a short account of the drowning, quoting Art, "I'm happy as hell just to be alive!"

He called to thank me and invited me over, sounding tired, but sober and clear. They had kept him in the hospital for three days, treating him for hypothermia. "I took the kids over to Jim's for a birthday party Sunday and we were out at the beach. Cal and Rafe were playing in the water. Then out of nowhere this bad riptide started to push them out to sea. Storm and I and Jim went in after them. Storm got the kids back to shore, but all three of us got caught by the current, we kept getting pushed farther and farther out. Three firemen saved us. The guy that rescued me got hit in the head by a surfboard, he had to go to the hospital along with us. When they pulled me out of the water I started shaking, I couldn't control it, I'd been in for

close to an hour without a wet suit. My temperature went down to
86. At UCSF, they put a special blanket on me. They said, 'The only
thing between that guy and death is this blanket!' When I heard that,
I really felt like it was serious. I let them do whatever they wanted to,
otherwise I might have died."

"Oh, Art."

"I know. It was a pretty close call."

The moment I was on Mohawk Avenue I felt the strongest sense of
fear. The house was hushed. On the dining room table stood the vase
of iris and daffodils I had sent, plus a long planter of pink and white
tulips. Art was lying in bed looking beautiful but ethereal, somehow
fading, like he was half in another world. I gave him a gentle kiss, and
he woke up and smiled. Then I lay down next to him.

He crawled on top of me and felt as light as a feather, "Do you
want this big dick?"

"Yes. More than anything."

Afterwards we were both very still. Being together again made us
realize how terrible it would have been for both of us if he had died.
He had come so close to dying. I held him.

"They put a tube up my dick for two days! They said the catheter
wouldn't hurt. But it hurt like hell. It didn't go in quite right, so I had
urine all over me, but I didn't tell them because I was afraid they'd do
it again, and I just couldn't stand it."

After Art fell asleep, I got up and did some dishes. I was terrified
but knew I shouldn't show it. Every so often I would walk softly back
down the hall to check on him; his breathing sounded so liquidy. I
was afraid he might stop breathing. He was so weak and thinner than
ever. It sounded like he had water in his lungs, still.

In the morning he pulled himself together, sounded somewhat
better, and to my horror announced he was going in to the O'Farrell
to work. "Don't you think you should get some rest for a few more

days?" I asked. "What did the doctors say when they let you go home?"

"They said I'm O.K."

"You know, if you just take a few days to get some rest now, I bet you'll be completely recovered from this much faster. It would be good to check with a specialist, just to see what they suggest. Gee, if it happened to *me*, I certainly would!"

"Now you're bitching at me." Art grinned whimsically, gave me a warm kiss, and left—to prove to himself, to Jim and to the world, that he was as tough as ever and very much co-owner of their businesses.

Near Ocean Beach at his house on 47th Avenue, the other Mitchell brother was getting ready to drive to the theater, too. Artie had so narrowly escaped death, Jim had to be wondering what life would be like without Art. What would it be like to be sole owner of the O'Farrell, Cinema 7, and Mitchell Brothers' Film Group?

I wanted to be with Art badly, but over the next few days, he didn't call. Maybe he's just resting, I hoped. Saturday an attorney hired me. His specialty was appealing death penalty cases. In the corner of his leather and mahogany-furnished office hung a skeleton wearing a T-shirt with an image of the gas chamber in an ugly shade of green. In a week, the first man in California in more than twenty years was scheduled to be executed.

Since I had so much reason to be worried about Art, I was quite concerned about how my working 9:00-6:00 would affect our relationship. But since at the moment he was seeing me sporadically, and the cash he had given me in November was diminishing fast, I had to take a job. Uncertain as to what would happen, and because I needed the extra money, I held onto my part-time gig with Vince, too. I would do his work at night and on the weekends.

I was beginning to get a fuller picture of the stigma attached to working in the sex industry. Not only did I have to come up with a story for my resume to cover the years I'd spent dancing, but I always had to guard against revealing too much about my past. This led to my never truly feeling comfortable, at the less than thrilling jobs I found.

Monday was my very first day with the attorney; somehow, I got through it. No clients came in, but a couple called from San Quentin's Death Row. Art spent the night with me. His breathing sounded just as alarming. I hated going to work in the morning; I could hardly leave him.

Since now I had to be in the city during the week, he invited me over on the weekends. Newly pinned up on his wall was the newspaper article on the California Supreme Court decision on Mitchell Brothers'. After eight years, the case had finally been resolved in Art and Jim's favor—they wouldn't have to serve time. Even the previous fall Art had still been worried, "If I have to go to jail, will you take care of my little kids, Simone?" he had asked. "You won't have to worry about me in there, though. If they ever get me, they'll think they're up against the ghost of Huey Newton!"

～

"Aaron has moved in with me," Art said in a few days. "He decided he doesn't want to live with Karen anymore. He hates her. He started crying and having tantrums, she can't handle him. When he turns twelve we'll go to court and I can get custody. I knew a long time ago he'd be with me. The male bonding happened when he was a real little kid. It won't be long before Cal's here, too. I guess I can't have all the kids with me. Jasmine likes Karen better, she is more like her. But I feel bad about leaving her with her crazy mother."

I sent Aaron a card: "Moved, Yes, and the New Address is 23 Mohawk Avenue." Much later, I realized Aaron must have sensed something that spring, too, when Art nearly drowned. He wanted to be with his father, and watch over him.

Sometimes Art stayed with me in the city, then days went by when I wouldn't hear from him. I had hoped that he'd slow down and take better care of himself since the drowning, but just the opposite happened—he was driven to blot out the awareness he was ill by getting high, and by maintaining his hard-partying reputation. Later I would realize there were other very serious reasons for alarm he was trying to blot out, too.

Even though I hadn't lost Art to the sea, sometimes it seemed like he was being swallowed up by the world I had left—the O'Farrell.

MAY 1, 1990

When I was still at the office at 5:00 p.m., Art called me, "Why don't you come down, we're having a party."

Standing around the poolroom was an entirely male group of sports writers and boxers. Art was shooting pool with one of the guests. In a moment, I realized Art seemed fifty times drunker than anyone in the room. On top of everything else, now he had the flu. Except for the guy he was trading shots with, all the men were staring at Art like ringside spectators just before a prizefight, sizing up a spirited but injured contender.

One of these guests looked familiar, so I said hello. "Substance abuse is really a bad thing," he commented embarrassingly loud, glancing at Art.

With a shrewd glimmer in his eyes and a touch of cruelty about his lips, political consultant Jack Davis sat down at the poker table. The phone rang and he picked it up. "It's Krystal," he said.

Art waved him off.

"Come on, Artie, talk to Krystal. Say a few words to Krystal."
How rude of him to do that right in my face. It was quite obvious Art
was with me. He was already plastered and very sick, the last thing he
needed was to go on a drug binge with her.

I walked the two or three steps it took me to get to Davis and
glared, "Put it down." He did, giving me an evil look. Then he left the
party.

After his game ended, Art threw a $100 bill down on the pool
table, trying to get people to play, acting the funny outrageous host. I
walked over near the jukebox to say "Hi" to Jim, and was surprised to
find him staring at Art with repulsion. "*Disgusting*, isn't it," Jim said
to me. "He's so petty." Just under Jim's sedate exterior was a glowing
rage; I had never seen him so angry.

"*Go home, Art*," Jim said. "You're lucky. You've got a ride."

Art ignored Jim's remark. Now he really didn't want to go. I felt
caught in the middle—frightened by Jim and afraid of trouble, I tried
to persuade Art to leave. Drunk as he was, Art knew to leave right
away would allow Jim to have the upper hand too easily. Who was
going to make him leave his own club?

Half an hour later, Art was feeling sicker and ready to go home.
Now leaving could seem like his personal choice. Ron was out in
the hallway and said, "It's a far, far better thing," meaning I was doing
everybody a favor by getting Art out of there. Years before I started
dancing at the O'Farrell, Art had been getting drunk. Why was
everyone reacting so differently to him now?

The mood in the poolroom was as cruel as an audience of Romans
relishing Artie being fed to a pack of lions. In keeping with this spirit,
and no doubt on Jim Mitchell's orders, Paulie escorted us to my car.

"Show ass," Art joked.

"Who, me?" said Paulie.

"No, her." Art pulled up my long, conservative skirt and gave me an affectionate swat through my slip.

Jim's anger, and the mood at that party would haunt me. No matter how he had to go about it, Jim wanted Art out of the O'Farrell, not just for one evening, but forever.

~

Never had I felt such a strong sense I needed to be with him. In the morning I phoned my job and took the week off—I wanted to see that he went to a doctor and got some rest. I drove him to Nick's clinic to make sure he actually walked in there. His old friend Nick, originally a gynecologist who was working as a GP at a clinic, was the only doctor Art would agree to see.

Half an hour later, he emerged with a prescription. Back in Marin, he went to bed. I picked up the pills, antibiotics, and he downed them. When I talked to Nick on the phone all he would say to me about Art's condition was, "He knows what to do."

At 1:00 p.m., Art had me call Jim at home to give him a message in O'Farrelleese: "If the party slows, that be the way it goes, compton, compton, compton. Definitely count me in for the Woody Creek run. Be rollin' by Friday. A. Fuckin Easy."

Hunter Thompson was facing serious charges—possession of drugs and explosives, and sexual assault. Art and Jim had been talking about making a trip to Aspen, Colorado during his court appearance there to show support. Art had to have been thinking having fun on the trip would smooth over his differences with his brother.

As I delivered this message, Jim listened in silence, then said, "Put Artie on the phone."

While they talked, I waited in the bedroom. When Art came back, he looked extremely hurt and exasperated. "Jim says he doesn't want to be partners anymore. I don't need HIM!"

Art was wounded and outraged. Being cast out of his beloved O'Farrell would have been a fate worse than death.

"I want you to call Mack Advertising," he said. "Tell them Art wants the ad for the newspapers changed. We're about to re-open the Cine Stage, I want to advertise it as open. The ad should say 'five live shows,' instead of four," he said authoritatively. That afternoon it was important to him to exert some power.

After I called, he said, "We deserve a vacation. Why don't you call Mexicana and find out what kind of rates they have for Zihuatanejo. We'll go down for a few days, about five is perfect. Does your boss know who I am?"

"Well, no."

"I'll talk to him. He's a fan. Everybody loves the brothers. I'll tell him I need to take my girl on a vacation."

I wanted to leave on the next plane with Art, but after I got the rates he had spun off thinking about Colorado and his brother again, "I need to find out when Jim and I are going to Woody Creek first to decide when you and I should go," he said. "It'll cheer Hunter up to see a few old warriors!"

The next afternoon I picked up some potting soil for Art's marijuana plants. When I got back, we sat by ourselves on the deck. "No wonder all the neighborhood kids are always over here," he said. "We're the nicest couple on the block!"

"When I look at my brother now it makes me sick, he's gotten so fat. I say to him, 'Is this contentment?' I'm really happy for him, though," he said. "Lisa's doing such a wonderful job with Jim's kids. Oh—she works him for what she can get out of him, I know, but she's right on top of it with his kids; they're doing their homework. Jim's finally found someone who can handle it!"

I felt jealous of the stability Lisa seemed to be enjoying with Jim. If Art hadn't gone back and forth with me so much, I could have been doing well with his children, too. Since we were spending weekends at the house in Moraga nearly two years earlier, I hadn't seen or heard from Lisa. Jim and Lisa seemed to have distanced themselves from our lives. "I think she's cold and calculating," I said, surprised Art couldn't see it.

"I wonder about some of Jim and Lisa's ideas," Art continued. "You know how Jim has Rafe dressed like Rambo so much? Now they're calling Rafe 'The Enforcer.' If any of the kids use swear words—even mine, when they're over there—Rafe is supposed to attack!"

"That's a terrible thing to encourage!"

Since Art was in such a warm, relaxed mood, I found myself saying, "I knew part of the reason you were with Missy and Krystal was you were doing drugs with them."

"No," he replied.

His answer surprised me. Why couldn't Art admit the part drugs played in his life to me?

"Saturday there's a fund-raiser for Jack Davis in the city I want to take you and the kids to," he said. "I have to go to pay the band. I'm afraid Davis won't come up with the $500 I promised them; that will be my contribution to Davis. You know what would really be boss—if you still have your nurse costume, it would be so funny if you wore it to the party. Everyone has heard I was in the hospital. If we go looking like you're my nurse, people will come up to me and say, oh, I heard you've been sick!"

It made me uneasy that Art was so conscious of feeling ill he wanted to draw attention to it. I didn't wear the costume.

Jack Davis had been accused recently of conspiracy to commit election fraud as one of the San Francisco 49er Ballpark Five, prompting the fund-raiser. On Saturday, Art put on a San Francisco Giants shirt, and under it another T-shirt: "Deep Trout" (a play on the famous 1972 porn film *Deep Throat*) printed beneath a large fish leaping out of a stream.

We took Aaron, Cal, and a couple of their buddies to the party, which was held on the rooftop of a building in downtown San Francisco. Art was quite sober. After paying the band, he stripped off his Giants shirt to reveal the Deep Trout shirt, and we danced with the floor to ourselves and an audience. Then he walked me over to the edge of the building, and as I resisted, pretended to try to push me off. "This is like I'm forcing you, like in *Green Door*," Art smiled. "What an uptight bunch of people!"

"I know, no one else is dancing," I said. "It was funny when you peeled off your shirt."

"I know all the moves, Simone. Your daddy knows all the moves."

Jack Davis looked grim. Art had a brief tete-a-tete with him, while I kept a casual eye on the kids.

"Davis is so disappointed," Art said as we were leaving. "He thought he'd get enough mileage from the ballpark thing to be able to run for mayor."

"*Mayor?* How could he have thought that?"

"I know. I told him he was dreaming."

I drove the kids back to Marin. "What did you guys think of the party?" I asked.

"It was O.K. Kinda boring, though," Aaron said.

A few miles up the road Cal piped up from the back seat, "Heather Hunter is my Dad's girlfriend!"

Heather Hunter was a young black porn star who had appeared at the O'Farrell late that February. I started to worry that if Cal knew about her, she was more than a one-night stand.

"If Heather Hunter is your Dad's girlfriend, do you think I'd be driving you chumps around?" I said.

"He's only kidding," Aaron said nervously.

When we were back, I mentioned it. Art said, "Cal—Cal will do anything to get you. Do you know what he did to me the other day? He came up right in back of me when I was resting and opened up a can so it popped right in my ear."

Maybe Heather is out of his life by now, I thought. A successful porn star wasn't likely to become one of Art's steady girlfriends anyway. He liked being the star.

"Happy?" Art asked when I got back. "Did you have a good time?"

"Yes." I beamed.

"Want anything else?"

"More of the same."

"I'm crazy about you. You're my woman. But I can never let you know that, I have to keep you guessing," he said. Do you know how many times I've tried not to love you? I can't not love you. . . . You stood by me even though everyone told you not to. I'm so glad you did. You know all those girls at the O'Farrell thought you were crazy."

"What do they know? I've always wanted you."

"In fact, just about everybody thinks you're crazy for loving me," he continued, "everyone except maybe Vince."

Why were Jim and the rest of the O'Farrell crowd now telling Art I was crazy for loving him? Art valued Jim's opinion more than anyone else's. I had thought Jim liked me, even if it was only because Art did fewer drugs when he was with me. Was there a reason Jim would prefer that I wasn't with Art?

Since the accident at Ocean Beach six weeks earlier, Art had been very ill. As he became weaker and more incapacitated by alcohol and drugs, Jim's opening to seize control of their business was growing wider and wider.

But that Saturday night we were happy, and I was blissfully hanging on Art's every word.

"Would you sign a cohabitation agreement, and live with me, be my woman?" he asked. "I've been trying to get Jim and his girlfriend to do that."

"Sure, I'll do it. I want to be with you, Art." I gave him a kiss and we walked outside in the moonlight. I felt such enchantment and hope.

~

In the morning, we watched the pair of ducks he had adopted glide serenely across the pool. "Art, can I bring my cat over?" I asked. "If I'm going to be staying with you I can't leave her in the city."

"It's not a good idea. I'm going to be taking off here pretty soon for the Hunter Thompson run and I'm not going to be around."

"Last night you were talking about *living together.*"

"I'm afraid you're too jealous."

I glared.

"Hey, take it easy. Do you know you have beautiful eyes. Take it easy, we'll make it. You need more sex," he said, pulling me down into the bed to try out yet another new move.

Half an hour later he asked, "So you really want to live here, do you?"

"I'll live with you, but it's only going to work if you're committed to making it work."

The phone rang and Art picked it up. "It's personal," he said, and went into Jasmine's room to take the call. I picked up the receiver anyway. It was *Heather Hunter.*

"Heather, this is Simone, Art's girlfriend."

In time to hear this, Art picked up the receiver. He walked back into the bedroom furious, "GET YOUR CLOTHES AND GET OUT. You and I are FINISHED."

"It was GODDAMN CONVENIENT for you for me to take off work and be up here for a whole week taking care of you when you were sick, WASN'T IT. But when some other girl calls you pretend I'm not your woman. I bet *Heather Hunter* wouldn't cook for your children!"

"I wouldn't expect it."

"You BASTARD!"

Art loved flirting—on the phone or off—he liked women to want him. In the heat of the moment, my tolerance evaporated. Why couldn't he respect me enough to just fool around on the side—not in my face?

Art walked out the front door, and I took a good long while packing my clothes. When I carried my bag out, he was sitting in his van silent and completely livid. Since he was typically unrepentant and wasn't talking, I got into my car and turned off sunny Mohawk Avenue, without the faintest suspicion I would never be there again.

Vince told me Art and Jim left for Colorado with a group of people and film equipment in two Winnebagos early Sunday morning, taking a red convertible Jim had restored to present to Hunter Thompson. Just two women went along: a dancer who had been at the theater for a couple of years, and a new girl, Julie Bajo. Once they were on the road Thompson's attorney called the O'Farrell to say, "Please don't send a caravan to Aspen. We're trying to avoid a circus-like atmosphere!"

Hunter had been charged with five felony counts of possession of illegal drugs and dynamite, and a fifteen-misdemeanor count of sexual assault against Gail Palmer-Slater. Tuesday, one of the drug possession charges against him was dismissed. Outside the courthouse, Hunter was photographed smiling and flashing victory signs. A few days later, all charges against him were dropped.

By the end of the week the brothers' caravan was back, and the Aspen papers found their way into Vince's office, with an article titled "Hunter's Friends, Fans Show Support." In the pictures, Jim and O'Neill looked half-bored, the rest were smiling. Art was with a brunette I didn't recognize, dangling one leg over his shoulder.

Vince told me to give both of the dancers who went to Colorado free stage fees for June and July.

"Did they film anything?" I asked Vince.

"No."

Over the last year the blocks of the Tenderloin surrounding Vince's building had become more and more dangerous. As a deterrent, a group of Guardian Angels with their red berets and young macho presence moved into an office in the basement and watched over the area, and the brothers started contributing to them regularly. A homeless shelter opened up in the big building across the street, so now a line of people waited to get in with their carts and blankets, while the usual mix of street hustlers, drug dealers and crazies hung out on our side of Polk, and as the population increased, the sound and feel of the street grew more and more reckless. Occasionally someone would yell "bitch," curse at me, try to sell me drugs—or once, even a hot case of motor oil. I chose times that seemed safest, when I could park close to the entrance and run a shorter gauntlet. I dashed in and out of Vince's office fast. The money I was making as a fulltime secretary was so much less than what I had earned as a dancer, I had to supplement it.

In the middle of the afternoon, Art called me at work. "Do you still have all those costumes?" he asked.

"You never get rid of those," I replied.

That evening at my apartment, I told him about the latest crisis at my job.

"You can still work," Art said. He meant I could come back and dance at the O'Farrell.

"Sorry, I can't do that."

"You got something against making money?" he sounded surprised. "You're the best!"

That was quite a compliment, but I took it in stride, "I know. But I'm too old to be working as a dancer."

"No, you're not!" he said.

"Do you have any idea how hard that last year was? I can't work at the theater when I'm your girlfriend. I'll go into the O'Farrell with you but otherwise I'm never going in there again. Ever."

"I know you're my girlfriend, Simone. How could I ever forget it!"

Since I wanted more power in our relationship, I could no longer maintain the mental distance from him that working at his theater required. Being back there for even an hour or two would have sent me stalking into the poolroom screaming at him the first time he did anything to test me. Art didn't realize that, because that theater was his world. For me, it was almost as though the O'Farrell walls had sealed themselves up and had become impassable, like in a fairy tale, and I stood permanently outside them.

Art was offended and hurt that I wouldn't come back, and I was insulted by his only staying for a couple of hours that evening.

In a few days, I had a dream. It was night in my apartment and I was alone. I heard a knock at my door, as often over the years Art would come over late at night and knock like that. Only this time, I knew he was dead, trying to knock and knock and knock, and couldn't get back in.

All summer long I felt edgy. I had the terrible sense that something awful—I didn't know what—was going to happen. Most of the time I felt dead serious, withdrawn, and braced for something bad to happen. Later that summer I had the dream again.

Just after Labor Day, I started a new full-time job, at an electrical engineering company. It took a couple of months to learn the job, and by that time I knew it was the worst fit in the world for me. Ironically, just around the corner was a massive orange and black billboard endorsing "Dianne (Feinstein) for Governor."

∾

Wearing a monkey tooth bracelet and a straw coolie hat, Art took a little .22 pistol out of his fanny pack, and laid it on my desk with great care. Then he rested his eyes on it keenly for a moment, as though the weapon was a friend he was acknowledging a bond with, so it wouldn't fail him. Never before had I seen him pack a gun. I felt a little uneasy.

"I saw Hunter last night," Art said. "It was so funny, I surprised him—I picked him up and threw him over a couch and hurt his back! He was so glad to see us when we went up to Colorado!"

Art's poor health had slowed him down from bouncing back and forth between girlfriends. Even though we hadn't been together for a couple of months, there was a warm bond of feeling between us that made me feel at ease, even though I had so many reasons to be upset with him. Making love reanimated that feeling.

His breathing still sounded bad, and he seemed weak. After breakfast, he pulled out a prescription bottle. "I'm taking thyroid now," he said. "I was feeling so tired. Nick said I need to take this for awhile, because of the hypothermia. I have trouble remembering to take it, though."

"How are you feeling?"

"I'm fine now. I'm a lot better."

"I went to see *Henry and June*, have you seen it?" I asked.

"No. The director's a real good friend of mine, though."

"We should go see it. It's good, I wouldn't mind seeing it again," I said. "I know you like Miller." Art had told me the most beautiful words ever written about love were Miller's description of feelings for Mona in *Tropic of Cancer*.

The look Art gave me told me he would never see that movie with me. I wondered why.

"The neighborhood around Vince's is much worse now," I said. "I hate going down there."

"Don't ever go there at night," he cautioned. "What you should do is pull up in front of the O'Farrell and drop his stuff off there. It's just too dangerous."

"I can't do that, though," I said. "I need to get in there."

"You heard about Rocky getting stabbed in the neck, didn't you?"

"No! When did that happen?"

"It happened months ago, back in December. You never heard about it? There are a lot of crazy, vicious people out there! Rocky packs a .38, too. I know he had it on him, but he didn't use it."

Jim and Art's cousin Rocky was still doing janitorial work at the theater after hours and saw Vince a lot. Vince should have told me about anything that serious. He probably didn't say anything because he didn't want me to quit.

"What you do is get a small gun. Go to the Gun Exchange, I know the owner, she will help you," Art urged. "Get a .22 pistol and keep it in a jacket pocket like an A's jacket, something like that. And if anybody hassles you, you shoot them, right through the jacket. And you walk away from it. Nobody cares if there's one less swine. Nobody's going to look into it. You just get out of there. And it's self-defense."

Art must have had a strong sense of danger to be packing a weapon himself, and to tell me to get a gun. He left me with such a sense of urgency, I felt I should learn how to defend myself.

Within a couple of weeks, Art spent the night again, and we felt more relaxed together. "It's so funny at work now," he said. "Jeff, and Mez and Jim—they want to burrow in and forget they're pornographers. It's like they're ashamed of the business and the shows—I'm not. Sleaze is my life!"

"Someday I'm going to take you with me forever, Simone. We'll always be together. You see, eventually you're going to be my wife—in a few years. Jasmine asks me, Where's Simone? She misses you."

In the morning he asked, "How do you like your new job?"

"I'm already bored. I'd like to go into business for myself."

"I think you should. You know if you're in business for yourself, you've got to steal," Art said. "I saw it with my in-laws when they opened up a gallery. I told them, but they didn't listen. And I watched them lose their business. It was a beautiful little business, too. The government expects you to take ten percent off the top. *We* take twenty-five percent!"

"We've got a low nut, you know. Business is good."

The O'Farrell was quite a cash cow. Most customers paid for their tickets in cash. The dancers paid their stage fees in cash, too. Even on the official books, in the late 80's and the beginning of the 90's, the O'Farrell was grossing over $3.3 million a year. That twenty-five percent skim of the actual gross was nothing to laugh at.

Art covered most of his daily living expenses with cash. Unless he was around to personally collect it, he couldn't count on getting his full share of the cash he needed to provide for his children, and for himself. No wonder it was never practical for him to leave town for any length of time. And entering a long term treatment plan for alcoholism would have seemed impossible to him—until the time came when he felt drinking could cost him his life.

Although the skim was invisible, and the O'Farrell records were immaculate after his death, Art's share no longer went in his direction. How convenient for Jim Mitchell that Art's children would have no way of touching any of this sizable hidden cash flow.

"It's hard to say what Jim spends his money on," Art added. "He's got bricks in his toilet to save on his water bill!"

What he said about the cash skimming was interesting, but I had other concerns. That morning I had no idea of the significance of what he had just told me. I had no notion what was brewing inside Jim Mitchell's mind.

~

These nights Art spent with me led me to believe he was on the verge of coming back. In a few days, I checked with Justine. She said he was fucking around with Julie Bajo, the new girl who had gone on the Colorado trip. I wanted to scream.

"Are they getting high together—drinking and doing coke?"

"Yeah. I'd say both."

"What's she like?"

"Honey, she's dangerous."

"*Dangerous?* What do you mean, *dangerous?*"

"She's kind of like Missy, only more intelligent. Julie knows just what to say and how to say it, where you can see the wheels turning. But he'll always come back to you," Justine said. "No matter what. He'll always come back. You guys have been going on too long together for that to change. Don't even worry about it!"

Charles was thinking about using one of the dancers who was working in the newly remodeled Cine Stage with Julie in a film, so he and Rita went to the O'Farrell to see a show they were doing, advertised as "Sweet Potato Pie."

"In the show they smeared all this disgusting food over themselves, chocolate syrup, whip cream, cheese whiz, and sprinkles, then one of them got down and used a cucumber, then a carrot as a dildo. After that they put a test tube up one girl's pussy, poured Kool-Aid in, and sucked it out with a straw," Rita explained. "At the end of the show they sponged off in a bucket and went out to sit on laps."

"After getting so sticky?"

"I know. When I went backstage afterwards, Julie was telling the other girls to go wash off the tray of props for the next show, and they gave her a look, like this bitch really likes to throw her weight around."

Even though I was seeing Art occasionally, and talking to Vince on the phone, the whole Mitchell Brothers' world had become distant. Was it still the same, or was it ever so surely changing?

Sometimes I felt I would find out something had happened to Art while I was at work. Other times I imagined him driving up in the street and yelling in his outrageous drawl I loved so much, for me to come with him.

Chapter 20:
Almost Like John Lennon

DECEMBER 26, 1990

Over the weekend I worked on the January schedule, so Vince could have it around Christmas. When I carried the schedule chart into Vince's building, some guy muttered, "I ought to slit that bitch's throat!"

I had abandoned Art's suggestion that I carry a gun when I went down there at night. When I was finally on the range I hated the sensation of firing my new weapon—it felt so overpowering and menacing in my hand. I pulled the magazine out, and put it away somewhere I thought was safe.

I thought Art would be occupied with his children, but the day after Christmas he called me. No matter what was going on in his life then, I wanted to reach out to him.

When Art got to my place, he was shaken. After laying down his .22 pistol, he said, "This weird thing happened. Just as I was leaving the theater, on my way out to the cab, some guy out in front of the building called out to me 'Artie!' Some—real creepy type of guy. It was a good thing there was this great big bouncer standing there who would have *just killed* the guy, 'cause there's no telling what he would have done! I got in the cab and came over here. It was so creepy. It was almost like just before they shot John Lennon!"

At the time, it sounded to me like he was just feeling paranoid. Later, I realized Art had to have felt a free-floating sense of danger and anxiety. Somebody was going to kill him, but who? Art would never

311

have allowed himself to suspect that his brother, whom he respected and trusted so much, would harm him.

All the years I worked at the O'Farrell, they never employed bouncers. Were they hired in 1990 to police and protect the mellow yuppie customers, or to provide a little extra muscle in case Jim wanted to overpower Art?

In the morning he was in a clear, relaxed mood. "Karen has just been acting totally nuts. And she's carrying a gun," he said. "Do you remember that letter my lawyer had me start sending, saying she should begin seeking employment?"

"Yes." Much as I disliked Karen for interfering with my relationship with Artie long after their divorce, it was hard to picture her going to work right now with five children and her twins only two years old.

"Karen's totally crazed behind it. She calls me up and says, 'Art, I've finally found the perfect career. I'm going to be a rock star!'"

"That's ridiculous! Has she ever done any singing before?"

"No. Never. So to prepare for it, she's hanging out at a club in Marin, the Sweetwater. But I think there's some other reason she's going there."

"She's driving a Jaguar now, and she's been calling the cops on me a lot," he said. "This one night I was at my house, fixing steak for the kids and Karen drives up in front and leans on her horn. Normally she picks the kids up at 6:00 p.m., but it was only 5:00. So I go out and ask her, can she come back in an hour after the kids eat dinner. She says, 'Absolutely not,' drives off, and calls the cops. So, in a little while the doorbell rings. I go to the front door, and because I had been cooking, I still had this little paring knife in my hand. And this cop says 'OK, first of all, *drop the knife!*' I busted out laughing, 'cause it was such a *little knife!* Then the cop asked the kids, 'What time do you go back to your mom's?' They all yelled out, '6:00 O'CLOCK!'"

"Why on earth is she calling the cops?" I asked.

"She's all uptight about her alimony ending, so she's taking me to court again. There will be a hearing. I'm not worried, about it, though. I made this *real cool move*. I'm hiring *Meredith* to represent me on it!" Art's first wife Meredith had a law practice in the East Bay.

"Are you sure that's a good idea? Wouldn't it be better to have someone do it who's impartial?" I asked.

"She says she'd do it for next to nothing. She's the perfect person. *No one* hates Karen more. Nobody understands my position, though, my wanting her to do it."

I thought it was craziness; there had been so much bitterness between them all in the past. Meredith's changing her kids' last name to Bradford from Mitchell a couple of years earlier was a sign all was not forgiven. What if something went wrong and Art lost? And if he won, having *her* involved would make Karen even more hostile. Art loved complicating situations, igniting fireworks, and stepping back to watch what would happen, but this sounded like real stupidity.

I spent December 31st with Rita and Charles, and went back on the 1st to share the Southern meal of ham hocks and black-eyed peas Charles had cooked, guaranteed to cast a charm of good luck onto the New Year.

JANUARY 2, 1991

At 9:00 p.m. Art called me, "Dress up for me, I want you to dress all in red."

Red. The color of passion, and fire, of Valentines, Christmas and heart's blood. Why red? Why, that last evening, red?

I didn't have anything much that was red. I put on a black silk chemise and red heels. Then I remembered that first afternoon, long ago. "Red is your color. You're so much of a woman," Art had said. "How about a kiss?"

In the street below, I heard a cab, then his footsteps climbed my stairs. As seductive as ever, Art embraced me. "*I told you* I wanted you in *red*. I never want you to wear black *again!*"

"I don't have anything red except—a real conservative dress."

"Go put it on!"

"I have your Christmas present," I said. I had just gotten some pictures back from a photographer, and had picked out two of them. In one I had posed on my black iron and brass bed in Art's favorite O'Farrell look—black lingerie and the S/M finery I'd had made for the Ultra Room by Jay Marsten of Hedonic Engineering—an elegant black

Christmas, 1990

leather collar and a red and black braided whip. In the other shot, I wore a black silk dress, smiling under an eighteenth century print in my living room, "Harlot's Progress," that I found in Rome. Lined up below it were a few books I'd chosen tongue-in-cheek: *Eros & Evil,* Hunter Thompson's *Generation of Swine,* Ken Kesey's *Demon Box,* Hawthorne's *The Scarlet Letter,* a couple of books by Sade I'd never been able to get through, *Marat/Sade,* and *The Adventures of Tom Jones.*

Ironically, in the Mission I had come across some stickers of Pancho Villa—an infamous bandit with bandoliers around both shoulders, holding a rifle. I had stuck one rifle-toting bandit on each side of the back of the double hinged frame, to decorate it. Then I had wrapped the frame in red foil.

"Don't you want to open your Christmas present?" I asked.

"No."

I moved towards my closet to change to the red dress and Art said, "You know this is a game, don't you?"

"Of course."

In a minute when I came back in red, he said, "I want you to dress conservative now!"

There was an urgency to the way Art was acting, that I had never seen before. He was so anxious. "You've proved it to me, you're the nicest person I've ever known, Simone. You've paid your dues. I'm coming back to you," he said. "I'll always come back to you. With *your* kind of luck, you'll have to put up with me all your life!"

This was exactly what I needed to hear, and I wanted so much to believe he was coming back, right away.

"I've always loved you," he said. "But I'm not like you. I can't do all the things you do, so I can never let you know."

"Well, you just do other things."

"How can you love me?"

"It's always different with you. You have a million moves."

He cackled with laughter. "*That's* funny. You've got a million moves, dude! How much do you love me?" he asked.

"More than anything, more than myself."

"I'm crazy about you," he said. "I'd love to marry you and make you my wife, but somehow I don't think you'd be up for that."

I laughed nervously. I wanted to marry him, but there was something edgy about him where I wasn't so sure it was possible right then. "Art, I've missed you so much I've been sleeping on the couch because I can't bear to be in this bed alone."

"Well, welcome home." He folded his arms around me. "Have you learned your lesson by now?"

"Yes," I said.

"You know what, you never did anything wrong, Simone, you never have!"

It was moving but mysterious to me, that Art was clarifying our relationship. Later I realized that because he knew he was in danger, he wanted to make his feelings very clear, once and for all. That night he said "I love you" over and over again.

In the morning, he told me, "I haven't been home in three days, I don't want to see that bitch who used to think she owned me!"

I didn't ask if he meant Julie or Karen.

"I have to go now, here's my work number, call me," I said. "I can fix you dinner tonight. I left your present right here."

"I have something for you too, do you want to wait so we can open them together?"

"No. Open it now."

I lingered a couple of minutes with him, and stared at him for a long, long moment, then I left.

When I got back to my apartment at 5:30 p.m. I found a note:

"Simone, Tx for the gift. You are a beautiful woman. I love you. XXOO, AJ."

At 1:00 a.m., he was back. "I'm gonna bring you some money for booze. You better *never, ever* run out of this," he said, sipping some vodka out of the freezer. "And I'm gonna give you some money to buy a humidifier."

"A humidifier?"

"Yeah. I don't know why, but at night I have trouble breathing."

"This rock and roll group came in tonight. I had to laugh! They were just overwhelmed. The girls were doing a little show—they put chocolate chips on their pussy, they were trying. I was so bored. It was silly!"

"There's a fortune to be made in L.A.! My brother can't see it, but there is. I want to open a club down there. Would you move down there with me?"

"Sure."

"I'm tired. This is an old tiger," Art said. "I'm forty-five years old."

I felt more secure, since it was the second night in a row, that he had come back. When it was light, he made love to me, for the last time.

"We're going to have a party for Crumb," he said. "We're calling it The Crumbs are Leaving the Country Party, so I have to get to work by 9:30 this morning. We're having a meeting."

He put on a new sweatshirt underground cartoonist R. Crumb had designed for them—Tiger Woman in a crouch, darting out her tongue. "We're trying to figure out the right color to print this on the shirts."

Once we got in my car, he seemed more distant.

"Could we go away somewhere together, for a couple of days?" I asked. "I've been working six days a week!"

"Well, yeah, we could. I've been thinking about making a little run down to Zihuatanejo."

"Call me," I said.

317

"I will." He gave me a kiss and got out of the car. At the front of the O'Farrell, he began talking to some new blonde who was trying to peer in through the mirrored glass door, waiting to get in.

In the middle of January, Rita's husband Charles flew to Las Vegas for a video trade show, and went to the Adult Video News awards presentation. Art was there with Jim, because they were being inducted into the Porno Hall of Fame.

"I bought them a drink," Charles told me. "Art was real fucked up, more fucked up than I've ever seen him. Jim looked so uptight, and dressed in this business suit, he looked like he was Art's lawyer, or his accountant. When they got up on stage, Art chewed up this piece of paper—it had been the award statement they gave him; he spat it out at the crowd. Then he said a few words. No one could understand what he was saying, or could make any sense out of why he did that. Later on I heard he'd done it to insult this porn distributor who's being prosecuted, who said he'll get out of the X-rated business if the cops will let him off, instead of fighting the charges he's up against."

"We were watching a legend, Simone. I've always admired Art's whole attitude of contempt and wildness!"

Three days after the AVN awards ceremony, the Gulf War began. Everyone's mood was anxious. How truly obscene it was that people were dying in another war.

At the end of January I asked Vince, "What's Art up to, is he back with Julie?"

"You've got it. She's in the neighborhood."

"Oh, God. The last time I saw him, he was saying he was taking me to Mexico!"

"Well, you know, in between the partying here and there, he's got so much going on!" Vince said in an upbeat tone, with admiration.

"Is he living with her?" I asked.

"Oh, no, they're maintaining separate residences. Julie just took some time off on her own because she's been working here so much."

∽

Through the first three weeks of February whenever my phone rang, I screened my calls. I was thinking, if I ignore Art for awhile, he'll get bored with Julie faster and come back to me sooner. But now, I could feel a barrier between us that had never been there before. I felt paralyzed and very depressed. I knew he was trying to reach me, and I wanted him badly, but he was only making a lukewarm effort.

No one I knew could tell me what was going on with him. Justine's number was disconnected. At this point, calling his house myself and getting another woman would have sent me over the edge. I thought about just driving over to his place some evening, but that night Missy Manners had walked into the Moraga house and tried to kick in his bedroom door put me off showing up unannounced at Artie's. If I had picked February 27, the evening Jim would choose to drop by, who knows what might have happened.

Art was just about due to come back to me, and I knew he would make a serious attempt to communicate when he was ready.

∽

Although I didn't see Art during the last few weeks of his life and would have only one more conversation with him during that time, I have based the following account of what took place on all I have read and heard since, and my own understanding of the players and events. I believe—in all my heart and mind—that this is what happened:

Art had to have been experiencing a whirlwind of emotions and a very real, increasing sense of danger. Looking back at what his January and February were like, it isn't surprising he wasn't communicating very well.

Since the court hearing on his visitation rights and the custody of his children was fast approaching, Art wanted to create a good impression in court and disprove Karen's charges he was an alcoholic. He was trying to quit drinking on his own and having withdrawal symptoms that were scary—because he was too physically dependent to dry out by himself. He was terrified of being hospitalized to detox, and afraid of being forced out of the business by Jim if he was gone for any amount of time.

During Jim's trial, some witnesses claimed there was talk about getting Art to go into a treatment program during January and February of 1991. No one making these claims understood alcoholism as a disease or took any positive steps to help. They said they complained about his drinking, made threats, and scolded Art.

As Art's alcoholism worsened, Jim had aligned himself with other upper management at the O'Farrell who had become accustomed to supporting his ideas and actions. If Art had detoxed and wanted to take an active role in the business again, Jim would have had to give up part of the control he had been enjoying for some time. Becoming sole owner of their business interests looked far more attractive.

Art signed his will naming Jim as his executor on February 14, 1991, less than two weeks before he would be killed.

Although things were uglier with Karen and she was taking Art to court, that had been her cyclical way of pressuring him for more money. At that moment, Karen was ready to fight—her alimony was scheduled to end on February 28.

On Tuesday, February 19, Art appeared in Contra Costa County court with Meredith, who was disqualified from representing him at Karen's request. The judge also granted the change of venue to Marin

County that Karen asked for. The date for hearing Karen's request for a restraining order against Art was set for the very next day—February 20. With no time to get another lawyer, Art represented himself, and lost heavily. His visitation rights with Aaron, Jasmine, and Cal were restricted to eight hours a weekend, to be supervised by a court-appointed monitor. After the hearing Art cried and held his head in his hands, saying, "I'm finished."

~

Over in San Francisco, Jim was completely swept up in a new project. After more than twenty years of being partners with Artie, in the last few weeks Jim had launched his first solo business venture, a newspaper called *War News*.

Jim funded *War News* to present the anti-war view of the Gulf War crisis, and leased a building in North Beach for its office. The first issue of *War News* was printed on January 31. It was a single 11" x 17" sheet with articles by Warren Hinckle and Bob Callahan on one of its sides, a cartoon strip by Dan O'Neill on the other. All three were on the staff, and a network of their writer/cartoonist acquaintances were contributors. *War News* had a rhetorical bent and an old fashioned severe look, like something a newsboy would hand out on a street corner in the 1900s. It would only have two issues. The second issue was printed after the Gulf War ended and Jim was in Marin County Jail for shooting Art to death.

~

Because the office where I worked was relatively close, I started driving home at lunchtime. Some days when I was home my phone would ring, be picked up by my answering machine, and there would be no message. I knew it was Art, hoping I would be around at his disposal—but I didn't know how ill he was, and how troubled his life had become.

FEBRUARY 25, 1991

Monday I drove home for lunch and the phone rang. This time I picked it up.

"Simone," Art said in a deeply intoxicated voice.

"Oh, hi. How are you?"

"Get another boyfriend. You like it too much. Some guys would die for you. You need some dick."

He was mad because I hadn't been answering my phone. But never had he said anything like "Some guys would die for you."

"I don't want another boyfriend," I said. "We've been over this before, many times. I love you very much, I want you."

"I've got a girlfriend."

"What, this Julie person?"

"Yeah."

"Art, you go through them."

"Yeah, you know what, you're right. I do. I'll probably always be with you. Sex, with you. . . ."

"You know, women, when they mature, when they love somebody they care about them, they want them, they don't want—it's not a question of dick! You want to be with the person you love," I said. "And that's what's happened with me."

"I'm moving out of the country, I'm moving to Mexico."

"You're not moving to Mexico, your kids are here!"

"Cal really *got me* Saturday," Art said. "He said, Dad, I sprained my finger. So I took him to the closest hospital, Kaiser-Marin, I took him there to the emergency room. I said, 'Do you take Blue Cross.' And they said they couldn't take it, so it was gonna cost $118. I said 'Money isn't one of my hassles,' and I slapped the money down. Then we had to wait *forever*, they just weren't taking care of Cal, and finally I went up and complained and they arrested me for disturbing the peace. They said I was drunk, but I wasn't. I wasn't drunk *then*, but I'm drunk *now*! But Saturday I wasn't. I didn't drink for ten days. They charged me with possession of drugs, but I told them that I didn't drive, that I took a cab there, so they couldn't search—they won't be able to get me on *that*. Then they put me in Marin County jail for four hours. In Marin they take your shoes."

"Why do they take your shoes?"

"Because you could *kill* someone with your shoes. They put me in this crowded cell, with a whole bunch of guys. There were two great big guys in there, one black guy and one Mexican, and they'd been fighting. One of them had four-inch tracks from shooting coke."

It was a little hard to follow what happened at the jail, and my mind was on how to break through the words, and touch his heart.

"I told the prisoners in the holding cell I was Artie Mitchell, Mitchell Brothers, and they said 'Hey, man really, we got nothing but respect for you,' and they all lined up to shake my hand!"

"When do I get to see you again? I love you. I want to see you so bad," I told him. "I miss you so much."

"How long are you going to be there?"

"I'm supposed to go back to work. I got you a humidifier," I said. "The expensive kind."

"Oh. . . . Say—Would you move to Mexico with me?"

"Yes."

"That's more like it!"

Art sounded so extraordinarily high and I sounded so sober. For the last five minutes, I had wanted to say, "I need you," but I was afraid it would make him paranoid. I didn't say it.

"So when are you coming over?" I asked.

I could hear someone interrupting on the other end.

"Hold on," Art said to me. "You'll get your chance."

∾

Something in his voice was very disturbing and urgent. When I got back to work, I phoned Vince. "Art called me, just called me and he sounds—is he real strung-out?"

"Gee, I hope not," Vince said. "Where was he calling from?"

"I don't know, I could hear people in the background. It sounded like a bar—it wasn't the O'Farrell or his house."

"I wonder if he was calling from the War News Club. . . . It's at Broadway and Montgomery. I wonder if Artie was calling from there—Jim is on his way down there. I hope they don't get into another argument. Art's really on a roll this time!"

"Did he go on a vacation?" I asked. "Has he gone to Mexico recently?" I figured Art would have been too paranoid to go during the Gulf War, because of what had been on the news about strict airport security.

"He hasn't gone to Mexico in the last week," Vince said, "but to me it seems he's the type of guy who's perpetually on vacation." That didn't sound like Vince—it sounded like Jim's point of view. Jim, who never went on vacations.

"I always hate to say anything, but I always assume you've just seen Art," Vince said.

"It varies. Mostly he's been getting my machine and then hanging up."

"Two or three weeks ago Art got really out of hand and fired some shots off in the poolroom, into the ceiling."

"Did it happen while the shows were going on?"

"No, at 2:00 or 3:00 in the morning. Jim got really mad at him then and said he had to stay away from the theater for six months."

Six months! Art would never stay away from his beloved O'Farrell for six months. Even if he was willing to, he couldn't, because he wouldn't get his fair share of the money. If Art was acting out in frustration, it was hardly surprising.

"He told me he was moving to Mexico and asked me to go with him, but I can't imagine him moving away from here."

"Well, he's been on this roller coaster ride in the last—especially the last two or three weeks, I've never seen it like this. Nobody knows what to do, and everybody's afraid something terrible is gonna happen."

We said goodbye, making a plan to have a drink together Friday. I had never heard so much concern in Vince's voice.

That night I talked to Rita and Charles, who had heard about the *War News* Club from a cartoonist he was working on a movie project with. Charles thought the brothers were going to have an opening party in a few days, on Thursday evening. Since Rita would be working, I could tag along with Charles to conveniently run into Art. "I'll be like the bad fairy," I joked to Rita. "Remember in the fairy tale, the uninvited guest who casts a spell on everyone?"

"It should be fun, Simone. Did you read the horoscopes for this week in the paper?"

"What did it say—better yet, read Art's. Did you know his sign is the same as Jim's?"

"Sagittarius—For many Sadges, the upcoming full moon floodlights the gunfight in the O.K. corral, careerwise. Either a breakthrough comes or else you walk. Whichever, whatever—you've seen the light. What's next? A whole new set of challenges. What did you expect?"

∾

Tuesday I wrote a steamy message for Art in a card, and mailed it to Mohawk Avenue on my way back to work after lunch.

At home in Marin, that day Artie got a disturbing call from Dennis Roberts, the attorney who had represented the brothers for years, telling him Jim wanted to end their partnership.

Art knew he would never receive his fair share of the true value of the business—to which he had every right. It had been his charisma, his warmth and his outrageous spirit of free-love, which he had all his life, that had done so much to get the business off the ground and maintain its mystique. Just when Art was feeling so much pain and sadness, Jim delivered a very cruel blow.

FEBRUARY 27, 1991

Wednesday, like millions of other Americans, I watched the news on television, since they were announcing that the Gulf War had just ended. I felt very tired. At 9:30 p.m. I fell asleep listening to the soft rain, unaware that the love of my life was just about to be shot to death.

While Lisa waited in the kitchen of their house near Ocean Beach, Jim Mitchell took a .22 rifle out of his gun case in the basement, and loaded it. He put on a shoulder holster, and placed a .38 Smith and Wesson pistol inside. Jim was an excellent shot, but just to be safe he stuck an extra box of .22 shells into his jacket pocket. Laying the rifle in the backseat of his new Ford Explorer van, he pulled away from 47th Avenue and headed over the Golden Gate Bridge for Marin County. Alone at the Ocean Beach house, Lisa did not warn anyone of this certain showdown—perhaps she was hoping that Jim would get the drop on Art and come out unharmed. Taking the Paradise Drive exit, Jim drove slowly past 23 Mohawk Avenue, and parked three quiet blocks away.

Hiding his rifle in an umbrella, Jim walked towards Art's little suburban house alone in the rain. Art's car was parked in the driveway; with a pocketknife, Jim punctured two of its tires.

Art had always been a fanatic about turning lights off—Jim knew that, since they had shared the Moraga house for two years as recently as 1988. Most nights that Art spent at home, he went to bed early, especially since he had become so ill. Predictably, the lights were off that evening, too. And, as usual, the front door was unlocked.

Jim hadn't gone to the house often; the last time he had been there was a few months earlier in the summer, for Art's daughter Liberty's birthday party. The floor plan was tight, and the bedrooms small. Artie's bed always stood just beyond his bedroom door, which was straight down the hall leading to the long living room, where Jim would begin firing to flush Art out of the bedroom.

Jim threw the front door open loud, then a door leading to the kitchen, startling Art and Julie, who had been in bed for several minutes talking. Without saying a word, Jim started firing the .22 Winchester rifle—the quietest firearm he could have chosen, without using a silencer.

Art and Julie both jumped up and switched on the light. She handed him a pair of green sweat pants to wear, but could find nothing but a studded belt for him to carry for protection. He picked up a half-empty Heineken bottle. Julie stepped into the far bedroom closet, then grabbed the phone and took it in with her, and dialed 911. The first minute of Julie's 911 call recorded her cries and the sharp, light cracks of five .22 gunshots, and would become crucial evidence. It was the last minute of Art's life.

Art stepped into the dark narrow hallway, unarmed. "What's going on?" he asked. "Who's out there?"

From the closet Julie sobbed, "Artie, don't go out there!" but it was too late. In the darkness of the living room, Jim was silent. Then bullets tore into Artie, aimed to kill. Grouping all but one of his eight shots tightly, within body-mass range, Jim fired at his brother, hitting him three times. The first bullet hit his belly. The second lodged in his shoulder. The fatal shot struck his right upper eyelid and entered his brain. Art collapsed into the hall bathroom in a fetal position, one arm outstretched, several feet away from the bedroom.

After stuffing the smoking rifle down his pantleg, Jim went out the front door, bloodstains on his pants, carrying his umbrella overhead.

The rain fell heavier now, dark clouds gathering into a relentless storm. My love lay dead in a pool of his blood. My fondest dreams were over.

Chapter 21:
State of Art

FEBRUARY 28, 1991

Knowing nothing about Art having been shot to death the night before, in the rainy gray morning I went to work. Someone heard the news on the radio and phoned Charles, who verified it with the O'Farrell. Then Rita called me at 9:30 a.m. "NO. NO!" I started sobbing uncontrollably. Rita and Charles came down and took me out of there. I spent the next four days with them, deeply in shock. They kept watch over me twenty-four hours a day and extracted the gun from my apartment, afraid I was a potential suicide.

I had to make endless calls to the O'Farrell to attend the funeral. The theater had taken on the mentality of the Alamo under siege. Since the police were only a block away from Art's house at the time Julie made her 911 call, Jim was arrested immediately as he hobbled up the street with the rifle down his pants, trying to escape. The new sole owner of Mitchell Brothers' was in jail for murder.

I never did see Art's body—the Mitchells made that impossible— so Art's death didn't seem entirely real to me. Vince told me the family had gone up to see his body and maybe Artie looked *too bad for a funeral.* When I wanted to send flowers I got a party line response—the family would prefer donations to your favorite charity. "Art was my lover for ten years," I said. "He deserves some fucking flowers," my voice was cracking.

Friday morning Jim was arraigned, while Karen Mitchell sat in the courtroom wearing a 19th-century looking costume—widow's weeds and a long black veil. Karen told reporters she had come to show Jim that he was still loved. In a couple of weeks, she would make a trip to L.A. to sell her story.

That evening cartoonist Dan O'Neill dropped by Rita and Charles' apartment to talk. Dan had been crashing at the *War News* Club while he worked on the paper and was very worried about the paper ending. Earlier that day, Lisa had held Issue No. 2 of *War News* in Jim's Marin County jail window to cheer him up.

It stormed all weekend. Saturday one of the managers said they were nervous about the funeral because Karen had been packing a gun, but I finally got permission to be there with my friends.

Sunday, March 3, was overcast and rainy. Very stunned, not really believing Art was dead, I made a trip back to my apartment to dress in a black suit, colored scarf, red heels Art was fond of. Rita, Charles, and two other friends went with me to a funeral home in Art and Jim's hometown Antioch, an hour's drive east of San Francisco. Since the funeral started at 2:00 p.m., we got to Antioch at 12:00 p.m. so I could have a little privacy, and the sight of masses of flowers at the front of the chapel as "I Did It My Way" played on the muzak destroyed me.

"There's one thing that's important to me, Simone, and it's not love and it's not anything else. It's freedom," I could almost hear Art say. He led the most uncompromising, relentless life.

By coincidence I had chosen the same floral piece as Art's mother, a heart shaped out of red roses and white carnations. Next to mine, stood a spray of flowers from Marilyn Chambers.

We left for a coffee shop at 12:30 p.m., returning just before the ceremony began. The chapel was crowded with a large group of family, many teenagers, Jim's children, friends, O'Farrell management, and some of Art's other women: Meredith, Karen, Krystal, Julie, and Missy—who was expecting her second child. Jeff Armstrong, formerly in charge of the brothers' video business, was at the helm of the O'Farrell now that Jim was in jail. He had his hair cut like Al Pacino and wore dark glasses, like he had stepped off one of the billboards scattered all over town promoting *Godfather III.* My friends and I sat in the middle of the packed chapel next to one of the owners of the Century and his girlfriend, a former O'Farrell dancer from Argentina. I made one trip up to the front.

"I'm so very sorry," I said to Georgia Mae.

"Thanks for sticking with us to the end," she replied. Georgia was glad I hadn't gone to the press. Karen had already been on television Friday.

I spoke to Art's daughters, Liberty and Mariah. I didn't see his younger children. Across the room, Storm was talking to someone. Seeing Lisa, I thought, You know a lot more about this than you are saying. She still had Jim but where the fuck was Art—I couldn't imagine *him* wearing a white robe and playing a harp somewhere and being any too happy about it.

The ceremony was distressing and a large red velveteen bag now stood on the altar, containing Art's ashes. Of course, it would have been upsetting to everyone for his bullet-ridden body to have been there. Surely, it would have been tougher for many people to stand a few feet away from Artie's corpse and say affectionate things about Jim into the microphone, even with notes. But with this bag, there seemed to be no problem at all. I wanted to fade into the wood pew.

As people milled about, I left with my friends. Art's ashes were buried next to his father J.R. Mitchell's grave, in the small valley town of Lodi, California, a hundred miles east of the Bay Area where Art lived his entire adult life.

~

All the years I danced at the O'Farrell during the legal battles, everyone knew what the cops didn't see certainly never happened. And a lot of things you did see it was better to ignore and deny. When I talked to people connected to the insulated world of the O'Farrell, the most condemning thing said was, 'It' (Art's death) was something that shouldn't have happened.

Warren Hinckle—who soon started writing a book on the Mitchells—described the killing as "Okie justice." Dan O'Neill, who had been a buddy of Art's (when he was alive) said, "We've lost one brother and we've got one brother to save." Translation—Jim is running things now, no one is going to get any more money out of Art, he's in Lodi, six feet under.

Vince tried hard to sound like Art had died of natural causes that were drug related—the first symptom of Art's demise had been his elbow swelling up after getting hit by that golf club. My God, I thought, he was shot at eight times and hit three.

I quit my part-time job with Vince, writing a resignation letter— saying out of respect for Art, I was cutting my last ties to the O'Farrell. Their point of view made me sick. If anyone else had shot Art, they all would have been jumping up and down demanding, "Lynch the assassin!"

People in the X-rated business with no connection to Mitchell Brothers' were shocked by the killing, and understood how bad it was for the industry's image. Things have always been out of control at the O'Farrell, I heard. Something there was bound to bubble up and burst, and destroy someone.

~

Although I was hurting severely, within a few weeks after Art's death, I began a long, slow process of healing. My friends were great, and granted me extreme patience and support. I threw myself into writing, beginning a first draft of this book. I had a total lack of interest in dating anyone. When I had spent much of my time with him, Artie was consuming and unwilling to compromise. Now I wanted to live my life as I chose to live it. The times I spent apart from

Artie when he was alive, and times we quarreled, had prepared me for the greater independence I needed now.

A friend would predict the technique that would be used to defend Jim—assassination of Artie's character. A huge amount of publicity was engineered by Jim's defense team to present Jim favorably, and to put Art on trial as a monster—although he was the victim. By the middle of March, the 911 tape with the gunshots was being played on TV. Two weeks later, the tabloid show "A Current Affair" staged a reenactment in which some actor playing Artie reached for a rifle under his bed—although the only object Artie had been carrying when he was killed was a beer bottle. He had never kept a loaded weapon lying around his house when I was there—not with the many children who might potentially wander in. Artie was so trusting, he didn't even lock his doors. This exploitation shocked me, but it was soon followed by more. I worried that an impartial jury wouldn't be able to be selected—but I was only starting to see how the opinion of the public would be warped.

Just before Easter, Lisa phoned me. It was the first time she had spoken to me in three years. She must have been calling to gauge my reaction to Art's being killed. At this point, I hadn't been able to get any details of how the shooting had happened yet, and Jim was still in Marin County Jail. "I went over to Vince's the other day and I had hoped to find you working there," she said. "There are some pictures I'd like you to have." In a few days, they arrived: three snapshots of Art and me with the children in Moraga. I wrote thanking Lisa, and asked for more photos, and a few personal things I had given Art as mementos. Lisa sent me a card decorated with a teddy bear, with a cool note saying everything was in storage.

In the weeks and months following the killing, I had a powerfully surreal, cut-off feeling from Artie, and a vast sense of loss. If anyone wanted to know how the shooting had occurred, I did. I read and watched every news account I could. For some reason, the San Francisco papers didn't run an extensive report of the shooting, but in a few weeks I was able to get the Marin papers, which gave more details. Eventually, I read the lengthy transcript of the grand jury testimony.

From the detailed accounts of the crime scene, it sounded like premeditated first-degree murder. Art was unarmed, but Jim entered the house with two loaded weapons and an extra box of ammunition. Art slept like a cat. Jim would have known if he had gotten any closer, it would have been exceedingly hard to murder him. Getting in and then out of Art's backyard without noise would have been too difficult, and getting in close enough to hold a gun to Art's head would have been impossible. Jim had killed his brother in a well-planned way, by flushing Art out of the bedroom into the dark narrow hall. The layout of the house gave Art no way to escape without crossing Jim's line of fire.

Art never would have called 911 if he had been there alone, like Jim most likely assumed. If the cops hadn't been nearby and Julie hadn't been cowering in a closet with a phone, Jim would have been at Art's funeral with the rest of us saying, "I'm *so* sorry. I just can't imagine *who* did it." It would have looked like a hit. Who would have suspected *Jim*?

The top investigator in the case, Mario Watkins, was interviewed by Donna Horowitz for the *Marin Independent Journal*. In her March 9, 1991 article, "Mitchell Slaying Called Premeditated," Detective Watkins said: "This was a premeditated murder and the suspect was involved in careful execution of the crime." He based his belief that the crime was premeditated and not carried out in a fit of rage on several factors, including: Jim parked at a distance to avoid connection with the shooting, and walked three blocks to Artie's house in the rain. Jim disabled his brother's car so he couldn't drive off, and positioned himself strategically in the house to prevent his brother's getting away. He explained that the .22-caliber rifle Jim used was a "favored weapon of assassins because it's so quiet. It's probably the quietest gun you can fire without using a silencer. The neighbors aren't going to hear it." If someone enters a home firing a noisier weapon, "you would dive under the bed. But with this rifle, all you hear is pop, pop, pop. ... This guy (Jim Mitchell) was cool, calm and collected when he got there. When the guy (Artie) came out of the bedroom, boom. He was nailed." Watkins also said he didn't necessarily think Jim Mitchell sat around for days plotting the crime, adding, "This is a scenario you could come up with by the time you left the city."

A peculiar explanation—heavy on denial—circulated around the theater. Karen Mitchell and other supporters of Jim referred to Art's death as "The Accident." Supposedly Jim intended to shoot up the house to frighten his brother, and didn't think Artie was home. But parking three blocks away, seeing Art's car parked in the driveway and puncturing the tires certainly indicated he believed Art was home. Why had Jim entered the house banging the doors loudly, if he thought Art was gone? After hearing his brother ask "What's going on. Who's out there?" and the sound of his falling, why continue firing and then flee? If this had been any kind of accident, the only decent thing to do would be to see how badly Art was hurt, call an ambulance and stay there with him. Opening fire into that dark house could have resulted in death or injury for anyone who just happened to be there, even in the death of one of Art's children.

Especially damning was the police account of Jim throwing down an umbrella he was carrying over his head, before pulling the smoking rifle out of his pant leg when he was apprehended. After murdering his brother, Jim concealed the weapon, and then had been coolly self-possessed enough to pause, at Artie's front door, to open an umbrella.

Jim had driven over at 9:30 in the evening, and shot Art to death at 10:20 p.m. If he hadn't been caught by the police, he could easily have made the thirty-minute drive back to the city, and had plenty of time to drop in somewhere public to cover his connection to the killing.

At this time, Karen was so disliked that much of the blame for Art's death was directed at her—although she hadn't shot him. The stress Karen had brought Artie, and her tendency to make impulsive statements, made her a convenient target. If the cops hadn't picked up Jim, Karen would have been the first person suspected. Karen had been acting crazed because her alimony was to end February 28. Earlier on February 27—the day Art was killed—Karen encountered Julie on the road up to her house and threatened her with a gun, saying, "If you ever come near my children, I will kill you." Julie reported this to the police, and Art had Julie call the O'Farrell to tell people there about the incident. It is likely that Jim heard about Karen's gun brandishing, and that it prompted him to act that night.

I remembered the Mitchell family secret Art shared with me years ago: "When I was ten or eleven years old my father told me, Son, if you ever kill someone, never tell anyone and you'll get away with it." I rather imagine Jim heard that one, too.

Soon I came across a quote from Jim Mitchell in Rusty Weston's article "Fatal Split," in the *San Jose Mercury News*, Sunday Magazine *West* (August 11, 1991), that expressed an attitude that is revealing:

"He (Jim and Art's father, J.R. Mitchell) sort of instilled in us, 'Don't go to jail, do good in school.' But really, sort of a deep hatred for the iniquities of the system. With that feeling, if you don't feel bad about what you're doing, *if you don't feel guilty, it's hard to be a criminal.*"

Jim took his outlaw attitude far over the line—to justify any action, even murdering a member of his family.

336

~

Several lawsuits were filed:

Julie Bajo sued Jim for wrongful death, stating she was suffering "extreme mental anguish" and "shock and injury to her nervous system."

Despite Art's having had a vasectomy in 1984, Karen Mitchell filed a paternity suit against Art's trust, claiming he had fathered her twins. She also began wrongful and accidental death suits against Jim on behalf of Aaron, Jasmine, and Caleb Mitchell. In the next months, Mariah, Storm and Liberty Bradford also filed wrongful death suits against their Uncle Jim.

Art had established a trust for his children, who inherited fifty percent of Cinema 7. Jim was named as trustee and as the executor of Art's estate in the will Art signed two weeks before he was killed. Since Jim could no longer serve in these capacities, Georgia Mae and Jim's accountant Ruby Richardson became co-trustees; Georgia became executor. As president of Cinema 7, Jim wanted to buy Art's kids' stock, but they didn't want to sell. Whether Georgia Mae and Ruby could sell the stock to Jim without the children's or their guardian's permission was to be decided in court.

~

Jim Mitchell only served two months in jail before he was released on $500,000.00 bail on April 30, 1991. In May, the TV show "Hard Copy" aired a police photo of Artie's crumpled body, a trickle of blood running down his forehead from a larger bloodied area at the crown of his head, arrows pointing to wounds. As shocking as it was, seeing Art's dead body on television made his killing much more real to me. This was followed by a barrage of stories that seemed to justify Art's being killed—that ran in everything from the *San Francisco Examiner Sunday Image Magazine* to *People*.

Soon I received an unusual invitation—Jim had scheduled a "Bereavement Ceremony" for Artie. The *Spectator* (August 2-8, 1991) ran this item, called "The Wake that Brutus Threw for Julius Caesar":

"It's not often an alleged murderer throws a wake for his victim, but that's what happened on June 23rd at the O'Farrell Theater. Jim Mitchell, accused of killing his brother and business partner Artie last February 27, held a bizarre memorial party at the San Francisco sex club the pair opened more than 20 years ago.

The guest list included state Senator Quentin Kopp, S.F. Supervisor Terence Hallinan, porn star Nina Hartley and the usual cast of house dancers, writers, lawyers and porn groupies. In spite of the entertainment, music, food and drink, the party lacked the O'Farrell's usual festive spirit.

'It was very strange seeing Jim talking to everyone and acting like nothing's wrong,' observed one guest. 'There's no reason to celebrate. How can you have a Mitchell Brothers' party without Artie?'

Another had this comment: 'I went to Artie's wake. I have not been to a wake like that since Brutus threw one for Caesar on 3/15/33 BC.'"

The whole idea of Jim throwing a party to build support for his defense outraged me. I pieced together a tape of Artie's voice from old answering machine messages to leave on Jim's home machine during the event: "Hello partner, this is Artie. I'm at the O'Farrell, it's today. Give me a call—very important business." But when I dialed Jim's number, it had been disconnected.

Dave Patrick of the Bay Area adult paper *Spectator* was the first reporter to write articles taking a courageously different view of the case. He urged me to write, and published two pieces of mine. Gene Ross of *Adult Video News (AVN)* also published my tribute piece,

"State of Art," in *Exposed*. I hadn't been away from the adult business for very long. I thought including a fair amount of hot content would ensure that my tribute piece about Artie would get into print in the adult papers, and win more attention for the first part of the piece, where I talked about his being killed. Now, I wish I had censored some of the material in this. Although it was intended for the adult readers of *Spectator* and *Exposed*, in 1992 journalist David McCumber would publish portions of my article in his book *X-Rated*. He hadn't asked my permission, although I had interviewed with him extensively. To add to his presumptions about my relationship with Artie and his other inaccuracies, McCumber quoted from some of the more explicit parts of the article, out-of-context. He omitted the section of my tribute piece where I discussed Art's killing, and gave a false impression of me.

∼

The wealth that Art and Jim earned together paid for Jim's team of defense attorneys, led by Ivanna Trump's lawyer, Michael Kennedy, who had handled cases for Artie and Jim years earlier. Maybe it wasn't the dream team, but Jim's defense cost $1.3 million. Twenty-two year old Liberty was called to testify. Artie's other children, who were all were younger than Liberty, were understandably silent in public. Artie's ex-wife Meredith was silent publicly as well, but the rest of the Mitchell family joined the network of acquaintances and politicians that Art and Jim had cultivated, in rallying to Jim's defense.

∼

Jim began funding the *Anderson Valley Advertiser*, a Northern California weekly. Journalist Warren Hinckle wrote clever, funny articles which excused Jim's actions and ridiculed the prosecution. Several underground cartoonists, including R. Crumb, drew satirical illustrations. Throughout the trial, newsracks of these papers were brazenly placed inside the courthouse.

Despite pressure from Jim's camp for silence, I wrote letters, continued talking to reporters, and to the prosecution during the investigation for Jim's murder trial. Jim and his supporters got a message to me via Dan O'Neill. "Everything's going terrible because of that goddamn Simone," Dan said. "Instead of comforting her after Art died, I should have taken Simone down to the ocean and drowned her."

Jim's trial began in January 1992 in the Marin County Courthouse, and lasted five long weeks. I was on the prosecution's backup witness list, but I wasn't called. In defending Jim, Michael Kennedy played on the jury's emotions. He called family members, including Art's daughter Liberty; Lisa; O'Farrell employees loyal to Jim; political consultant Jack Davis; professional experts; and other witnesses who praised Jim and condemned Art. Prosecutor John Posey based his case on the physical evidence, presenting technical experts and a computerized animation of the shooting—the first ever used in a murder case. Posey was outgunned by Jim's team of attorneys and investigators, and handicapped by the massive support Jim received.

Jim's lead defense attorney put quite a spin on the brothers' accident at Ocean Beach. Art was saved by the Surf Rescue Squad, but Michael Kennedy claimed Jim rescued his brother: "Jim Mitchell was the only one who cared enough about his brother to risk his own life to save him. Just as surely as Art was drowning in a surf off Ocean Beach on March 18, 1990, Artie was drowning in alcohol on February 27, 1991." Kennedy said the killing was a tragic accident that occurred when Jim's mission of mercy to calm down an alcohol-crazed and violent Artie and take away his guns "went awry."

Lisa Adams and Jim testified that Artie left two threatening messages on Lisa's answering machine the day of the shooting.

Conveniently, they claimed the messages had been erased. Even if Art did leave the messages, he had a tendency to bluster when he was upset, and everyone close to him knew that. I doubt that Jim or Lisa thought Art was malevolent enough to actually harm them.

The defense tried to have an answering machine tape, of Artie berating former O'Farrell dancer Lady T. after their run-in in December 1988, admitted into evidence. The judge ruled it irrelevant. In 1990 when Lady T. was dancing at the Century, she became despondent over a love affair and took an overdose of pills. Unfairly, Jim's attorneys suggested she committed suicide shortly after listening to Artie's message. Over time, Lady T. had developed some wonderful shows. She was overly serious. I had suspected she was a little strange when I saw her on the New York stage years earlier, dancing naked with a butcher knife.

To diminish the idea of Jim having cold-bloodedly planned and carried out his attack on Art alone, the defense briefly put Jim and Art's cousin Rocky on the stand. But they would not agree to let him testify unless the prosecution granted him immunity—which they would not. If Rocky had been granted immunity, he could have testified that he had shot Artie himself. Although there were no witnesses and no evidence to support that Rocky had been at 23 Mohawk the night Art was killed, Jim's attorneys were claiming Rocky had met Jim there. The defense had considered Rocky too unconvincing a witness to risk presenting before the grand jury. But at the trial, they succeeded in letting the jury see Rocky being called to the stand—to suggest he had knowledge of the killing, and for some reason unknown to them, would not be allowed to testify in court.

Protecting her only remaining son, Georgia Mae testified Artie had said he wanted to shoot Jim. Georgia told a reporter that she had consulted a psychic, who said Jim did everyone a favor by shooting his brother to death—because Artie had been on the verge of killing the entire Mitchell family.

Julie had been in the closet and had not seen Jim. Her memories of the shooting were inconsistent, and she had known Art and Jim less than one year. She had sold her story to two television shows, "Hard Copy," and "Inside Edition." Prosecutor Posey questioned Julie about what she was paid, and about her posing in a g-string sprawled across a pool table for *People* magazine.

Julie was criticized as being mercenary, but Jim Mitchell wasn't—although he stood to profit considerably from Art's death. As President of Cinema 7, Jim was the beneficiary of Art's one-million-dollar insurance policy. The theater's records were so clean it was impossible to prove Art and Jim were skimming cash. After his death Artie's share of the O'Farrell skim, which could have amounted to a half-million dollars each year, was no longer going to him; neither was his salary.

Dressed in a tweed jacket and looking sedate, Jim testified he had driven over to Art's house to "settle Art down" and "pick up all of his guns." Claiming he met Rocky near 23 Mohawk, Jim said the two of them approached the house, Jim concealing his rifle in an umbrella to avoid one of the neighbors spotting it and calling the police. After Jim and Rocky checked the doors to 23 Mohawk and found them locked, they concluded Art wasn't home—even though Art's car was parked in the driveway. Jim said he told Rocky to leave and make a call to the theater to check if Art was there, and a call to Lisa to warn her to stay away from their door in case Art showed up. After Rocky was gone, Jim said he became uncomfortable about neighbors thinking he was a prowler; he punctured the tires on Art's car in anger, and kicked in Art's front door. Contradicting Julie's testimony, other evidence, *and* the 911 tape, Jim said he started screaming when he entered the house, and said Art had come out of the bedroom fast, aggressive, with a gun aimed at Jim, yelling, "Okay, motherfucker, I'm going to blow your fucking brains out!"

Jim claimed he only remembered firing one shot until the police flashed a bright light in his face outside. Michael Kennedy called psychiatrist David Kessler to theorize Jim had amnesia. Posey called psychologist Sherryl Skidmore, who accused Kessler of a breach of ethics for giving his opinion even though he had not examined Jim. In his closing argument, John Posey said the killing amounted to "an execution."

I believe that Jim's greed, anger, and the desire to control their businesses were his motives for murdering Art. The shooting was too calculated to be a crime of passion or a bungled intervention.

The verdict was announced on February 19, 1992—the jury convicted Jim of voluntary manslaughter, not murder. Pending sentencing, Jim was allowed to remain free on bond. I was heartsick.

Psychiatric tests were ordered for Jim. He had no history of mental problems, and his attorneys hadn't developed a psychological defense during the trial. Court-appointed psychologist Bruce Pither said that Jim exhibited "strong antisocial, paranoid, and narcissistic personality features," and is "rigid and inflexible with an ability to deal with stressful situations only when there is adequate structure." Jim told the psychologist that at the time of the killing he imagined himself to be Travis Bickle, the disturbed, but well-meaning shooter in the movie *Taxi Driver*.

Following John Hinckley's assassination attempt on President Reagan, Hinckley said he was influenced by *Taxi Driver*. The jury at Hinckley's trial declared he was insane, and found him not guilty of attempted murder. Later Hinckley was placed in a mental institution. It's likely Jim's lawyers thought if Jim claimed he had a mental lapse spurred on by the same movie, he would look more sympathetic.

Godfather II was the all-time favorite film of the O'Farrell upper management, so much so that they could quote from it by heart, Artie had said. If Jim was identifying with a movie at the time of the killing, he would have been imagining himself as the don played by Al Pacino in *Godfather II*, who strengthens his position as head of his family by murdering *his* brother.

Over the years Art and Jim had established local political connections, cultivated journalists, and contributed to many campaigns and causes. They wined, dined, and extensively entertained a steady stream of VIPs. The wealth and the political and social connections that both Mitchells established paid off for the survivor.

After Art's death, Jim was a contributor to Frank Jordan's campaign for mayor, managed by Jack Davis. Davis was considered the most successful and most feared political consultant in Northern California—and he had recently testified in support of Jim. Just before the sentencing, more than one hundred letters pleading for leniency on Jim's behalf were sent to Judge Breiner. San Francisco's Mayor Frank Jordan, Sheriff Michael Hennessey, soon-to-be District Attorney Terence Hallinan, Police Chief Richard Hongisto, and California State Senators John Burton and Quentin Kopp were among those who wrote on Jim's behalf. Most praised Jim for his contributions to community welfare. Mayor Jordan's letter, quoted in the April 24, 1992 *San Francisco Examiner* editorial, "Soliciting for Jim Mitchell," was typical:

> "Although I do not condone the nature of his business, Jim Mitchell is known in San Francisco as of a supporter of charitable and civic causes."

It gave me the greatest sense of despair to learn that many public officials representing the city I lived in, including those administering law enforcement, were rallying to support a convicted killer.

On April 24, 1992, Jim was sentenced by Judge Breiner to serve a six-year prison term, and was allowed to remain free on bond pending appeal. Jim would remain free, running the O'Farrell, for the next two and a half years.

For good PR, Jim started the Artie Fund, a non-profit charity to raise funds for the Center Point Rehabilitation Center and the San Francisco Surf Rescue Squad. Eventually, Artie's children would write about Jim's hypocrisy in starting this fund, and express the bitterness and loss they experienced because of their father's murder on a website, Artiefund.com.

As if the trial wasn't ordeal enough, weeks after the verdict a satirical *comedy* based on the Mitchell brothers' murder opened at San Francisco's Magic Theater, and played to packed audiences. "XXX Love Act" was a superficial parody, full of clever jokes. It was uncomfortable for me to watch. The Artie character sold his soul to the devil, got shot on stage, and was led in his bloody sheet to the next world by a couple of campy angels.

~

Artie's life insurance company, Summit National, refused to pay his one-million-dollar benefits to Cinema 7. How disgraceful it was that the President of Cinema 7, Jim, could potentially use this money to pay his criminal defense fees for murdering his brother. Summit filed suit on the grounds that Art misrepresented himself as a light social drinker at the time he applied for the policy. To prove Jim was entitled to the money, his lawyers had begun claiming that Artie hadn't become an alcoholic until 1990—contradicting the murder trial testimony and medical evidence. During the suit about this, Jim subpoenaed my journal. After two unpleasant depositions, I had to go to federal court to fight to keep it. This case would be settled out of court in December 1992, before I had to surrender sections of my journal that described Art drinking or getting high.

The murder, the awful publicity about it, and the long period of legal proceedings were draining. And it made me tense that a killer with so many resources—whom I risked speaking against—remained free in my hometown. Before Art's death, my life was centered on passion. Now it would be about survival.

∾

Two journalists, David McCumber—who had been Hunter Thompson's editor—and John Hubner, began compiling books on the brothers soon after Art was killed. Interviewing with them let me express some of what actually had taken place. When their books came out, I was horrified. Some information was true, but far too much of the interview material, quotes and dialogue was inaccurate, twisted or invented. Hubner seemed to have no affinity for adult entertainment, and revealed in the Acknowledgements of his book, *Bottom-Feeders,* that he was the son of a minister. David McCumber had hung out with Jim and Art, and spent some time at the O'Farrell before the killing. He was fairer to me in his book, *X-Rated,* than Hubner was, but many of the distortions and misquotes he printed were ghastly. Almost no one wanted to anger Jim Mitchell by presenting him as guilty of murdering Art, since Jim was dangerously out of jail and also likely to sue. I hoped these books would never be adapted into sensational, grim movies with the theme that being involved with the sex business has to lead to tragedy.

By the spring of 1992, I had asked a few local agents about my manuscript, but there was little interest since two books were already coming out. I kept writing because I had fallen in love with the process. In June 1993, I finished my first draft, and kept trying to have it published. Later I would get an agent (in 2000), but he was unable to sell the project.

I met a doctor from Alaska in the summer of 1993, and we had a long distance relationship for six months. Although we didn't have enough in common and I didn't want to move there, I will always remember traveling to Denali National Park and seeing some of the wildlife and the beauty of Alaska.

In the spring of 1994, my 83-year old father became very ill. Since my mother's death in 1981, we had visited a few times a year, and called each other weekly. But we had not been close, especially in recent years, since he had remarried—to a very religious woman. My stepmother was beginning to develop Alzheimer's dementia. I looked after my father's care until he died in July. That summer, I was injured doing too much computer keyboarding and had to leave work. I began a long course of treatment, and would have to choose a new occupation. For five years, I was not able to type or work on my manuscript. After my dad's death, I watched over my stepmother's care until she died several years later. Having Artie's death followed by more turmoil like this was difficult. I felt a lot of anger and despair, but having to "parent" my parents made me stronger. Fate has a funny way of providing special people when you most need them. During this time I met a man—successful in his field and a non-conformist in his own right—who has been a true, supportive friend and lover, able to accept the independence I need. I have never again wanted to become involved with anyone with so much power over my life as Artie.

∾

On April 13, 1994, a hearing of Jim's appeal was held at the California State Court of Appeals in San Francisco. Jim attended with several lawyers on his defense team. That day Jim was represented by University of Texas law professor Michael Tigar, who later represented Oklahoma City bombing defendant Terry Nichols. Tigar argued that Jim's conviction had been based on "junk science" built on speculative and unreliable analyses. Justice Anthony Kline disagreed, stating that despite the evidence being disputed that "This record is replete

Picketing at Jim Mitchell's hearing at the California State Court of Appeals, in April, 1994.

with evidence of intent to kill," including the fact that Jim went to his brother's home in Corte Madera carrying two loaded guns and a knife. Outside the hearing, to the surprise and annoyance of Jim and his entourage, I carried a sign with a photo of Art, with a caption that read "Justice for Art Mitchell." A written decision was issued by Justice Kline on May 27, 1994. Jim's conviction was upheld.

On October 26, 1994, Jim was scheduled to appear before Judge Breiner in Marin Superior Court. In front of the courthouse in the autumn sunshine, I picketed again. From the mood of the Mitchell insiders who passed me on their way into the building, I knew something was brewing. Attorneys Dennis Roberts, Michael Kennedy, and his wife glared at me and looked grim. Last Gasp publisher Ron Turner was serious. Dr. Nick was thoughtful; "That picture of Art looks good, Simone," he said. Then a cab pulled up with petite Julie

Bajo, who was living in Hawaii and dancing in clubs there. Julie wore a mini dress and spike heels, a contrast to my more demure black dress and pumps. She gave a thumb's up to my "Justice for Art Mitchell" sign.

"Julie!" I said.

"Simone," she said. We hugged.

"He was a wonderful man. The best man I've ever known," she declared, glancing at Art's picture. "Everyone felt that way."

"Jim needs to go to prison. It's been so long," I said.

"Oh, he does. He really does. Hopefully, it'll happen today. I'm going to see my Victim Witness counselor and tell her how I've transformed my life through dance!"

That afternoon, Jim *was* taken into custody and sent to San Quentin. I felt relieved yet stunned. After so much time and anguish, Jim's going to prison for what was expected to be three years hardly felt like a conclusion. Eventually, I would hear that around the theater, there were rumors about how soft Jim's treatment and living situation was at San Quentin.

⁓

Early in October 1997, with credit for time served and good behavior, Jim was released from prison. In the October 4, 1997 *San Francisco Examiner* article, "Mitchell Returns to Home, Family," his attorney Nancy Clarence said:

> "His children are coming from all over the Bay Area and Southern California to reunite. This is a real opportunity for the family to move forward and heal."

Thankfully, some other opinions were expressed. Twin Cities Police Chief Phil Green, whose department handled Jim's murder case, said in a KPIX Eyewitness News television interview with Hank Plante on October 3, 1997, that he was outraged:

"I do feel it's a travesty of justice. I think to begin with at the minimum he (Jim Mitchell) should have received life in prison, and being out after three years is kind of a joke for the system... . There is a similarity between the Mitchell brothers' case and that of O.J. Simpson, where a high-profile type individual—Mitchell being well-known in the Bay Area communities and having enough money to obtain high-priced lawyers and beat the system."

Artie's daughter Mariah Bradford, who by then was 23, gave an interview in the *San Francisco Chronicle* in an October 4, 1997 article by Susan Sward titled "Niece of Paroled Porn King Unable to Forgive, Forget":

"People are talking about this man coming back to the embrace of his family. My dad is never going to return to the embrace of his family." Her uncle, Jim Mitchell, who fired three shots into her father, has never uttered a word of apology to the family and has shown no remorse for his actions, she said.... "If it were an accident, I would expect a lot of remorse. 'How can I make it up to you?' I would expect an apology. We never had one—not even an attempt." Bradford said she was motivated to talk about her family's sentiments because she was tired of reading sympathetic accounts about her uncle in the wake of his release. The stories that irk her the most, she said, seem to emphasize "Jim needing to take care of my dad—as if Jim hadn't killed him, my dad would have killed someone else. As if this was a service to society." Over the years, she said she has "struggled and struggled" with how her uncle... could have reached a point where he could have ... kicked in his door and killed him.

"The nearest I come is that it could have been for money because it's very obvious his story (of why he killed Artie) wasn't true," Bradford said. Artie Mitchell's six children filed wrongful death suits against their uncle; the suits were settled out of court. Each child will be paid a monthly settlement until the year 2000. She said the children settled for a sum "less than we knew he had, but we couldn't prove it. He knew where the money was. We didn't. He hasn't offered to help us with any support other than the settlement where he has to."

Georgia Mae Mitchell, the brothers' mother, said that she felt Bradford and two of Artie's other older children, Liberty and Storm, were "coming from guilt. All of these years they did not treat Art like a father. Those kids ignored him until they wanted money."

Bradford discounted her grandmother's contents, saying, "It must be easier for her to think of her grandchildren as greedy that it is for her to think that her son is a murderer."

Rob Morse's October 7, 1997 *San Francisco Examiner* column was called "Behind the kicked-in door":

"Imagine you loaded a rifle and a handgun, drove to your brother's house, parked three blocks away, slashed his tires, then kicked in the door and shot him to death. You can bet you wouldn't be out of the joint in three years. You'd at least expect to be a bit of a pariah in your community. Jim Mitchell did exactly that, and after three years in San Quentin, he's out.... There's a different standard of justice for San Francisco characters with powerful friends.... Rich celebrities are allowed to hire good lawyers and get off easy. It's as American as O.J.... Every few years murders occur showing that San Francisco sits on moral landfill. Dan White, Jim Jones and Jim Mitchell were all well-connected to political powers in The City.... Unlike corrupt places like New York and Providence, here you have to listen to sanctimony about healing, living with your crime for the rest of your life and the stress of the porn business.... Please no more of this healing crap. We need closure. If it's too late for a cell door, how about closure of some mealy yaps."

The Mitchell brothers' story was too juicy to be ignored for long. In April 1994, *X-Rated* author David McCumber brought Bob Rafelson, who directed *Five Easy Pieces* and the 1981 version of *The Postman Always Rings Twice,* among other films, and Norm Snider, who wrote the screenplay for *Dead Ringers,* to my apartment. They interviewed me for a screenplay for an HBO film on the Mitchells. Although the books had been so disappointing, I was still concerned about how the story would be told. This project never materialized, but *Rated X,* a cheaply-produced Showtime original movie loosely based on McCumber's book, premiered on cable TV in May 2000. Oddly cast with Charlie Sheen playing slender Artie and the shorter, more slight Emilio Estevez as Jim, the film was directed by Estevez and shot in Toronto. It fictionalized the Mitchells' history, highlighted their early successes, glossed over the 80's, and made the O'Farrell look like a dive. It also added some terrible, false notes to some scenes, and exaggerated Art's worst qualities to the max. In Justin Berton's article "Caleb's Cage," in the *East Bay Express* (July 3-9, 2002) Artie's youngest son commented on the books about his family and the movie, "All of these stories are justifications for why my uncle murdered my father," says Caleb (Mitchell). "They're told from my uncle's side. Any time they had a chance to make my uncle look good, they did. Any time they had a chance to make my dad look bad, they did." Charlie Sheen's own history of substance abuse and clashes with his brother Emilio were considered promising background. In his *San Francisco Examiner* review of the film, "Sex, Drugs, Murder—and Boredom," Tim Goodman wrote, "The central fault may be that despite all the elements, the writers haven't been able to elevate this brother vs. brother tale above the obvious—sex, drugs, sibling rivalry and murder. The 'why?' is missing. If it was Artie who was completely out of control and unpredictable—an increasing danger to those around him—why was it Jim who did the killing?"

It wasn't until the fall of 2002 when the E! Entertainment cable channel began to tape interviews for a two-hour "E-True Hollywood Story" on the Mitchell brothers, that Artie's oldest son Storm Bradford, Julie Bajo, and about a dozen other people close to the story including me were able to express more of our views. This program, which was shown for the first time in March 2003, was the fairest, best production that has been done yet—although some misrepresentations were made—by omission, and by John Hubner.

I was surprised that even Hunter Thompson participated in this show. Unlike most others who knew Art and Jim, Hunter never made any public statements about Artie's being killed. In the sound bites they recorded, he said:

> "I was the night manager. That was my job description … a consultant, really. My job was to make the O'Farrell the Carnegie Hall of public sex. They had to be made hip. The Carnegie Hall thing was exactly what they needed to be portrayed sympathetically. Like Berlin in '37, it had a decadent quality. There were always a hundred hits of acid within arms' reach in those days."

Of Jim and Art's trip to visit him during his hearing, he said:

> "It was like seeing the cavalry coming over the hill when they came to picket the courthouse. That's what friends are for. My lawyer flipped out at the idea these naked people were going to surround the courthouse in the morning and the judge would see them. Just their presence in town meant they were on the front

page. It leant an edge of humor and weirdness and fun to the otherwise very hostile proceedings."

Artie's son Storm, who had never made any public statements about his dad's death before, made these comments on Jim's trial:

"I think more could have been done. And the fact is that my uncle got away with murder. He's out of jail, he still owns the place, and you know people don't like to talk about it. But the fact is that you know it's wrong."

Speaking of the Showtime movie he said, "They paint my father like an out-of-control monster. That's simply not the case, he was a loving man."

"I think about him every day. I think about the way things could have been. I'd like to think that I've gotten over and I'm able to go on with my own life. I would not want to spend the rest of my life pining for something that's not there. You've got to kind of take what you can get, you know. Life is like a movie."

On parole after his release, Jim kept a low profile and ran the O'Farrell Theater. Eventually, he bought a ranch in Petaluma, and raised horses with Lisa, who had become his wife. He played a less active role in the business as his children began working at the theater, which recently celebrated its thirty-eighth-year anniversary. On July 12, 2007, he died of a heart attack at home. He was 63.

One week later, three hundred people gathered for a memorial service including former mayor Willie Brown, Jim's defense attorney Michael Kennedy, Warren Hinckle, and Jack Davis. Jim was praised for his generosity, and some of the same lies about Art's death being an accident were repeated. "Artie was the f — lunatic — he was doing more cocaine and alcohol," Kennedy said in his eulogy. "Why in the hell would Jimmy want to kill his brother?" Jim was buried right next to Art and their father J.R.—like there had never been any bloodshed.

In the face of such injustice and loss, grief and anger are small words. At my heart's core, I will always have a sense of longing for Art, although he was not easy to be involved with. His murder changed me forever. It limited my dreams and left me empty. I have had to become tenacious, and learn to feel pleasure and affection again

~

Six weeks after Art's funeral I took a long drive east, through little delta towns and miles of quiet countryside. Calling the cemetery was eerie. "Artie Mitchell, yes, he's here, he's over in the Garden of Memories." Christ, I thought, I couldn't imagine a more unlikely place for one of the last true outlaws of the Western World to be.

It was Saturday, and buying the last six long stemmed red roses they had, daisies and a green bow—he always did like green—I drove out not wanting to find a grave that was Art's. Hopefully, this was some nightmare or a hoax and Art was really sucking back a Pacifico somewhere South of the Border. How could this have happened? I still had his underwear in my drawer, Cristall in the freezer. That day I could almost hear him, "There are only four or five real men left and I'm one of them, Simone. You never wanted a stockbroker. You chose me, you know."

The graveyard office was locked until Sunday, and a creepy old man helped me look for a fresh grave. I carried my bouquet as he and I, and then I walked over what seemed like hundreds of graves not finding Art's. What a relief, I thought, he can't be dead. I never *had* seen his body—maybe he wasn't gone in some absolute, irretrievable way, after all.

When I called Rita she thought I should wait until the office opened, to find out for sure if he was buried there, so I checked into the Lodi Motor Inn with the roses. In the morning an attendant walked me right over, immediately dug out a metal cylinder for flowers and held it up. "Art Mitchell" it said, in plastic marking tape on the bottom of the tin container, and I burst into tears. Several rows over, two little old ladies looked up. "Art was shot by his brother," I told the attendant. "He was murdered. His family would have said it was an accident."

"I talked to Jim," a "friend" of Art's had said to me a couple of days before, his voice dripping with sentimentality. "Well, I've seen what's left of Art," I could tell him, "and it's a raised area in the ground about two' by three.'"

Nearby stood a statue of some comforting saint, and a plaque engraved, "I think that I shall never see a poem as lovely as a tree..." What an odd place for one of the hottest and most flamboyant pornographers of all time. I looked around my lover's new address—a quiet grassy plain dotted with markers, yew trees in the distance. Artie was far away from complications now, light years from the O'Farrell.

To show Art respect, the attendant walked over, splashed some water into the container by the fence, and carried it back to me. It looked cloudy but the surface shone in the sun. I put the flowers in.

Then I remembered . . . At the airport I saw that Art had first class tickets made out to Mr. and Mrs. A. Mitchell. "On the tickets you're my wife," he said. "I know you won't like that."

I laughed and kissed him. The airport bar was nearly deserted, except for us. Art had a shot of tequila.

. . . At Al Goldstein's party Art spoke up loudly, "You mean I came three-thousand miles for this thing and you're not even going to speak! Speech, Al, Speech! Come on, Al—Speech!" Goldstein didn't respond. There were only eight people in the room by then. Art delivered a little speech of his own saying, "Well, you made it. You lasted twenty goddamn years. Despite the pigs, despite everything, you lasted. I take my hat off to you, Al. Anybody that lasts twenty goddamn years has to be pretty tough, and pretty special, in this business."

. . . It was very dark. When I got down to the bottom of the stairs and walked over, at first I couldn't quite see Art, then I looked behind a box and Art was standing there, a lit joint in his mouth, his pants unzipped. Just standing there against some stuff, sort of leaning back like a Mexican against a fence.

I put my hairbrush on top of a stack of truck tires, my pearls inside my shoes.

It was dark and smelled of dust.

I stepped back to look at my flowers against the green, flat graveyard, on the edge of town, as flat and still and eerie as the wide gray limitless sea at night off the cliffs of Zihuatanejo, not even a horizon, beyond the balcony of our room at the Sotovento, and suddenly the whole world was flat and silent and empty and there was no Art—anywhere, at all.

"I'll always be with you, Simone. I'll be fucking you when you're eighty. And there will be times when you won't see me for a long, long time and think I'm never coming back to you but I always will, because I love you. I just want you to experience all the angles. Simone . . ." I can almost hear Art say, you see, I can almost hear Art say that, because now, I can't.

EPILOGUE

Since the eventful decade when I was wrapped up with Artie Mitchell, my life has changed dramatically. I cut my connections with the O'Farrell when I took a different stance on Jim's guilt. There is no closure—but my friends, writing, and time has helped me work through much of my grief. Although he possessed qualities I loved, Art was a difficult, demanding man, and I will always wonder how our lives and our relationship would have developed, had he lived. I linked great sex with love, and prized eroticism, excitement, and independence more than a stable relationship. I was able to share these values with a charismatic lover whose needs meshed with my own, for 9 ½ years. Now I realize that nothing lasts forever, and to open my mind and heart to what lies ahead. Life is full of distractions, yet I can't help following, from a distance, how the sex industry is evolving.

Take a leisurely walk through San Francisco's alluring old Italian neighborhood, North Beach, in the evening, and the landscape is changed. No longer is the corner of Broadway and Columbus dwarfed by the massive sign of a woman with pulsing light bulb nipples, promoting the Condor—which now has a tame neon sign. Continue two blocks along Broadway, past the sparkling sidewalk in front of Showgirls, and across the street at Montgomery you'll see how Jim Mitchell's former War News Club has been transformed by his chief competitor—first into an elegant gentlemen's club called Centerfolds, then into a Déjà Vu. The Déjà Vu chain, based in Michigan, has revamped several other San Francisco clubs to its own lucrative format. Larry Flynt's Hustler club is slightly downhill from Broadway, on Kearny Street. Flynt—known of late for his political principles and his articulate interviews on television—made a special visit in his gold-plated wheelchair at the opening, which was attended by then-Mayor Willie Brown and Frances Ford Coppola, while outside a couple of anti-porn feminists picketed.

The debate about women working in the sex business became more sophisticated and more public, beginning in the mid-90's. More articles on the subject have been in newspapers, in journals and magazines, and on the Internet. The Sex Worker Film and Arts Festival has been held yearly in San Francisco, since 2002. Some women academics have written on the subject, including NYU law school professor and ACLU President Nadine Strossen, whose book, *Defending Pornography,* came out in 1995. San Francisco Attorney Heidi Machen, who had interned on a local case against Jim Mitchell's corporation, published an article, "Women's Work: Attitudes, Regulation, and Lack of Power within the Sex Industry," in *The Hastings Women's Law Journal* in 1996. Tad Friend's article, "Naked Profits," ran in *The New Yorker,* in 2004. *Spread,* a magazine with articles and features for sex-workers, began publishing in 2005.

Next door to the Hustler, is the first and still only American strip club to successfully unionize, the Lusty Lady peep show. A popular independent film was made by one of its dancers, Julia Query, and Vicky Funari, titled *Live Nude Girls, Unite!* When the Lusty Lady was in danger of closing in 2003, their dancers bought their club. Since then, they have been trying to balance paying the dancers' wages with upkeep of their place, which faces tough competition.

All around town since the mid-90's, there has again been a trend toward permitting more contact between customers and dancers. The O'Farrell took the glass out of the Ultra Room, dimmed the lights in the Kopenhagen, and provided more places for customers to be alone with dancers, including private curtained "Cabana Booths." Requiring dancers to pay escalating stage fees, or meet quotas and split their tip money with their club has been a trend in strip clubs nationwide. Dancers who have become activists have said the increased financial pressure and competition with other women leads dancers to perform "extras" with customers. Lawsuits alleging unfair business practices have been brought against some club owners. Others have said that everyone, dancers and owners, are now making less money because of increased scrutiny, changing regulations, and lawsuits. In 1998, a $2 million settlement fund was ordered for the more than five hundred O'Farrell dancers who were part of the class action suit in *Vickery v. Cinema 7, Inc.* (Jim Mitchell's corporation). Another class action suit brought by a group of dancers against Cinema 7 is now pending. In recent years, the quotas that were required to be met by the dancers, then split with the club, rose to $240 on a weekday shift and $400 on a Friday or Saturday night.

The Exotic Dancers Alliance was formed by Laddawan Passer and Johanna Breyer to work for changes in the clubs. Together with COYOTE (a prostitutes' rights group founded by Margo St. James in 1973), they also obtained funding from the City and established a clinic on Mission Street for local sex workers, the St. James Infirmary.

Near downtown San Francisco are the Market St. Cinema, LA Girls, the Crazy Horse, and the Gold Club. And close to where this history began, The New Century glitters and vies with the O'Farrell. In her book *Strip City*, Lily Burana (who was a named plaintiff in the first class action suit against Cinema 7) describes the O'Farrell Theater as the "crown jewel of San Francisco strip clubs":

> "If the Lusty Lady is college—ideals, self-discovery, political consciousness, then Mitchell Brothers is the real world, a sophisticated venue that requires dedication and discipline. I love to sit in the front row in New York Live, the room with the big stage, and watch the show. Such range! Such talent! … As I watch these

women, each of whom exudes the supreme confidence of a sexual adventuress, I wonder, will I ever ascend to that level?"

Since the days when Artie and Jim were partners, more and more films, television shows, books, and plays have been done about adult entertainment. *Boogie Nights, The People vs. Larry Flynt, Exotica,* and the documentary, *Inside Deep Throat,* were significant films. "Family Business" had a two-year run on Showtime. Jenna Jameson wrote a best-selling memoir, *How to Make Love Like a Pornstar.* Lily Burana's book, *Strip City,* received a starred review in *Publishers' Weekly,* while Diablo Cody's memoir, *Candy Girl,* led to her appearing on David Letterman. But despite this increased exposure, most Americans consider adult entertainment and sex work to be socially unacceptable subcultures, no matter how sexualized mainstream show business and advertising have become. When you are making a transition to a "straight" occupation, having been involved with the renegade porn industry, or having worked as a stripper, remains risky to admit to anyone outside that world.

Women prominent in the adult business have become articulate advocates, including porn star Nina Hartley, and AIM Healthcare director and former star Sharon Mitchell, proactive in providing HIV testing and counseling for AIDS-prevention to the industry. Many other performers have moved into other areas of the adult business, are successful working conventional jobs, or have become entertainers, writers and artists. Post-porn modernist Annie Sprinkle is now a performance artist, gifted photographer, film producer, and author. Former stripper Carol Queen is an activist, writer, performer, and founder of the Center for Sex and Culture. Ex-O'Farrell dancers Linda Serbu, and Danielle Willis (the same Danielle who fought with Artie) each wrote and performed their unique plays locally. The list of adult entertainers involved in creative work goes on and on.

Along with Art *and* Jim, some other people I knew during my
O'Farrell years are now dead. I heard a few rumors that women I
worked with had died, but after I stopped dancing it was hard to be
certain. I was saddened by the loss of Hunter Thompson, when he
shot himself to death, after being in poor health for two years. A
couple of months later, I took part in a tribute to Hunter that was
held at the San Francisco Public Library. How ironic that an English
major like me would get to meet the most original, gifted writer of our
generation because I went to work at a notorious San Francisco strip
club. I am fortunate to have crossed paths with—as Hunter called
himself—this "road man for the lords of karma."

It was hard for me to believe that Vince Stanich, my boss at
Dancers' Guild and the general manager of the O'Farrell, who
skillfully oversaw the running of the club for more than thirty years,
died of cancer. How many secrets died with this pragmatic, clever
man?

Although neither of us is still in the business, my closest friend
is a former O'Farrell dancer. Rita completed an MA in clinical
psychology, and is now working as a licensed psychotherapist. For
the last nineteen years, she has been happily married to Charles De
Santos. After my stubborn computer keyboarding injury, I am still in
transition, searching for another career that will pay the rent but be
compelling. And although I am happy being independent, I am still
captivated with the caring, intelligent man I met ten years ago.

My years "behind the green door" seem almost like a fantastical
dream. I have the capricious O'Farrell Theater to thank for my being
able to lead part of my life like a novel. Although I have moved on, I
do miss the sex business, the ironic touches, the dark irreverent humor
of it all. In the end, I would trade none of the spangles, sensuality, and
dressing room drama for any safer, less passionate destiny.

CPSIA information can be obtained at www.ICGtesting.com
Printed in the USA
LVOW06s1359030813

346127LV00002B/760/A